A Practical Guide to SAP® S/4HANA Financial Accounting

Oona Flanagan

Thank you for purchasing this book from Espresso Tutorials!

Like a cup of espresso coffee, Espresso Tutorials SAP books are concise and effective. We know that your time is valuable and we deliver information in a succinct and straightforward manner. It only takes our readers a short amount of time to consume SAP concepts. Our books are well recognized in the industry for leveraging tutorial-style instruction and videos to show you step by step how to successfully work with SAP.

Check out our YouTube channel to watch our videos at
https://www.youtube.com/user/EspressoTutorials.

If you are interested in SAP Finance and Controlling, join us at *http://www.fico-forum.com/forum2/* to get your SAP questions answered and contribute to discussions.

Related titles from Espresso Tutorials:

▶ Anurag Barua: **First Steps in SAP® Fiori**
  http://5126.espresso-tutorials.com

▶ Ann Cacciottolli: **First Steps in SAP® FI Configuration**
  http://5137.espresso-tutorials.com

▶ Janet Salmon & Claus Wild: **First Steps in SAP® S/4HANA Finance**
  http://5149.espresso-tutorials.com

▶ M.Larry McKinney, Reinhard Müller, Frank Rothhaas: **Practical Guide to SAP® FI-RA—Revenue Accounting and Reporting**
  http://5174.espresso-tutorials.com

▶ Mary Loughran, Lennart Ullmann: **Guide to SAP® In-House Cash (ICH)**
  http://5191.espresso-tutorials.com

▶ Mary Loughran, Praveen Gupta: **Cash Management in SAP® S/4HANA**
  http://5281.espresso-tutorials.com

▶ Marjorie Wright: **Credit Management in SAP® S/4HANA**
  http://5300.espresso-tutorials.com

▶ Oona Flanagan: **Delta from SAP ERP Financials to SAP® S/4HANA Finance**
  http://5321.espresso-tutorials.com

Oona Flanagan
A Practical Guide to SAP® S/4HANA Financial Accounting

ISBN:	978-3-96012-140-4
Editor:	Lisa Jackson
Cover Design:	Philip Esch
Cover Photo:	© SkyLine, 94193283 – stock.adobe.com
Interior Book Design:	Johann-Christian Hanke

1st Edition 2019, Gleichen

© 2019 by Espresso Tutorials GmbH

URL: *www.espresso-tutorials.com*

Feedback
We greatly appreciate any feedback you may have concerning this book. Please send your feedback via email to: *info@espresso-tutorials.com*.

Table of Contents

Preface

This book is aimed at existing and prospective users of SAP S/4HANA who want to understand how the basic financial accounting processes work in SAP S/4HANA, according to SAP Best Practices.

Although there are many differences between the various SAP S/4HANA editions, in most cases the best practice processes, definitions, and trans-actions are fairly similar. New innovations and functionality are being re-leased faster than ever before, but at different times for each edition of SAP S/4HANA, so the biggest challenge while writing the book was to ensure that we cover the most relevant functionality. The book is based mainly on the 1709 and 1809 releases of SAP S/4HANA, using the new SAP Fiori interface, although we include some exciting new apps available only in the cloud on the assumption that they will soon be available for all editions.

There is a huge amount of information on the internet: guides, best prac-tices, blogs, product information pages, and so on. Yet, at the end of the day, it is not always straightforward to find answers in one place to questions such as: what are the different versions of SAP S/4HANA, what is the asset technical clearing account for, what is the GR/IR, why are there so many G/L accounts for one physical bank account, and so on. This book aims to bring things together, give a little bit of background on SAP S/4HANA, and answer some of these questions.

SAP provides plenty of training material and step-by-step tutorials as part of the implementation plans; this book is intended to supplement rather than replicate those resources. We concentrate on explaining the context behind each process, the typical SAP Fiori apps used, and the things to look out for. We summarize the key parts of a transaction and sometimes go into a bit more detail of the more-complicated steps and provide useful tips where we can.

The book commences with a bit of background on what SAP S/4HANA is and how it came about along with the implementation methodology. If you are more interested in how it works, you can dive straight into Chapter 2 where we introduce SAP Fiori, before going on to explain the organi-zational structure and the key financial master data. We then go into the basic financial processes followed during a typical day with examples of key transactions and finish with reporting and closing. We try to use SAP

Fiori apps to cover most of the transactions, but on occasion may use GUI transactions, where we feel it would be of benefit.

No prior experience of SAP or SAP S/4HANA is required. Managers considering an SAP S/4HANA or an SAP Fiori implementation (if already on SAP S/4HANA) may also benefit from this book, to see how existing processes will look with SAP Fiori on SAP S/4HANA and to help build their business case for SAP S/4HANA.

We have added a few icons to highlight important information. These include:

Tips

Tips highlight information that provides more details about the subject being described and/or additional background information.

Examples

Examples help illustrate a topic better by relating it to real world scenarios.

Attention

Attention notices highlight information that you should be aware of when you go through the examples in this book on your own.

Finally, a note concerning the copyright: all screenshots printed in this book are the copyright of SAP SE. All rights are reserved by SAP SE. Copyright pertains to all SAP images in this publication. For the sake of simplicity, we do not mention this specifically underneath every screenshot.

1 Introducing SAP S/4HANA and SAP S/4HANA Cloud

This chapter introduces the concept of SAP S/4HANA and how it improves on the previous SAP ERP versions. There are two main editions, SAP S/4HANA and SAP S/4HANA Cloud, with a number of differences between them, especially related to the customizing options. More and more companies want to move away from the numerous custom pieces in their existing systems and use the standard SAP Best Practices to simplify and streamline their business processes—SAP S/4HANA is specifically designed to do this, and SAP S/4HANA Cloud even more so.

1.1 SAP S/4HANA background

SAP is a German-based enterprise software company, founded in 1972 and historically well-known for its flexibility. Customers could configure the standard systems exactly how they wanted and even write their own custom pieces of code whenever the standard program didn't fit their requirements. However, this flexibility came at a price, with systems growing ever-more complex to cope with all the different permutations that customers came up with and bringing a steep learning curve for new employees.

Historically, organizations used to maintain development, quality, and productive systems as a minimum, and often additional sandboxes, testing, and training systems to better manage everything that was going on. Some even had parallel sets of systems in order to separate out projects and business-as-usual (BAU) streams. All of which came at a cost for the hardware, maintenance, and time spent keeping all the systems up-to-date.

Although the initial implementation might have been well-documented, often that documentation was not kept up-to-date, especially for enhancements and minor changes to standard. Experienced SAP consultants struggled when transactions didn't behave as standard, and regression testing, whenever there was a new release or new functionality, became a nightmare.

Financial markets demanded faster and more detailed information and as organizations got bigger, it became harder to analyze the data efficiently in the operational system. Frequently, there was so much complex data that transfers had to be made overnight to *online analytical processing (OLAP)* systems for reporting as the operational systems were *online transaction processing (OLTP)* systems and designed to facilitate data entry, not reporting.

Eventually, the price of memory dropped, so more data could be held in-memory, cache was improved, powerful multicore processors allowed parallel processing, and new database designs meant faster data retrieval. SAP was able to redesign their existing solution to take advantage of new technology, turn things around, and work towards a simpler but more efficient solution.

The first step was the new *SAP HANA database* itself, and then subsequently, SAP rewrote the finance programs to produce *Simple Finance*. Then more improvements to the rest of business suite programs followed (procurement, manufacturing, sales, and so on) to optimize the new capabilities of the database and redesign the underlying table structure, and eventually the current *SAP S/4HANA* came about.

1.1.1 SAP S/4HANA Cloud

SAP wanted to reduce complexity and have consistent best practices for as many processes as possible, allowing the organizations to become more harmonized and efficient. *SAP S/4HANA Cloud* is a *multi-tenant public cloud* solution where a single cloud system is shared, via a public network, amongst a number of organizations on a subscription basis, known as *software as a service (SaaS)*. SAP S/4HANA Cloud is sometimes known as the SAP S/4HANA public cloud or *multi-tenant edition (MTE)* and consists of two systems—a quality testing system and the live productive system— managed by SAP. (There is an initial cloud starter system, but this is for evaluation and is not kept).

Organizations using SAP S/4HANA Cloud no longer require large amounts of hardware and software, a large IT department to manage everything, and different SAP expertise to cover the different applications. Custom programs would affect other users of the public cloud and require extensive regression testing, so the approach to extensibility is different (see section 1.5), making it easier to upgrade to new releases.

With the multi-tenant cloud, releases are quarterly and mandatory, so organizations automatically have the latest updates, new functionality, and any new regulations.

New releases also bring huge increases in scope and increased automation of core processes. They are named after the year and month they are released in, for example, 1905 (May 2019) and 1908 (August 2019). And there is very little downtime during the upgrade, which is usually launched over a weekend.

When we mention SAP S/4HANA Cloud in this book we always refer to the aforementioned multi-tenant public cloud. Recently however, a new SAP S/4HANA *single tenant edition (STE),* became available, to allow customers to get the feel of the cloud model but with the flexibility of the on-premise model covered in the next section. The STE is particularly attractive where customers need more flexibility with upgrades (only two per year), and customizing, and it supports industries and countries that are not currently supported by the multi-tenant cloud.

Where customers want even more flexibility, or are in industries with specific security or privacy requirements, there is another option, officially called *SAP S/4HANA.*

1.1.2 SAP S/4HANA

Whereas SAP S/4HANA Cloud refers to the subscription-based editions with very standard processes and a single-user interface, the other option, SAP S/4HANA is different. Although it may also be physically in a cloud, the term *on-premise* was originally used to highlight the fact that it was controlled by the organization as if physically on premise and we will often use the term on-premise in this book to highlight the distinction between the two. SAP S/4HANA on-premise allows the organization to host as many sandboxes and development, quality, testing, and training systems as it wants, and where it wants. An organization can host it themselves, with a third party, or with SAP privately on the *SAP HANA Enterprise Cloud (HEC),* giving the organization complete freedom on what to implement and when.

All editions have the same code line, but the SAP S/4HANA Cloud (multi-tenant) leads with new functionality on a quarterly basis, which is then rolled up into the annual on-premise releases for SAP S/4HANA on-premise. These are also named after the year and month of their release, for example 1709 (September 2017), and 1809 (September 2018).

All options are based on best practices (which we will explain in section 1.3), but SAP S/4HANA allows a lot more leeway to configure the system differently if required and to implement custom code. The new user interface, SAP Fiori, (see Chapter 2), is mandatory for SAP S/4HANA Cloud, but optional for SAP S/4HANA.

1.1.3 Other options

Other options are a hybrid or *two-tier* setup, perhaps with smaller subsidiaries that have consistent processes on SAP S/4HANA Cloud and corporate or more complex processes on-premise, or whatever combination makes sense for the organization.

The least disruptive option if you have a number of SAP and non-SAP systems, is to use *Central Finance*. Using the *SAP landscape transformation replication server (SLT)* you can remap and repost all finance documents from the source systems to Central Finance on an SAP S/4HANA system, where you can centrally manage, for example, payments, clearing, credit and dispute management, dunning, foreign exchange revaluations, and so on.

Both SAP S/4HANA and SAP S/4HANA Cloud natively connect with other cloud offerings from SAP, such as *SAP Concur* for travel and expense management; *Ariba Network* for sourcing and procurement; *SAP Hybris* for customer sales, service, and marketing; *SAP SuccessFactors* for human capital management; *SAP Fieldglass* for the management of the contingent workforce; and *SAP Leonardo for the Internet of Things (IoT).*

1.2   SAP Activate

Historically, a move to SAP tended to be quite lengthy and expensive. After the initial project preparation, a lot of time was spent on the *business blueprint,* which was effectively the client's wish list. In the next phase, *realization*, the application experts would configure each item, often manipulating SAP with additional (chargeable) custom programs in order to fit the blueprint.

With *SAP Activate,* a combination of methodology, best practices, and guided configuration tools, it is the other way around—the organization adapts its existing processes to match standard SAP Best Practices. Implementation is quick and inexpensive, particularly for SAP S/4HANA Cloud customers, who can also test drive a starter system to understand how the standard best practices solution works and to validate that this solution will work for their organization in the *fit-to-standard* workshops. Emphasis is on self-enablement and learning tools to speed up the training process and there are a number of standard *accelerators* that the organization can benefit from such as project plans, templates, process flows, test scripts, and other tools.

An SAP Activate project should be well controlled with qualified consultants following the published guidelines. It should be much faster and cheaper than a standard implementation, as there is less initial outlay, no design stage, little additional configuration, and all the aforementioned accelerators.

1.3   SAP Best Practices

A best practice package consists of a number of scope items, which can be found in *SAP Best Practices Explorer, https://rapid.sap.com/bp/.* SAP Best Practices Explorer contains both cloud and on-premise best practices for a number of different countries. Although best practices are usually similar for the cloud and on-premise versions, there are some differences, especially in availability, so make sure to select the correct version and country. The scope items are divided into groups, for example, finance, human resources, sales, manufacturing, sourcing and procurement, and so on. There are also best practices for migration, integration, analytics, master data, and so on, as well as the actual functional topics.

SAP user ID

You will need an SAP user ID to access the tutorials and test scripts in SAP Best Practices Explorer.

Each scope item contains an overview, key process flows, process models, and test scripts, and some contain video tutorials and additional documents. The test scripts include the roles required to run those transactions. SAP Best Practices Explorer also contains detailed configuration documents for each on-premise scope item.

Scope item example

In both SAP S/4HANA and SAP S/4HANA Cloud best practices solution packages, you can select the country and drill down to the detailed item in the solution scope, for example FINANCE • FINANCIAL OPERATIONS • ACCOUNTS PAYABLE (J60). Scope item J60 describes the accounts payable business benefits and key process flows and also provides a test script and process flow diagrams. Currently, only the cloud package has tutorial videos.

We include an explanation about some of the most-common best practices scope items. We don't replicate every detail from the scope item; we concentrate on supplementing the SAP Best Practices Explorer. As scope items are an integral part of any SAP S/4HANA implementation and follow a similar logic, we reference related scope items where relevant, so you can look up further information. We also sometimes refer to sample master data scripts found in a separate section of SAP Best Practices Explorer on-premise (and also in the cloud scope item 1I5).

Best practice scope items for finance processes covered in this book are:

▶ 1GA—Accounting & financial close—group ledger IFRS

▶ 1GB—Asset accounting—group ledger IFRS

▶ 1GF—Asset under construction—group ledger IFRS

▶ 1GO—Cash journal

▶ 19M—Direct debit

▶ 2JB—SAP Fiori analytical apps for financial accounting

▶ 2QY—SAP Fiori analytical apps for asset accounting in finance

▶ BD6—Credit management

- ▶ BFA—Basic bank account management
- ▶ BFB—Basic cash operations
- ▶ BFH—Asset under construction
- ▶ J58—Accounting and financial close
- ▶ J59—Accounts receivable
- ▶ J60—Accounts payable
- ▶ J62—Asset accounting

Scope items referred to, but not covered in detail:

- ▶ 1EG—Bank integration with file interface
- ▶ 1I5—Master data catalog for SAP S/4HANA Cloud
- ▶ 1LQ—Output management
- ▶ 1J2—Advance compliance reporting
- ▶ 16R—Bank integration with SAP multi-bank connectivity
- ▶ 1N9—In-app extensibility (SAP S/4HANA Cloud)
- ▶ 1QM—Advanced credit management
- ▶ 2V8—Advanced financial closing
- ▶ 22Z—Procurement of services
- ▶ BEV—Internal order—actual (SAP S/4HANA on-premise)
- ▶ BGC—Fiori analytical apps for G/L accounting in finance
- ▶ J77—Advanced bank account management
- ▶ J78—Advanced cash operations

Other resources

Another useful resource is the *Roadmap Viewer* which contains accelerators for the implementation team. It can be found at: *https://go.support.sap.com/roadmapviewer/*. Note that you need an SAP user id to access some content.

1.4 Initial configuration and setup

With SAP S/4HANA on-premise, as standard you can convert your existing system inclusive of your configuration and transaction history (known as a *brownfield* implementation). Or, a *greenfield* implementation is possible, where you start with a blank system, and then either enable the best practices or manually configure the system how you wish. There are other options offered in between (even bluefield), by third parties. You transport changes as required, from a development system, via quality testing systems, to production. Consultants working with on-premise systems keep the same access to the configuration they had in SAP ERP, i.e., using the *IMG* (customizing menu) to access configuration.

With SAP S/4HANA Cloud (MTE), only a greenfield implementation is possible as you are using a shared system. You have access to two systems, quality and production. At the start of the project, you request a preconfigured *cloud starter system* with some master data included, to explore the best practices business processes, but you will only have this for a limited time.

Prior to requesting the quality system, you have to decide on the scope items, (some may require an additional license), and complete the organization structure and the chart of accounts mapping. The next step, once you receive the system, is to ensure the relevant scope items are activated. This updates the configuration automatically, and once this is complete, the project team will be able to make any manual adjustments if required.

In early cloud versions, there was little access to any configuration for the implementation and support teams, but the self-service configuration user interface (SSCUI), the equivalent of the on-premise IMG, has expanded considerably and continues to do so. The MANAGE YOUR SOLUTION (see Figure 1.1) app contains a section called CONFIGURE YOUR SOLUTION for the implementation and support teams, although certain changes still require *expert configuration*, which means creating a support ticket with SAP. Other changes are slowly moving into the hands of the key users in the form of specific SAP Fiori apps, for example, for house-banks, taxes, accounting clerks, and some account determinations.

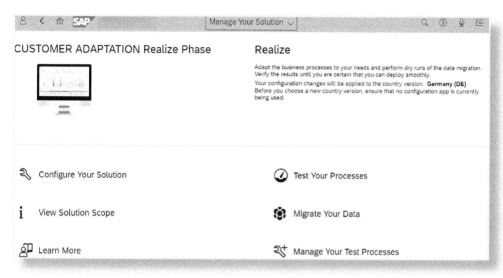

Figure 1.1: App F1241—manage your solution

1.5   Extensibility in the cloud

Extensibility means non-standard or custom changes, in other words, anything not part of the standard configuration. On-premise, it is still relatively easy for ABAP programmers to make amendments to the SAP standard programs by way of various enhancement options in the SAP GUI, or using new SAP Fiori apps such as F1481 Custom Fields and Logic or F1712 Custom Business Objects.

In SAP S/4HANA Cloud, program changes may affect other clients in the same system, but simple changes, such as adding custom fields can be made in the app itself, and other changes can be found in SAP Fiori app F2866 Extensibility Cockpit (cloud only) This is known as *in-app extensibility* (best practice scope item 1N9 In-App Extensibility for SAP S/4HANA Cloud with tutorials). For more complex changes, organizations can use the *side-by-side extensibility* from *SAP Cloud Platform* to build applications or extend existing functionality. SAP Extensibility Explorer provides more information about this at the following link: *https://extensibilityexplorer.cfapps. eu10.hana.ondemand.com/ExtensibilityExplorer/.*

2 SAP Fiori basics

This chapter introduces the new SAP *user experience* called *SAP Fiori*, with its launchpad and apps, designed to reduce complexity and make working with SAP S/4HANA easier and faster than with the traditional SAP GUI.

2.1 The SAP Fiori launchpad

Using the classic SAP GUI was not easy. Menu paths were complicated, the screen old-fashioned, and transactions only accessible on a desktop or laptop. You needed extensive training and often had to scroll through multiple screens to action a single item.

SAP has replaced the traditional menu and *graphical user interface (GUI)* with a *consumer-grade user experience* called *SAP Fiori*. SAP Fiori is web-based and consists of a dashboard or *launchpad* with a number of tiles which contain only the apps relevant to each user. The tiles are simpler, more intuitive to use than the GUI menu, more in line with apps on a Smartphone or tablet, and can be used on any device.

Apps can be transactional, analytical, or factsheets, and many of the analytical apps show key figures on the face of the tile itself. For example, apps for approving purchase orders or staff leave may contain the number of outstanding approvals on the face of the tile; bank apps may show the bank balance; and bank statement monitors may show the number of successful and unsuccessful bank statements processed. There are some examples of these smart apps shown in Figure 2.1.

In many apps, you see an overview screen showing all customers, suppliers, or other items and you can then either drill down to display or edit the details, or create new items.

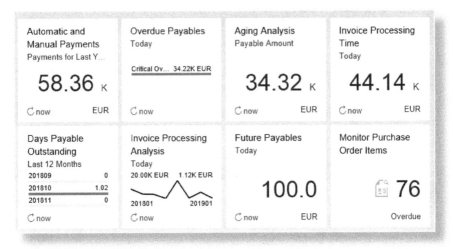

Figure 2.1: Smart SAP Fiori apps on the SAP Fiori launchpad

You can tailor the launchpad and arrange your apps into groups, or mini-dashboards, perhaps with the most-used apps at the top. In the top left of the screen (above the apps), there is a small button, 🧍, which takes you to the ME area where you can change settings, edit your home page, or sign out. If you select the APP FINDER, the apps are listed by catalog and you can also search for them by name. Click on 📌 at the bottom of an app in the app finder to create a new group or add the app to an existing group.

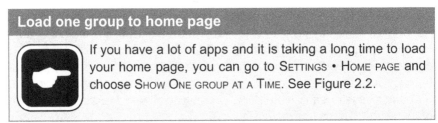

Load one group to home page

If you have a lot of apps and it is taking a long time to load your home page, you can go to SETTINGS • HOME PAGE and choose SHOW ONE GROUP AT A TIME. See Figure 2.2.

Also, under SETTINGS, you can change various settings such as the color of the screen, and set defaults, which we will explain later. EDIT HOME PAGE allows you to rearrange the tiles and create your own groups. See Figure 2.2.

If you have used an app recently, you can see it in RECENT ACTIVITIES when you click on the ME button. There is also a neat search option at the top right of the launchpad, the *enterprise search*, where you can specify where to search, as well as what to search for. For example, if you have a reference but are not sure what it refers to (e.g., a document or master data), you can search using ALL, which will return every location the reference appears. Alternatively, you can use the dropdown to restrict the search to a specific area such as apps, specific master data, documents, etc.

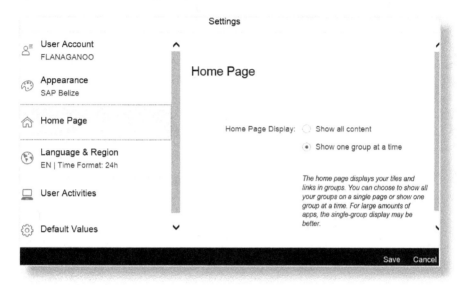

Figure 2.2: SAP Fiori settings for home page display

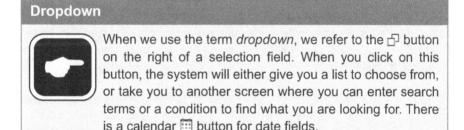

Dropdown

When we use the term *dropdown*, we refer to the ⊡ button on the right of a selection field. When you click on this button, the system will either give you a list to choose from, or take you to another screen where you can enter search terms or a condition to find what you are looking for. There is a calendar ▦ button for date fields.

In Figure 2.3, we searched ALL for the number *12345*, and the system returned journal entries with that reference, batch numbers of stock items, customers, and a number of other items to choose from. You can restrict the search to billing documents, cost centers, employees, or a number of other items in the dropdown list, and you can also restrict it to apps, and use the search function instead of the app finder, or export the results to a spreadsheet. You have a 🝖 button at the top left of the results screen, (not shown in the figure), where you can filter further.

Figure 2.3: SAP Fiori enterprise search

2.2 SAP Fiori apps

SAP Fiori apps look and feel similar to each other and are consistent across different platforms and devices. They are simple, intuitive, and role-based so that users are not faced with a number or fields or screens that are not relevant to them.

Although you can still use the traditional GUI transactions, as well as or instead of the SAP Fiori apps in SAP S/4HANA on-premise, the SAP Fiori apps are the only way for users to access the transactions in SAP S/4HANA Cloud. In some cases, the apps are based on (or similar to), the GUI transaction and the fields that need to be filled in will be similar (if not the same), although many apps are completely new or have been rewritten with additional functionality. If we describe an app as *based on* a GUI transaction, it means that we will probably use the app in associated figures, but everything applies equally whether you are using the app or the GUI transaction.

As the apps are simple and intuitive, with plenty of onscreen help and tutorials available, this book concentrates more on the process itself, explains more about the key fields, and highlights the key features of mentioned apps. Often, the figures may not be identical to what you see in your system as the functionality is changing so quickly. New functionality is usually available first in the cloud and later on-premise.

Switching on the help functionality

To see the help functionality in SAP S/4HANA Cloud, you can click the ⑦ button or F1 key, which indicates where further help is available. See Figure 2.4. In the latest versions of SAP S/4HANA Cloud, you may see a pop-up to advise you of new features and sometimes you can launch a video from the initial screen to see how to perform the transaction and follow links to related topics.

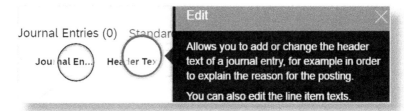

Figure 2.4: SAP Fiori help functionality

In many apps, you can create your own layout variants to see the fields most relevant to you, and you can save an app as a new tile containing the specific range of accounts, banks, or company codes that you use the most.

Not all apps are available in every release and descriptions sometimes change, so, where possible, we will precede apps with their five- or six-digit code beginning with F, which you can search for in the SAP Fiori app library, and compare with the app in your system.

Many apps allow you to jump to other apps, for example, while in the F0731 MANAGE G/L ACCOUNT MASTER DATA app you can jump directly to the F3297 DEFINE FINANCIAL STATEMENTS ITEMS app. Some of overview apps contain quite a bit of information on the first screen in the form of a number of larger cards with graphical displays. See Figure 2.5, App F2769—OVERVIEW INVENTORY MANAGEMENT.

There are many types of financial overview page apps, such as G/L, accounts payable, accounts receivable, projects, and treasury. Best practices scope item 2JB SAP FIORI ANALYTICAL APPS FOR FINANCIAL ACCOUNTING covers the accounts payable and accounts receivable overviews in detail, but the scope item is only available in SAP S/4HANA Cloud at the moment.

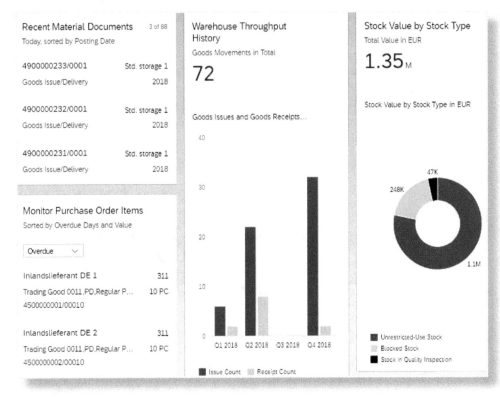

Figure 2.5: App F2769—overview inventory management

If you go into an SAP Fiori app and click ⌂, you will see an information button, which gives either the app number for some SAP Fiori apps, or other information. You can use this information to search or double-check the app number in the SAP Fiori library, if you don't find the exact name. The link to the SAP Fiori apps library, *https://fioriappslibrary.hana.ondemand. com*, allows you to find out more information about a specific app and check which apps are available for which release.

SAP Fiori app numbering

Multidimensional reporting apps have the generic Design Studios app ID F1035, in the system, but their own app number in the library. Some key performance indicator (*KPI*) apps only have a technical name instead of a number, and apps based on a GUI transaction use the GUI transaction code.

In the example illustrated in Figure 2.6, we searched for the F1579 CLEAR G/L ACCOUNT app in the SAP Fiori apps library, which returned three results. The first and third are what we will call *GUI-based apps*. They have an SAP Fiori look and GUI transactions F-03 and FB1SL underneath. The middle result is app F1579. Make sure you have selected either SAP S/4HANA or SAP S/4HANA Cloud (whichever is relevant for you). Part of the way down, you will see two tabs. PRODUCT FEATURES gives you information about the functionality of the app and occasionally a link to a video tutorial and the IMPLEMENTATION INFORMATION tab. In the IMPLEMENTATION INFORMATION tab, select the dropdown box to see if the app is available for your release. Under CONFIGURATION on the IMPLEMENTATION INFORMATION tab, there is information about which roles, groups, and catalogs apply as well as the technical information (under INSTALLATION) to set up the app.

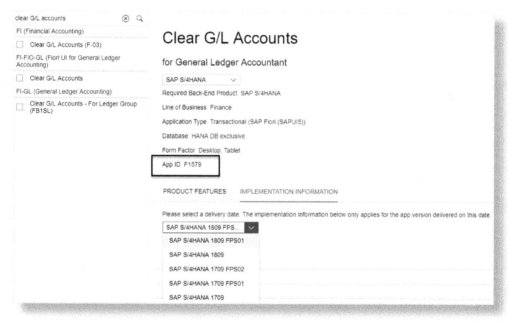

Figure 2.6: SAP Fiori app library: App F1579—clear G/L accounts

3 Organizational structure

This chapter goes through the key organizational objects used in SAP S/4HANA and explains how the other modules feed into Financial Accounting. It covers the different structures that co-exist for financial reporting, management reporting, and profitability analysis, and the concept of different ledgers, currencies, and accounting principles.

Accounting data generally serves two purposes. Audited accounts are reported to or relied on by various authorities, tax departments, shareholders, banks, and so on. This is known as *financial accounting (FI)*. *Management accounting* or *controlling (CO)* includes cost object controlling and profitability analysis. Historically, postings in SAP ERP could be made differently to financial accounting, controlling, and profitability analysis which sometimes entailed complicated reconciliations to ensure that all three were correct.

In SAP S/4HANA, these different areas have been partially merged, so that all postings now appear in a single table (ACDOCA) and there is no need to reconcile the results of the different modules at the end of each period. Some of the old tables still exist for various reasons, but nearly everything can now be found in ACDOCA.

3.1 Organizational structure

Cloud restrictions

 We have given the full definition of the various organizational objects in the next section based on on-premise capabilities, but please note that there may be some restrictions, for example, only one operating concern and one controlling area are currently available in the multi-tenant SAP S/4HANA Cloud.

3.1.1 Finance

In SAP S/4HANA, you would normally set up one *company code* for each independent legal entity. There are a number of additional organizational objects that are optional and will depend on the structure of your enterprise and the reporting requirements.

A *company* (as opposed to a company code) can represent one or more company codes and can be used for consolidation.

A *functional area* is used to report costs and revenues according to a functional area, for example, for cost of sales accounting. Common functional areas are sales, production, marketing, administration, and research and development. The functional area can be entered in the master data in objects such as the cost center, cost center category, internal order, internal order type, or G/L account. You can also create a substitution rule to derive the functional area. (A substitution rule automatically inserts or replaces the correct code according to specific rules, for example, a particular tax code or cost center when you enter a certain G/L account).

A *business area* is an operational area, or area of responsibility within an organization, but it can also be across company codes. Financial statements can be run by business area for internal purposes. The business area can be entered when posting a transaction or it can be derived from other objects, such as the cost center. Unlike functional areas, you can also run a balance sheet and profit and loss statement by business area.

If you want to assign credit limits and carry out credit control across several company codes, you use a *credit control area,* with *credit segments* for different *sales areas.*

3.1.2 Controlling and profitability

Since controlling is now partially merged with financial accounting, it is impossible not to mention some aspects of controlling, for example, where controlling fields have to be completed with cost objects as part of a financial accounting transaction. Please note that this book is primarily about financial accounting processes.

Controlling is the area in SAP S/4HANA which deals with areas such as controlling overhead costs, product costing, and profitability analysis. As controlling is used for internal or management accounting, it is not restricted by company code and instead reporting is by *controlling area*, defined as a closed unit for costs which reflect the management accounting structure of the organization.

Usually, only values from the leading ledger are posted to CO in the ledger approach and all values are posted to CO in the accounts approach, but you can choose to define a different ledger for the CO version. Each company code must be assigned to one controlling area. If you want to manage and allocate costs across several company codes with the same accounting structure and fiscal year, you can assign several company codes to the same controlling area (this may differ in the cloud). Companies within a controlling area must have the same operating chart of accounts. You set the controlling area in some apps by clicking ⌂ and choosing SET CONTROLLING, or choosing SETTINGS, and then DEFAULT VALUES.

The *operating concern* is the highest reporting level for *profitability analysis (CO-PA)* and can contain one, or more (on-premise) controlling areas. Generally, CO-PA receives postings from other areas in SAP S/4HANA and analyzes them according to different market segments, customer types, product groups, etc. Typically, CO-PA is associated with InfoCube diagrams depicting the slicing and dicing of information in different ways, something like the cube shown in Figure 3.1.

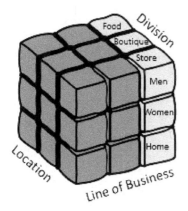

Figure 3.1: Example of an InfoCube (slice and dice approach)

CO-PA can analyze the sales or operating profit for different market and profitability segments. The market segments are defined by characteristics such as customer type and product group, and the amounts by value fields such as revenues, costs, and discounts.

3.1.3 Other

You may also come across the following non-finance organizational objects.

A *plant* is an organizational unit in logistics, but it is shared across many areas—finance, sales, production, procurement, etc.—and refers to an operating area within a company, for example a factory or production area. Some companies may set up regional offices or branches as plants for indirect purchasing. A plant has its own address and can have storage locations and shipping points assigned to it. A plant has its own material master data, and stocks, production, material requirements planning (MRP), and plant maintenance can be managed by a plant.

The *sales organization* is the selling unit and can only be attached to one company code, although one company code can be linked to several sales organizations. A sales organization can have one or more plants assigned to it and be further divided into other objects such as sales area and distribution channels.

The *purchasing organization* is based on the procurement requirement to negotiate terms and conditions with suppliers. Unlike the sales organization, the purchasing organization can be assigned to one or many company codes or not be assigned to a company code at all (as the plant is assigned to a company code and the purchasing organization can therefore be determined that way).

3.2 Ledgers and currencies

SAP S/4HANA uses only the *new general ledger* functionality, although the word *new* has since been dropped and the official terminology is *SAP S/4HANA General Ledger*, (we'll use general ledger or G/L going forward). This functionality allows you to set up additional ledgers to run in parallel for different *accounting principles,* and *document splitting* to balance accounts by profit center or segment in addition to the G/L account (see Chapter 4.1.4).

3.2.1 Ledgers

SAP S/4HANA always has a *leading ledger* to which all company codes are automatically assigned. If the enterprise only needs to report one set of books for each company code, or there are minimal differences between the two sets of books, one ledger may be sufficient. However, many multinational organizations may require more than one set of books. For example, there may be a need to report by *International Financial Reporting Standards (IFRS),* as well as local *Generally Accepted Accounting Principles (GAAP),* or their group reporting may be different to the local legal requirements and additional ledgers may be required for other purposes.

There are several approaches to maintaining several sets of books. A second *non-leading ledger* can be set up, in which case most postings will be made to both ledgers at once, with adjustments usually posted to the non-leading ledger. To run a complete set of books for each ledger, you simply select the relevant ledger. With this approach, called the *ledger approach*, you can also report for a different timeframe, for example, your group accounts may be made up to 30th June, but for local reporting you need to file accounts according to calendar year, i.e., to 31st December.

A second approach is the *accounts approach*, where only one physical ledger is posted to, but separate ranges of G/L accounts are used for the delta postings when reporting additional sets of books. Finally, an extension ledger is possible. It contains only the delta postings, but is linked to an existing full ledger and when reports are run, both ledgers are automatically included.

Most transactions automatically post to all ledgers, but some have a field where you can choose the *ledger group*. You technically post to a ledger group containing the relevant ledger rather than the ledger itself. If the ledger group field is blank, it means it will post to all ledgers anyway.

3.2.2 Currencies

Postings can be recorded in a number of different currencies. The *company code currency* (or local currency) is fixed and is the currency that the company operates in. Although this is normally the currency of the country where the company is registered, this is not always the case. If a company does most of its trading, for example, in U.S. dollars, but is based elsewhere, it may decide to keeps its books in U.S. dollars.

The *document currency* (or transaction currency) can vary, for example, if a purchase or sale is made in another currency. The enterprise may also require companies to record transactions in the *group currency* if their local currency differs from that of their head office. From SAP S/4HANA on-premise 1610 you can also define up to 8 eight additional freely defined currency types.

4 Master data

In this chapter, we look at financial master data. Master data tends to be static—you create it once and then use it for years, whereas transactional data is a one-off recording of a specific transaction such as an invoice, payment, or goods movement. You need master data in order to post transactions in the system. For example, you need customer and supplier master data to post invoices and payments, but you also need G/L accounts as well as cost and revenue objects to be able to report on and analyze the data.

4.1 General ledger master data

When a transaction is recorded in the general ledger, it can be classified in several ways. We will start with the G/L account, which is used to identify the type of expenditure or income.

4.1.1 Chart of accounts definitions

An organization can have as many G/L accounts as required in order to record and analyze the financial postings of daily activities. Each G/L account feeds into the appropriate line of a *financial statement version* (FSV) which produces the financial statements of the company, such as the balance sheet, income statement (profit and loss), and cash flow.

The chart of accounts (COA) is the overall grouping for a set of G/L accounts. A company code must be assigned an *operating chart of accounts* in order to record financial transactions, but it can also have up to two additional charts of accounts.

Some countries, by law, require accounts to be prepared according to a specific numbering convention, for example, France. If the organization resides in only one country, it uses this numbering for their operating chart of accounts. However, if the organization wants a harmonized operating chart of accounts across companies in different countries, it can assign an additional, country-specific *alternative chart of accounts* for those countries that are legally required to report according to their local chart of accounts.

Each individual account in the operating chart of accounts is then assigned to a G/L account in the alternative local chart of accounts, usually 1:1.

A *group chart of accounts* can be used for consolidation where different regions have different charts of accounts, or where only a summarized chart of accounts is required at the group level, in which case you would normally have N:1 (i.e., many operating G/L accounts to one group G/L account).

Each FSV is a different layout of a set of financial statements. Typically, you may have one version for your IFRS accounts and others for each local country's legal requirements. In the app F0763A MANAGE CHART OF ACCOUNTS, you can choose to view your different charts of accounts as a sequential list or in the format of any of the financial statement versions. Figure 4.1 shows the G/L account master data list, in an FSV format.

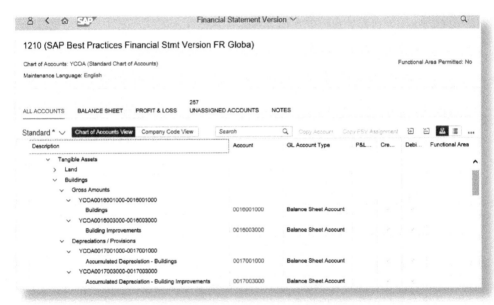

Figure 4.1: App F0763A—extract of chart of accounts in FSV format

Whether you choose the FSV layout or the sequential chart of accounts layout, you can then drill down to the individual accounts and jump to the F0731A MANAGE G/L ACCOUNT MASTER DATA app to display or maintain the detail. Further information on using and configuring the FSV is in section 10.2.2.

4.1.2   G/L account master record

Master data has its own area in SAP BEST PRACTICES EXPLORER (see Chapter 1.3). If you navigate to CREATE YOUR OWN MASTER DATA, you will see the list of master data scripts which tell you how to create the relevant sample master data using the correct app or transaction for your version of SAP S/4HANA. Figure 4.2 shows an extract from a master data list on the SAP BEST PRACTICE EXPLORER site, where you can see BNG is CREATE G/L ACCOUNT AND COST ELEMENT, for example.

Your Master Data

SAP Best Practices for SAP S/4HANA Cloud provides sample master data that can be used to test the preconfigured business processes. You can also create your own master data by following the master data scripts below.

Master Data Scripts

BND	Create Customer Master - MDS	Master data script
BNE	Create Supplier Master - MDS	Master data script
BNF	Create Product Master of type "Trading Good" - MDS	Master data script
BNR	Create Product Master of type "Raw Material" - MDS	Master data script
BNS	Create Product Master of type "Semi-Finished Good" - MDS	Master data script
BNT	Create Product Master of type "Finished Good" - MDS	Master data script
BNG	Create G/L Account and Cost Element - MDS	Master data script

Figure 4.2: Example of best practice scripts for master data

Master data is an area which can rapidly get out of sync between different systems if the maintenance is not centralized. Users may create most data only in production, particularly for on-premise setups where there may be a number of training, testing, and quality systems. Some organizations create the data manually or use *master data governance (MDG)* to coordinate master data requests and then push the completed master data out to all systems. In SAP S/4HANA Cloud, G/L account master data is created in the quality system and then moved automatically to production.

Manage G/L account master

In the app F0731A MANAGE G/L ACCOUNT MASTER DATA, you can choose a chart of accounts to review and then drill down to display or amend individual accounts. You can copy or add new accounts from the initial screen, or you can perform mass changes on existing accounts. Each G/L account master record consists of three parts. Figure 4.3 shows the global chart of accounts view, but you can also select company code view, or controlling area view.

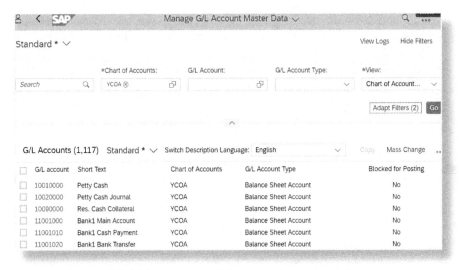

Figure 4.3: App F0731A—manage G/L account master data

The first part (COA view), contains global information relating to all organizations and must exist before you can create the other two views. You only need to extend an account into the company codes that are going to use it, although sometimes all accounts are extended to all company codes for ease of maintenance. Each account section contains its own change history. The next sections cover some of the key fields.

Chart of accounts view

The chart of accounts view contains general, global information such as descriptions and related translations, a functional area if required (see Chapter 3.1.1), G/L account type, and account group, as shown in Figure 4.4.

The *G/L account type* must be one of the following four types: BALANCE SHEET, NON-OPERATING EXPENSE OR INCOME, PRIMARY COSTS OR REVENUE, or SECONDARY COSTS. If an account is assigned a primary or secondary cost account type it will appear in controlling. You mostly post to primary costs when posting invoices, salaries, depreciation, and expenses. Secondary costs are used for value flows in controlling.

The *account group* determines what fields need to be completed when you create a new G/L account master record in the company code. It also determines the number interval for the account number, for example, only reconciliation account groups allow you to enter a reconciliation account type, and a liquid funds account group would allow you to enter relevant bank data or relevant cash flow data.

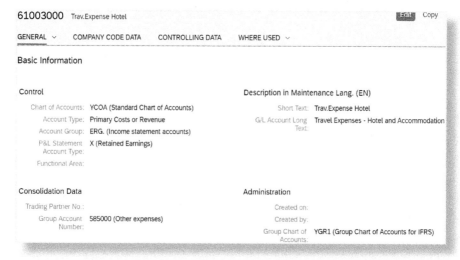

Figure 4.4: G/L account master data record, general data

Company code data

The *account currency* will nearly always be the company code currency, usually the local currency. The main exception would be cash or bank accounts held in different currencies.

The *tax category* symbols, < and >, are only used for the actual VAT account that is posted to automatically. The—only allows postings with input tax, so would be used for most expense accounts; + only allows postings with output tax accounts, so would be used for revenue accounts; and * is used for accounts where both income and expenses may be posted. The other option is to restrict a G/L account to one specific tax code, but this is rarely used as most countries have more than one tax rate that could be posted to a G/L account.

A *reconciliation account* is the umbrella account in the general ledger used for subledgers such as customers, suppliers, and fixed assets.

The *alternative account number* is used if you are using a shared operating chart of accounts and need to report according to a specific numbering convention due to local legal requirements.

Clearing specific to ledger groups is used if you have an open item account with different postings for the leading ledger and parallel ledger and you have different clearing requirements.

The *sort key* is used for clearing as well as sorting. Your GR/IR account, for example, usually has a purchase order sort key, as you would tend to group postings by purchase order when reconciling the account and clearing invoices against goods receipts.

When entering a document, there are a lot of possible entry fields, not all of which will be applicable to every account, therefore, each field can be mandatory, optional, or suppressed for a specific account. A *field status group* combines accounts with similar requirements.

The *post automatically only* indicator is necessary for accounts usually posted to automatically, but which can be supplemented with manual postings.

Figure 4.5 shows the company code and controlling area sections of a primary cost G/L account.

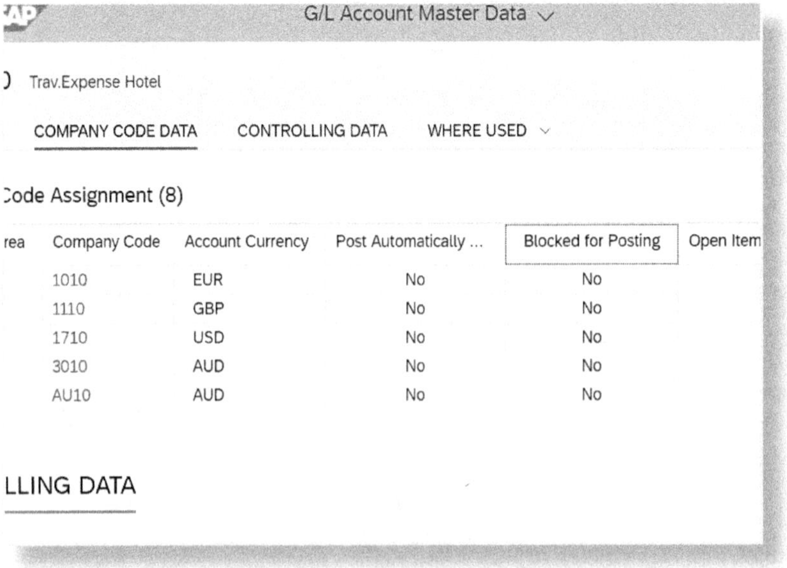

SAP   G/L Account Master Data ∨

) Trav.Expense Hotel

COMPANY CODE DATA   CONTROLLING DATA   WHERE USED ∨

Code Assignment (8)

rea	Company Code	Account Currency	Post Automatically ...	Blocked for Posting	Open Item
	1010	EUR	No	No	
	1110	GBP	No	No	
	1710	USD	No	No	
	3010	AUD	No	No	
	AU10	AUD	No	No	

LLING DATA

Figure 4.5: G/L account master—company code and controlling data

Controlling area data

This is only relevant for primary and secondary costs, not balance sheet or non-operating expenses. The available *cost element categories*, (field: CE-LEM CATEGORY), will vary depending on the account type. For primary costs and revenues, it is usually *01* or *11*, but other categories may be used for accruals, deductions, and external settlements. For secondary costs, there are different categories for internal settlements, allocations, order/project/ results analysis, and so on. The category affects whether they appear with a negative sign in CO-PA and which processes they can be used with in controlling. Figure 4.6 shows app F0731A G/L ACCOUNT MASTER DATA, with the CONTROLLING AREA VIEW selected in the filter to show the list of cost elements used.

A *cost element* used to be a separate object in controlling prior to SAP S/4HANA, but has since been merged into the G/L account master record. However, you can still create *cost element groups*, which you can use to combine similar costs together in reports and selection screens, rather than listing the individual cost element numbers.

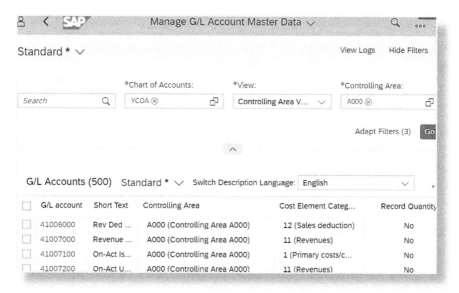

Figure 4.6: App F0731A—G/L account master data controlling data

Where used

App F0731A MANAGE G/L ACCOUNT MASTER DATA has a WHERE USED section which shows which financial statements use the account, (see Figure 4.7).

MAINTAINED IN AUTOMATIC ACCOUNT DETERMINATION APP is available since on-premise release 1809.

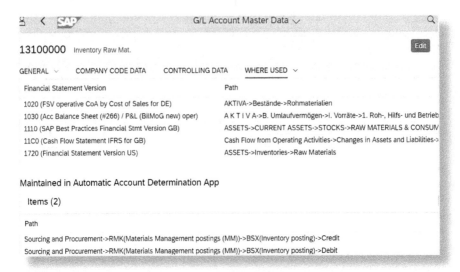

Figure 4.7: App F0731A—manage G/L account master data, where used

Manage chart of accounts

The app F0763A MANAGE CHART OF ACCOUNTS is another way of managing the G/L accounts. On the first screen, you choose the tab to display the accounts in FINANCIAL STATEMENT VERSIONS format or the tab for CHART OF ACCOUNTS. See Figure 4.8.

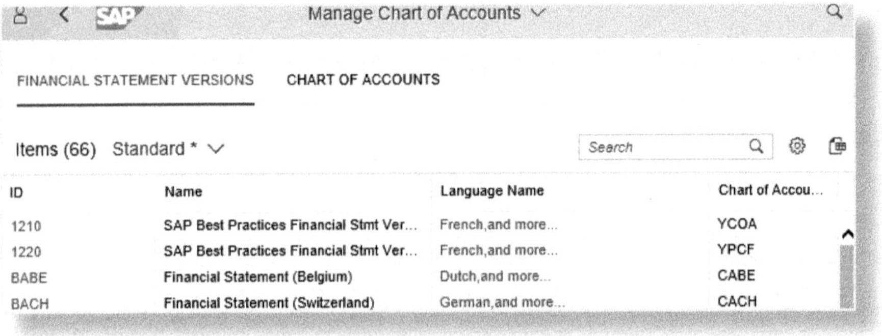

Figure 4.8: App F0763A—manage COA by financial statement versions

If you choose CHART OF ACCOUNTS and select the required chart, in the CHART OF ACCOUNTS VIEW tab you will then see a list of accounts to choose from, as in Figure 4.9.

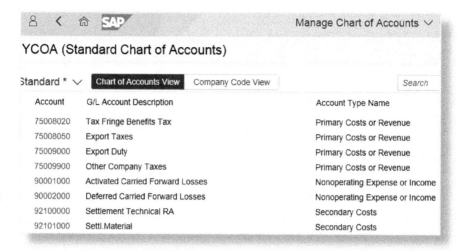

Figure 4.9: App F0763A—manage chart of accounts (COA) view, global

Clicking on the column heading gives a dropdown by which you can sort in ascending or descending order, or filter. See Figure 4.10 which shows the company codes that G/L account 75009900 has been extended into.

75009900 Other Company Taxes

GENERAL ∨   COMPANY CODE DATA   CONTROLLING DATA   WHERE USED ∨

Company Code Assignment (4)

Controlling Ar...	Company Code	Company Name	Account C...	Marked for Deletion	Open Item Manag...	Post Automatic...	Block..
A000	1010	Company Co...	EUR	No		No	No
A000	1110	Company Co...	GBP	No		No	No
A000	DE10	Company Co...	EUR	No		No	No

Figure 4.10: G/L account master data company code data view

G/L account maintenance

The SAP S/4HANA Cloud test script directs you to the same apps, but via CONFIGURE YOUR SOLUTION when creating new G/L accounts. This enables consistency in the cloud releases by creating the account in the quality system and moving it to production.

4.1.3　Cost and revenue objects

A *cost object* is the collective name for cost objects such as cost centers, internal orders, and work breakdown structure (WBS) elements, which can identify the area of responsibility for controlling costs. You can also link a transaction to a profit center assigned to a plant, region, brand, or other unit to identify how profitable that area is, or you can use internal orders and WBS elements (which are part of projects) to group costs and revenue in other ways.

If you want to post costs to a G/L account that has been set up as a primary or secondary cost account type, you have to add a cost object such as a cost center, internal order, WBS element, or CO-PA segment. Revenue accounts generally require profit centers.

You must have one true or *real posting* in controlling but you can have several additional *statistical postings*. Profit centers are always statistical. Only real costs can be reallocated, and real and statistical postings show up in different ways on certain reports.

Cost center

The related master data item for creating sample data is BNM CREATE COST CENTER AND COST CENTER GROUP. A *cost center* is an area of responsibility for costs in controlling and can be rolled up into a profit center by entering the profit center in the cost center master data. A posting to a cost center is usually a real posting, but it can be a statistical posting if there is another object that takes real postings, such as a real internal order or a WBS element in the posting. Postings on real controlling objects can be allocated to other real controlling objects, but statistical postings cannot be allocated.

You can post to a cost center by entering it during a transaction, or the cost center can be derived from the master data. For example, when running the fixed asset depreciation, the cost centers come from the asset master data. For automatic postings, such as exchange rate differences or bank charges, a default cost center must be entered in the configuration against the appropriate account (e.g., exchange rate gains or losses).

Cost centers must be assigned to a standard hierarchy, but can be assigned to other hierarchies or groups, including *flexible hierarchies,* which will be explained in section 4.1.3.

You can review, create, edit, and delete cost centers with the F1443A MA-NAGE COST CENTER app, as shown in Figure 4.11. This app also gives you information on where the cost center is used (in customizing, activity types, allocation cycles, etc.), who is responsible for it, and how long it is valid for. To see more, you can add fields by using the ⚙ button or you can click on the arrow on the right of a specific cost center to drill down into it.

Figure 4.11: App F1443A—manage cost centers overview screen

You can use the + sign to create a new cost center or drill down to display or amend an existing cost center, as shown in Figure 4.12. You can create new validity periods if you want changes to apply only going forward, for example Mr. X is responsible for postings until the end of December and then Mr. Y is responsible from January onwards.

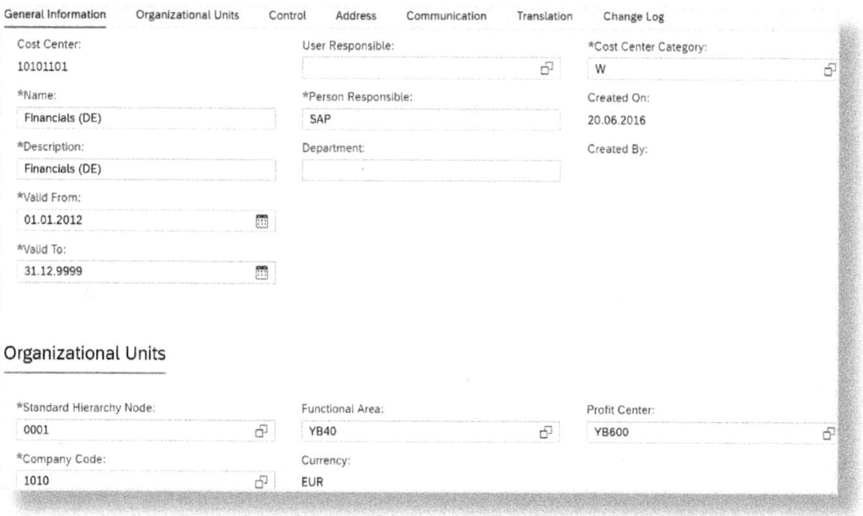

Figure 4.12: App F1443A—manage cost centers detail screen

Profit center (scope item BNH)

A profit center is an area of responsibility for profits, i.e., the balance of the costs and revenues for that area. This will vary according to how the organization is structured, but could be a geographical or organizational location such as a plant, division, or line of business; a brand, product group, or anything else that makes sense for the business. You can also arrange the profit centers in groups or hierarchies, including flexible hierarchies.

Profit centers can be manually entered in a transaction or set in the configuration, but are usually derived from another object. This can be a related cost object such as a cost center, internal order, WBS element, or a material (product) master record for revenues and stock movements. A posting to a profit center is always statistical.

The profit center overview screen for the on-premise version is shown in Figure 4.13. There is also a different app, F3516 MANAGE PROFIT CENTERS (VERSION 2), in SAP S/4HANA Cloud which has slightly more information shown in the detail screen, similar to app F1443A for cost centers.

Figure 4.13: App F1444—manage profit centers overview screen

Flexible hierarchies

Every cost and profit center must form part of a *standard hierarchy*, but organizations frequently want to rearrange the hierarchies or use different hierarchies for different purposes. The standard hierarchies are numbered and objects are manually assigned to them, but *flexible hierarchies* assign objects to the appropriate hierarchy node automatically, based on the master data fields linked to each flexible hierarchy.

Let's say that your profit center represents a division of the company and you want a report by cost center arranged by division. You can achieve this with app F2759 MANAGE FLEXIBLE HIERARCHIES, by using the master data field in the cost center that is filled with the profit center, to create your cost center flexible hierarchy. To create a new hierarchy, choose a HIERARCHY ID and DESCRIPTION in the first of the three sections of the initial screen, as shown in Figure 4.14.

Figure 4.14: App F2759—creation of flexible hierarchy structure

In the second section, choose a type, such as a cost center or profit center hierarchy (or company code in later versions). You also need a validity date (can be past, current, or future) and controlling area, and you can choose whether or not to restrict the hierarchy to a specific range of cost centers.

In the third section, create the structure by choosing from a range of fields and putting them in the order of the hierarchy using the up and down buttons. So, for example, you might choose company code first, then functional area, then cost center category, or you could have category first and functional area next, whatever makes sense for your organization. Finally, you can click on the preview button to see if you like the way it looks and click on the arrows to expand it, as shown in Figure 4.15. This is the hierarchy structure. To see the figures, you need to pull the hierarchy into a report—covered in section 10.1.2.

Figure 4.15: App F2759—preview flexible cost center hierarchy structure

Internal orders, projects, and WBS elements

Internal orders can be real or statistical. If they are real, costs are collected on an internal order for a specific purpose and then later settled to another cost object. If they are statistical, the costs are collected in parallel with the real cost object.

An internal order can be used statistically, so that in addition to recording the type of cost on a G/L account and the department responsible on a cost center, you could also record the cost by employee on a statistical internal order. Alternatively, you could set up real internal orders for events or marketing campaigns, posting to the internal order initially and then settling to a cost center at the end of the period.

Another type of real internal order is an investment order. If you are building a new factory, large plant, or machine made up of different parts, labor, architects fees, and so on, you can post the different invoices against an investment order and then settle those costs to an asset under construction

(AUC) at the end of the month. When the capital expenditure is complete, the costs are transferred from the AUC to the final asset.

Internal orders to be phased out

Internal orders (best practices scope item BEV) are still available on-premise at the time of writing, but are replaced by scope item INT—Project Financial Control in SAP S/4HANA Cloud.

Projects are similar to internal orders, but can also be used for more complex requirements, and both allow planning, budgeting, and availability control. Costs are collected on *work breakdown structure* or *WBS elements* which can be created in a hierarchical structure under the umbrella of the project, along with more complex recording and planning activities. Similar to internal orders, projects can be settled to a final destination. Unlike cost centers, both real internal orders and WBS elements have various system statuses during their lives, such as created, released, technically complete, and closed, which control what can be entered when. You can also set up user-defined statuses.

Segment

IFRS 8 and some local GAAPs require an organization to report by operating segment when an organization has different business activities. In SAP S/4HANA, a *segment* is used for this purpose. Segments are generally derived from profit centers (by entering the segment in the profit center master data).

Costs are posted to cost centers which can be linked to a profit center. If you enter a segment in the profit center master record you can see all costs and revenues by segment. In order to run accurate financial statements by segment, you need to implement document splitting, (this is the default setting in SAP S/4HANA Cloud). You can always run reports to see the profit and loss by profit center, but if you want to run a balance sheet by profit center or segment you also need to implement document splitting.

4.1.4 Document splitting

Document splitting can be implemented when there is a requirement to have financial statements at a lower granularity than the company code, such as by segment or profit center and you need to adjust some of the balance sheet postings so that the accounts balance back to zero by segment or profit center.

Document splitting

 A US$1,000 training invoice is to be split 40:60 between cost centers A and B, each linked by a different profit center to different segments. With document splitting enabled, the invoice is entered in the same way, and will show as a single amount on the supplier account, but in the background, there will be an additional finance posting, splitting the supplier amount in two, accordingly. It is this split that will appear in the financial statements and the general ledger view of the line item display report.

4.2 Material master data

Most products (and services) a company makes, buys, or sells will be set up as *material master* records which contain general data, such as the material number, description, and material type and also department-specific data where relevant. As SAP S/4HANA is a fully integrated system, the same material master record can be used in purchasing, sales, inventory, manufacturing, accounting, costing, foreign trade declarations, and other areas.

There are far too many fields to go into detail about each one, but some key fields for finance include the valuation class (which links to the account determination for goods movements), the cost, and whether the material is valued at moving average or standard price. The tax data in the sales section, combined with the tax data in the customer master, determines the type of tax that should be charged.

The material group indirectly dictates the G/L account when purchasing the material, for example, stock of finished goods, raw materials, trading goods, semi-finished goods, etc. A material may also be non-valuated, i.e., expensed when purchased rather than held on the balance sheet. It is also possible to hold spare parts for fixed assets in stock and only capitalize them when used.

There are a number of different master data scripts in SAP Best Practices Explorer (BNF, BNR, BNS, BNT) to set up trading goods, raw materials, semi-finished, and finished goods. These scripts give examples of the typical values for each material type.

Material or product master?

 Historically, the term *material* was used for the name of the master record, and this is still used in the GUI, but some newer apps use the term *product*, such as in app F1602 Manage Product Master.

From the initial screen of the app F1602 Manage Product Master Data, you can select the range of products to display, copy, or edit, or you can create new products. You can mass-process items or show them in a hierarchy structure. See Figure 4.16.

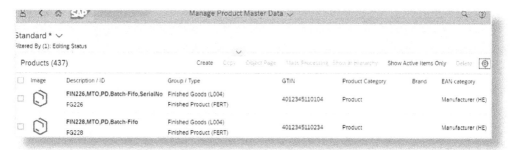

Figure 4.16: App F1602—manage product master data

If you use the app based on GUI transaction MM03, you can see a number of different views for the different departments. Figure 4.17 shows the first tab—Basic Data 1.

Figure 4.17: Transaction MM03—basic data 1 tab

In Figure 4.18, you can see some more tabs, including the accounting and costing tabs.

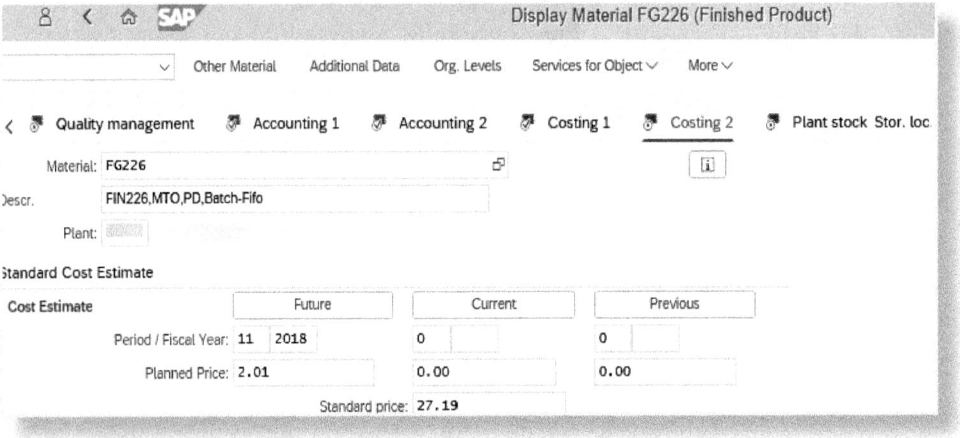

Figure 4.18: Transaction MM03—costing 2 tab

4.3 Business partners

A business partner can be a person, an organization, or a group of persons related to the company. The bulk of the business partners are likely to be suppliers and customers, but you can also have a variety of other partners such as contact persons, banks, financial services, tax offices, etc. You can use the business partner apps based on the whole business partner, or there are a number of other apps which take you to a part of the business partner, for example, the customer master, supplier master, or credit master depending on how the different tasks are assigned in your organization. You can find master data scripts BND—CREATE CUSTOMER MASTER and BNE—CREATE SUPPLIER MASTER in SAP Best Practices Explorer.

4.3.1 Business partner functionality and apps

App F3163 MANAGE BUSINESS PARTNER MASTER DATA, shown in Figure 4.19, is only available from on-premise 1809 and in SAP S/4HANA Cloud, and once you select a customer or supplier, the next screen is similar to F0850A MANAGE CUSTOMER MASTER shown in Figure 4.25, and fairly self-explanatory (once you select EDIT in the customer screen, the fields are available to add, copy, or edit).

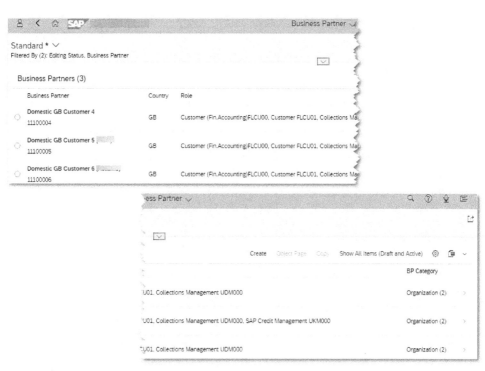

Figure 4.19: App F3163—manage business partner overview

The earlier business partner app for on-premise was based on GUI trans-action BP; it contains the same fields in a slightly different layout. In the initial screen of the GUI-based MAINTAIN BUSINESS PARTNER app (transaction BP), you can search for existing business partners by various criteria, as shown in Figure 4.20. The search term can be an abbreviation of the name, or perhaps a legacy system number, or any term that helps you find a part-ner quickly.

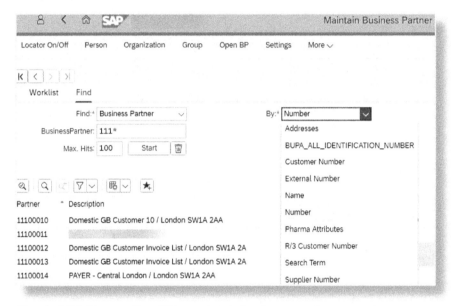

Figure 4.20: Transaction BP—maintain business partner search

When creating a customer or vendor with the MAINTAIN BUSINESS PARTNER APP, you can start with the BUSINESS PARTNER (GEN.) role, containing infor-mation applicable to all company codes such as name and address, and corporate and banking data. Then you can add the company-code-specific financial roles plus purchasing, sales, credit management, and collections management roles where applicable. Figure 4.21 shows the data found on the business partner screen. You can toggle between display and change by clicking the SWITCH BETWEEN DISPLAY AND CHANGE button, or switch to dif-ferent areas by choosing a different role and switching between tabs. You can use the SETTINGS button to set the initial screen, for example, with the search screen narrow, full screen, or hidden, and the transaction defaulting to display, change, or the last selected setting.

Figure 4.21: Transaction BP—maintain business partner general data

You can link business partners together by clicking on the relationship button and then display those relationships in a table, as shown in Figure 4.22, or in a hierarchy.

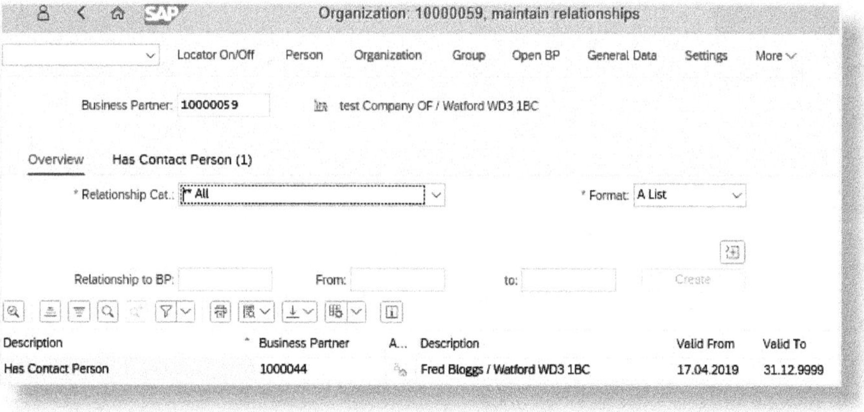

Figure 4.22: Transaction BP—maintain relationships

To review the customer information, you can use app F2640 Display Customer List, (shown in Figure 4.23), or F1861 Display Supplier List for suppliers. You can drill down to amend existing customers or edit, copy, or create new ones with F0850A Manage Customer Master Data. This contains essentially the same fields as the business partner, laid out slightly differently. F1053A Manage Supplier Master Data is the equivalent for suppliers.

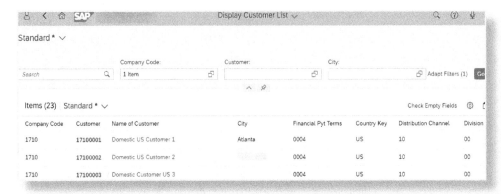

Figure 4.23: App F2640—display customer list initial screen

You can also search for customers (or suppliers with the relevant app) according to specific criteria, such as VIP or UNDESIRABLE CUSTOMER. In Figure 4.24, the criteria to find every customer with the VAT registration number is equal to blank, using the CHECK EMPTY FIELDS button.

Figure 4.24: App F2640—customers missing VAT registration numbers

In Figure 4.25, app F0850A MANAGE CUSTOMER MASTER DATA, the customer is also a supplier and has a general business partner role as well as company-code-specific financial accounting roles, purchasing- and sales-organization-specific roles, and a credit management role. He could also have collections management roles and other roles.

Figure 4.26 shows the F1053A MANAGE SUPPLIER MASTER DATA app's initial overview screen, where you can drill down to the supplier master data. Selecting a supplier and clicking OBJECT PAGE takes you to app F0354 SUPPLIER FOR PURCHASER, which is the supplier factsheet (see section 6.7.2) and has additional purchasing information, including charts for spend, contract, and off-contract spend and other transactional information as well as master data.

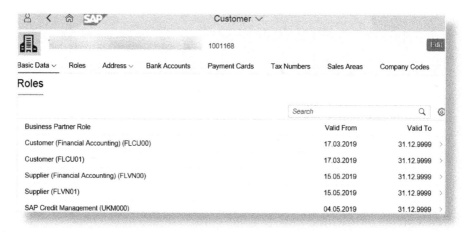

Figure 4.25: App F0850A—manage customer master data—roles section

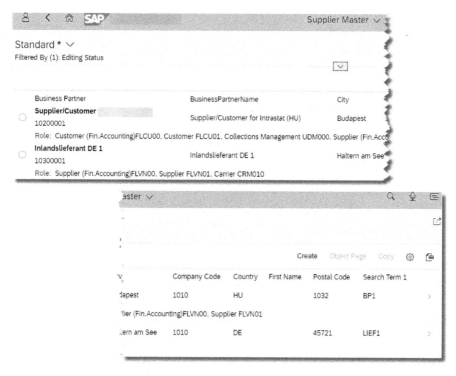

Figure 4.26: App F1053A—manage supplier master data

Figure 4.27 shows the initial overview screen of app F1861 DISPLAY SUP-
PLIER LIST.

Figure 4.27: App F1861—display supplier list

As with most SAP Fiori apps, you can export information to a Microsoft Excel spreadsheet, which, in this case, makes some of the information more manageable. The export is almost identical for customers, and you can see both customers and suppliers in one list if you select the relevant roles.

4.3.2 Customer and supplier master data fields

We will explain a little about the key fields relevant to finance, as there are too many fields to be able to cover them all in this book.

VAT registration and tax numbers

Under general data, applicable globally, you can enter a TAX CATEGORY and related numbers such as an EU VAT registration number, U.S. tax ID, UK company registration number, and so on. These numbers, apart from being legally required for the VAT register in many European countries, can also be used to identify if the customer or supplier already exists in the system. Particularly in the EU, VAT registration numbers are necessary in order for the system to identify whether VAT is chargeable on EU sales or not.

Bank information

If you are making automatic payments or collecting direct debits, you need to enter a BANK ACCOUNT NUMBER and VALIDITY date. Depending on the country, you may need to enter an IBAN (International Bank Account Number), or a SWIFT/BIC (Bank Identification Code). Rather than entering the same bank data multiple times if several business partners use the same bank, banks are created in a separate app (see section 8.1.1), and selected from a dropdown using the Bank Key field. The Bank Key can be the sort-code (UK), the BLZ or Bankleitzahl (DE and AT), SWIFT/BIC, or any other relevant identification to uniquely identify a bank. You can also have Alternate Payees, for example head offices or financing companies, and you can set up payment cards.

Company code fields

A Reconciliation Account is required for subledgers to identify where in the balance sheet you want the business partner to appear, for example, under foreign or domestic, or affiliated companies. You may use the Planning Group field for liquidity planning and forecasting. You can also set up a Dunning Procedure and a Dunning Clerk for customers and your reference number at the customer/supplier site, (Account at Customer or Account at Supplier), as well as withholding tax information.

In addition to the bank data, for each company code you will need to enter a Payment Method such as BACS, SEPA, check, bank transfer, and so on. Payment Terms, which dictate the due date and any cash discount allowed for paying early, can be at the company code level or sales/purchasing organization level.

Payment terms

Payment terms entered at sales or purchasing organization levels are used by invoices relating to sales or purchase orders, whereas terms entered at company code level are used by finance invoices without a sales or purchase order.

Purchasing fields

Key fields here are copied into the purchase order (and in some cases can be changed) and include the Order Currency, Payment Terms, Incoterms and some invoice settings, such as Goods (or service)-based invoice verification.

Sales fields

Key finance-related fields are found under Billing and include Payment Term, Incoterm, and output tax information. You cannot assign a single tax code to a customer as the final code depends on other criteria, such as the combination of country, customer type, and product type. Instead, you maintain a Tax Category (i.e., the relevant country tax) and a Tax Classification in both the customer and material, such as *0* (tax exempt) for a charity and *1* (Liable for tax) for a company, plus additional codes in the material for low or full tax rates. A separate table maps the actual tax code, based on the combination and geographical location. If between two EU countries, it will also check if a VAT registration exists before allowing an exemption from VAT under EU rules.

Partner functions

Typical customer partner functions usually set up include *Sold to Party, Bill to Party, Payer,* and *Ship to Party, Goods Supplier, Ordering Address, Invoicing Party,* and *Manufacturer* for suppliers.

5 General ledger

In this chapter, we introduce the SAP S/4HANA general ledger and explain what the Universal Journal is. We also run through some of the operational transactions relating specifically to the general ledger.

5.1 Introduction to the general ledger

The *general ledger* is the area in finance where postings, including those initiated outside of finance, are recorded in G/L accounts. Sometimes the original transaction may have its own document, perhaps with different numbering, for example, a customer sale will generate a billing document and a financial document. Similarly, purchase invoices, goods receipts, and goods issues will have both material documents and financial documents.

There may be circumstances when certain types of expenses and revenues are posted directly in finance without a sales or purchase order and there are other postings made only in the general ledger, such as accruals, provisions, and adjustments.

The related best practices scope item for SAP S/4HANA Cloud, J58 Accounting and Financial Close, contains over 60 video tutorials covering these different processes step by step. If you have activated additional ledgers, there is also scope item 1GA Accounting and Financial Close—Group Ledger, plus country-specific ones such as 2VA Accounting and Financial Close—Group Ledger US GAAP.

5.1.1 Universal Journal

The changes brought in by SAP S/4HANA allowed SAP to replace many of the historical tables with one single table in finance and to introduce the concept of the *Universal Journal*. The Universal Journal is a powerful financial document, which allows the finance department to run financial reports by many different dimensions in addition to the standard finance objects. For example, you could run the trial balance and other financial reports by asset or material, or using cost or profit centers or their hierarchies.

Journal or document

 Best Practices and GUI transactions still use the term **document** and SAP Fiori apps often use the term **journal**. The terms are almost interchangeable where there is a financial posting, but non-finance documents, such as material documents, are generally documents rather than journals.

5.1.2   Document structure and dates

Each document (or Universal Journal) in SAP S/4HANA has a *header* and *line items*. See Figure 5.1. Fields in the header, such as document type, user, dates, and currencies will apply to the whole document, whereas data such as G/L account, cost object, or debit/credit indicator will be relevant only to a specific line item.

Document Header

Dates	Currency	Document (Journal Entry) Type
Reference (Invoice Number)	Company Code	Ledger Group
Document Header text	Fiscal Period/Year	Document Number (assigned automatically)

Document Line Items

G/L Account Number	Item Number
Debit/Credit Indicator	Posting Key
Tax Information	Company Code (for Cross-Company)
Cost Object (Cost/Profit Centre/WBS Element)	Asset Information
Assignment	Line Item Text

Figure 5.1: Document layout

Each document has a two-digit *document type* to indicate its purpose (sometimes called *journal entry type* in SAP Fiori). Sales invoices, sales credit notes, purchase invoices, purchase credit notes, accrual journals, and asset postings each have a different document type. The document type appears in the document header and dictates, for example, the document number range, intercompany settings, which account types it can be used with, and the document type to be used if the document is reversed. Most transactions have a default document type, for example, the default document type for most general journal entry transactions is SA.

A document can have several different dates. The system will assign an ENTRY DATE, but you have to enter the JOURNAL ENTRY DATE, (or DOCUMENT DATE where GUI-related), and also a POSTING DATE. The JOURNAL/DOCUMENT DATE is usually related to when the transaction occurred. The POSTING DATE dictates which period the transaction will be recorded. If, for example, you physically enter a journal at the beginning of April, but want it to appear in the March reports, you enter a POSTING DATE such as March 31, assuming you have calendar periods, or if not, the equivalent period end date for the March period.

The *posting key* is a 2-digit code indicating the type of posting as well as whether it is a debit or credit, for example, *31* is used for a supplier invoice and *25* for a supplier payment. In most cases, the posting keys are assigned automatically, but it is still useful to be familiar with them as they may be used for reporting, especially if you are using the GUI transactions and they are still currently required for some transactions, such as certain fixed assets acquisitions and disposals. Figure 5.2 shows some of the finance keys you might use with accounts receivable, accounts payable, and asset accounting, but others exist for stock movements and price differences, for example.

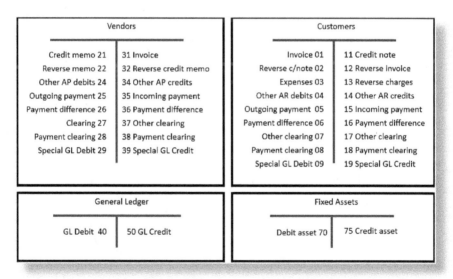

Vendors	
Credit memo 21	31 Invoice
Reverse memo 22	32 Reverse credit memo
Other AP debits 24	34 Other AP credits
Outgoing payment 25	35 Incoming payment
Payment difference 26	36 Payment difference
Clearing 27	37 Other clearing
Payment clearing 28	38 Payment clearing
Special GL Debit 29	39 Special GL Credit

Customers	
Invoice 01	11 Credit note
Reverse c/note 02	12 Reverse invoice
Expenses 03	13 Reverse charges
Other AR debits 04	14 Other AR credits
Outgoing payment 05	15 Incoming payment
Payment difference 06	16 Payment difference
Other clearing 07	17 Other clearing
Payment clearing 08	18 Payment clearing
Special GL Debit 09	19 Special GL Credit

General Ledger	
GL Debit 40	50 GL Credit

Fixed Assets	
Debit asset 70	75 Credit asset

Figure 5.2: Finance posting keys

5.1.3 Exchange rates

Exchange rates are maintained at the client level—in other words, one rate applies to all company codes, but you can set up different exchange rate types. SAP Best Practices uses Exchange Rate Type = M as the standard for most day-to-day transactions and P for planning, but you may create new exchange rate types as required.

Exchange rates have a validity start date which ends when the next exchange rate is entered. The exchange rate is selected based on the posting date of the document, but can be manually amended if necessary.

The key points to take care of include:

▶ Ensure that you use the correct direct/indirect quotation.

▶ Check that you have the correct exchange rate ratio in SAP to match your bank or exchange rate source. Avoid entering or changing exchange rates historically

---

Example of direct and indirect quotations

 Direct quotation means quoting one unit of foreign currency in terms of the local currency, so if your local currency is U.S. dollars, then a direct quotation for the euro means €1 = US$1.10 and an indirect quotation would be US$1 = €1.14.

Some organizations download the daily exchange rates via an interface, but others still upload the rates manually. While there are manual transactions in the GUI to do this and also a worklist you can set up, there is an SAP Fiori app which allows you to import a Microsoft Excel spreadsheet with the current exchange rates.

You simply click on Download Template at the bottom right of app F2092 Import Foreign Exchange Rates, (see Figure 5.3), choose whether to use comma-separated or semi-colon format, and then fill the resulting Microsoft Excel spreadsheet with the relevant exchange rates. Finally, click on Browse to find and upload the completed Microsoft Excel template. Any errors will be shown immediately; otherwise the rates will be uploaded.

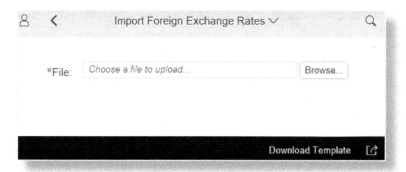

Figure 5.3: App F2092—import foreign exchange rates app

App F3616 CURRENCY EXCHANGE RATES gives you an overview of the existing rates and allows you to add, copy, delete, or export the rates and change the layout of the columns. In Figure 5.4 we clicked on + and the side panel on the right appeared for us to complete the details and show the rate trend. Clicking on CURRENCY CONVERTER in the later versions allows you to check a specific amount of a currency pair on a specific date.

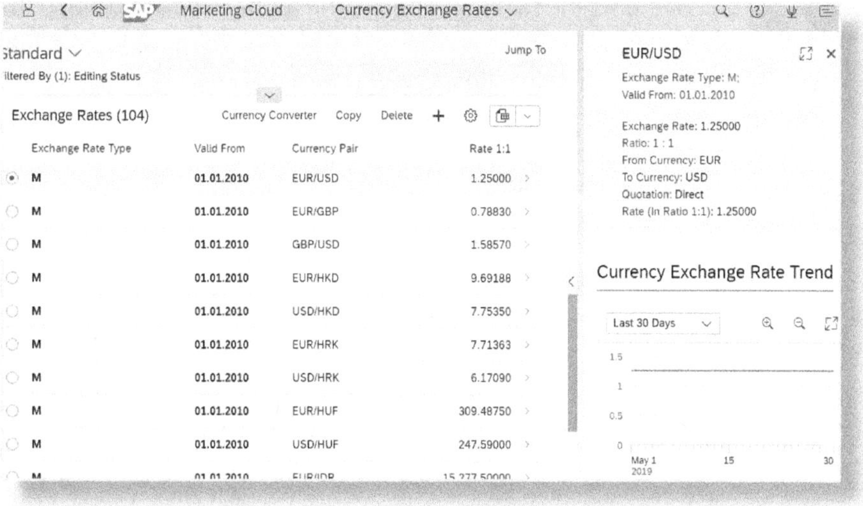

Figure 5.4: App F3616—currency exchange rates

You can still enter and view exchange rates manually in the GUI or app based on GUI transaction OB08, as shown in Figure 5.5.

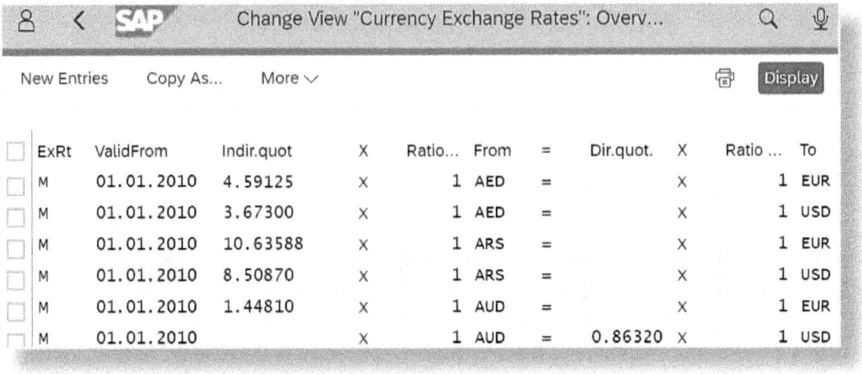

Figure 5.5: Transaction OB08—foreign currency exchange rate

5.1.4 User settings

App F2130 EDIT OPTIONS FOR JOURNAL ENTRIES—MY SETTINGS allows you to set some defaults prior to entering journals; for example, if you do not have an accounting year based on calendar periods, it can be useful to display the period number when entering a journal to check that the posting date you have chosen is in the correct period, see Figure 5.6.

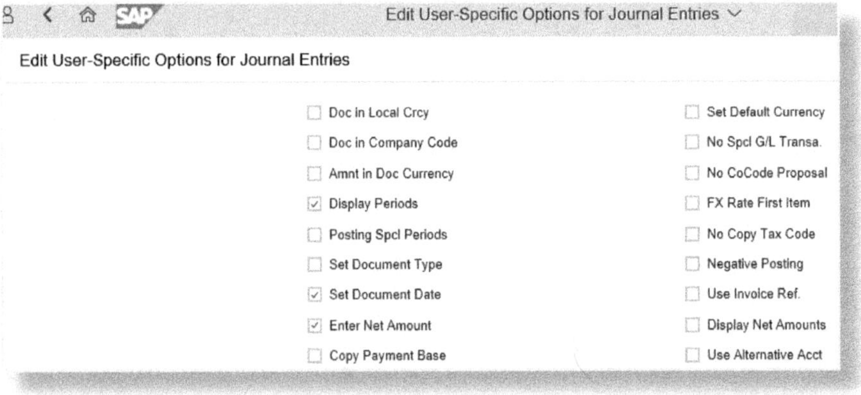

Figure 5.6: App F2130—edit options for journal entries—my settings

You can set more defaults if you go to your user settings (under the ME button) and then select default values. This is useful to save you manually entering, for example, the same controlling area or cost center each time. Figure 5.7 shows the first section, which are the default values for CON-TROLLING.

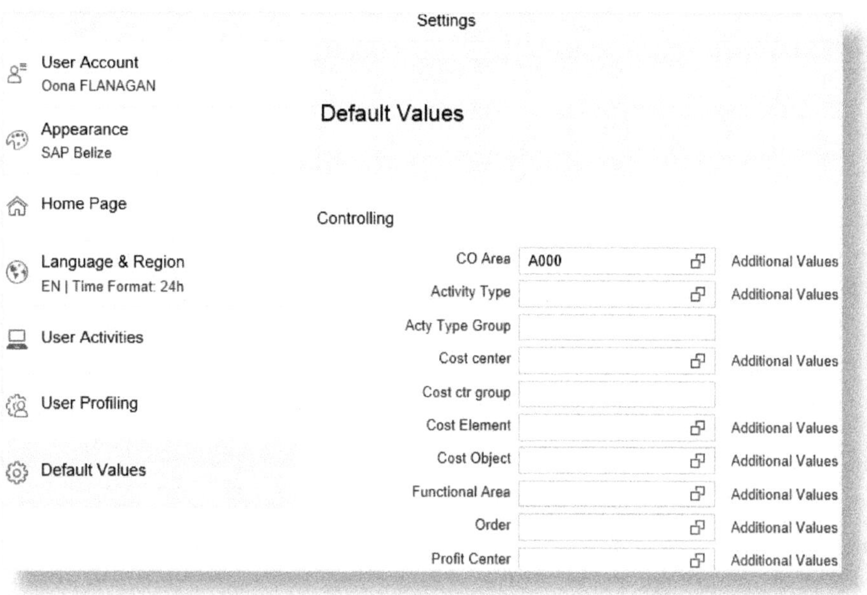

Figure 5.7: User default settings for SAP Fiori—default values

If you scroll further down, you will see FINANCIAL ACCOUNTING defaults such as company code, ledger, journal entry type, and many more. Below that, you have the FINANCIAL SUPPLY CHAIN MANAGEMENT defaults, including the banks as well as the credit segments. Then LOGISTICS EXECUTION, MATERIALS MANAGEMENT, and finally SALES AND BILLING. In the same area, you can see other settings such as appearance, display color, and so on.

5.2 General journals

5.2.1 Journal entry apps

There are a number of different apps that you can use to create and display a journal depending on the process that your company has decided on. You may enter and post a journal directly, or submit a journal for somebody else to verify. You can hold or park a journal and return to it later or upload one or more journals at one time from a Microsoft Excel spreadsheet. You can reverse a journal entry.

The apps listed below are covered in this section. Chapter 10, (reporting) also covers some journal reports.

- ▶ F0717 MANAGE JOURNAL ENTRIES

- ▶ F0718 POST GENERAL JOURNAL ENTRIES

- ▶ F2548 UPLOAD GENERAL JOURNAL ENTRIES

- ▶ F3664 DISPLAY JOURNAL ENTRIES IN T-ACCOUNT VIEW (SAP S/4HANA CLOUD ONLY)

5.2.2   Manage journal entries

App F0717 MANAGE JOURNAL ENTRIES is a good app to review existing journals according to various selection criteria or filters and to see any related documents. ⚙ allows you to add additional columns, which you can drag and drop in whichever order you want, sort the columns, or export to a spreadsheet. See Figure 5.8.

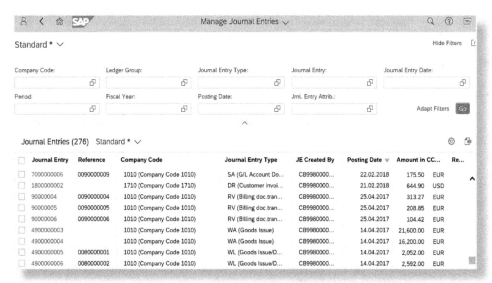

Figure 5.8: App F0717—manage journal entries initial overview screen

You can view the journal by clicking on the journal number, and in the pop-up screen, selecting the journal number or MANAGE JOURNAL ENTRIES. Or, you can jump to other apps, such as DISPLAY JOURNAL ENTRIES or JOURNAL ENTRY ANALYZER.

More links

 Usually where you see a figure in blue in an app, for example, a document number, you can click on it and choose an option in the pop-up to jump to. If you select the MORE LINKS button, you will see additional options and you can add or remove buttons from the original pop-up depending on what you use most frequently. Figure 5.9 demonstrates this with the first pop-up screen showing three apps, including the MANAGE JOURNAL ENTRY app, which takes you to the detail of the journal number.

Journal Entri 90000038

Journal Ent	Manage Journal Entry
90000038	
90000039	Display Journal Entries
90000040	Journal Entry Analyzer
90000035	More Links

Figure 5.9: App F0717—manage journal entry app with link to other apps

Displaying any journal document in F0717 MANAGE JOURNAL ENTRIES allows you to see (and drill down to) all related items in the RELATED DOCUMENTS tab, for example, goods issues or receipts, purchase or sales order, controlling documents, material documents, reversals, and so on. See Figure 5.10.

Journal Entry (90000038) - Entry View ⊙

	0	0	7	
HEADER	ATTACHMENTS	NOTES	RELATED DOCUMENTS	

Document	Object Type	Company Code	Fiscal Year	Logical system	Journal Entry Type	Ref. Docum
0090000068	CustIndivBillingDoc					
A000 A00000KW00	Controlling Document					
0080000058	Outbound Delivery					
0000000107	Sales Order					
4900000386 2019	Material Document					
4900000144	Accounting document		2019		Goods Issue/Delivery	Material doc
A000 A00000KV00	Controlling Document					

Figure 5.10: App F0717—related documents to a logistics invoice

5.2.3 Creating a general journal entry

Regardless of which app you use to enter a journal, you will need to fill in certain fields. After entering the transaction date and the posting date, the period should default in automatically. If you want to use one of the year-end adjustment periods, you will need to enter a posting date from the last period of the fiscal year in order to enter the adjustment period number.

If you only work with one company code, your user ID may automatically default in the COMPANY CODE, otherwise you will need to enter a company code as well as the CURRENCY that you want to use. (You can set this in the ME area under SETTINGS • DEFAULT VALUES). The EXCHANGE RATE will normally default in based on the posting date, but can be overridden.

If you leave the LEDGER GROUP field blank, the journal will be posted automatically to all ledgers if you have more than one, otherwise if you want to make an adjustment that is only relevant to a specific ledger you will need to enter the relevant ledger group.

If you want to enter a description, you can enter it in the document HEADER TEXT or the line ITEM TEXT, depending on whether it applies to the whole document or not. There is also a slightly shorter REFERENCE field in the header, which is mandatory for certain document types that need a specific numeric or alphanumeric reference, such as an invoice or document number.

For each line item, you will need to specify a G/L ACCOUNT and a DEBIT or CREDIT amount. Usually, tax is only posted when posting an invoice or credit note, so if you are making an adjustment between two G/L accounts, you would probably not include tax, but you may nevertheless need to enter a zero or exempt TAX CODE if tax codes are mandatory for that account.

Each line item may have different mandatory fields, for example, if you are posting to a primary cost account, you will need to add a cost object such as a COST CENTER, internal ORDER, or WBS ELEMENT.

Once a document has been posted, only certain fields can be changed. These are usually text fields, such as the line item text, document header text, payment terms, or method, but never dates or items that could already be included in reporting, such as a G/L account, tax code, supplier account, or cost objects. If such fields are incorrect, you either have to reverse the journal and repost it correctly, or if the amount is incorrect, you could post the difference as an adjustment.

Screen variant

At the top left of the journal entry screen, you can choose a different Screen Variant, depending on which fields you fill in the most.

5.2.4 Post general journal entries

Figure 5.11 shows the key fields in the Post General Journal Entries app F0718, as discussed in section 5.2.3. The line items can be expanded to show more fields. When complete, you have the option to Simulate, Hold Journal Entry, Post, or Submit the journal. (Submit goes to someone else to verify). Simulate will add any automatically created lines, for example, where the tax is calculated automatically, and will check for missing or incorrectly filled fields.

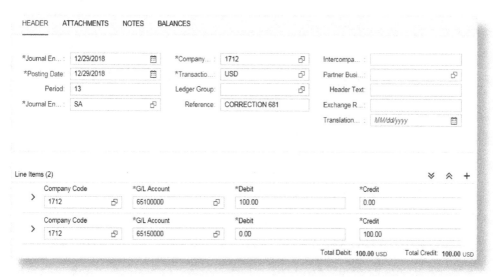

Figure 5.11: App F0718—entry screen for post general journal entry

The total debits and credits must balance in order to post the document, but you can put it on hold if it is incomplete, or if you are unsure of something, and then retrieve it later. To retrieve it, you click on the Hold Journal Entry button and select *View*. A pop-up will appear with the held journals and you can select, delete, or open the held journal and continue working on it. You can add notes or an attachment, and there is a link to app F2548 UPLOAD JOURNAL.

Message types

 SAP Fiori apps, like the GUI, have three message types. A red circle ①, identifies a blocking error message and means you cannot continue until the error has been corrected. A yellow or amber triangle ⚠ is a warning message that you must read and understand, but you are able to complete what you are doing. A green tick ☑ is information, for example, the number of the document you posted. You can view further details of the error by clicking on VIEW DETAILS, which is usually next to the message, as shown in Figure 5.12.

Figure 5.12: Example of an information message

App F3803 MANAGE JOURNAL ENTRY TEMPLATES is new in the Cloud release and allows you to create a journal template. You can prefill some of the values (e.g., G/L accounts and cost objects) if you post a similar journal each month. When creating a journal, at the bottom of the initial screen, there is a SELECT TEMPLATES button which will then prefill the screen with the data from the template.

5.2.5 Upload general journal entries

Journals can be uploaded individually or several together, but currently you can only upload postings to G/L accounts and not to supplier, customer, or asset accounts, (although there is now a new, similar app F3041 IMPORT SUPPLIER INVOICES). You can review the journal before posting it, or you can submit it to be verified by somebody else.

When you use the F2548 UPLOAD GENERAL JOURNAL ENTRIES app for the first time, you will need to click on the DOWNLOAD TEMPLATE button to download a Microsoft Excel template (see Figure 5.13) which you can then fill with the relevant details.

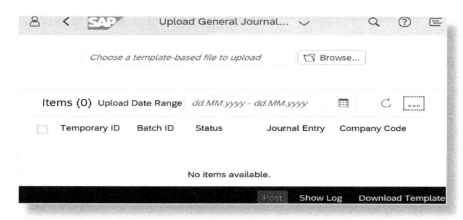

Figure 5.13: App F2548—download journal entry template screen

The fields will be the same as those in the journal entry program. You can choose to use CSV (comma-separated values) format, but Microsoft Excel is more user-friendly. If you are uploading more than one journal, you will need to add a blank row and a separate header with a unique number before each journal. Figure 5.14 shows part of a completed Microsoft Excel template.

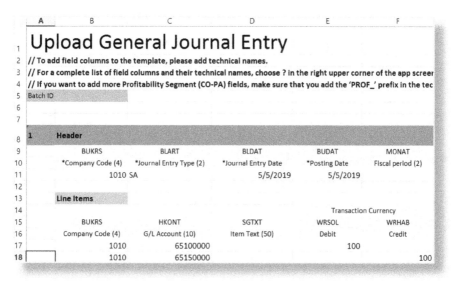

Figure 5.14: App F2548—Microsoft Excel journal upload template extract

When you have completed and saved the spreadsheet journal, you go back to the app and select BROWSE to find the file and upload it. You will then see the relevant message with the option to select SHOW LOG to view further details. Figure 5.15 shows a red ⓘ blocking error.

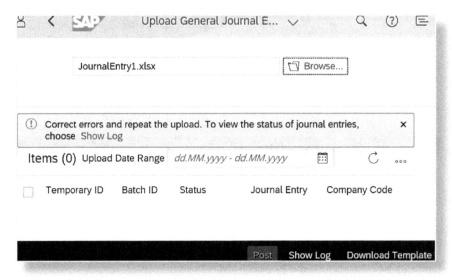

Figure 5.15: App F2548—journal entry upload format error

SHOW LOG will take you to the application logs where you can select the error and drill down to the detail. You can see that in the example in Figure 5.16, a date in cell D11 was entered in the incorrect format, so the journal could not be uploaded.

Log Details Standard ∨			Search		
Severity	Description				Time Stamp
ⓘ Error	Please follow the date format (line 11, column D).				29.05.2019, 20:56

Figure 5.16: App F2548—journal entry upload error log showing date error

In Figure 5.17, you see the upload of the journal was successful because the format of the spreadsheet was correct, but there is still a ⚠ warning error when the system tries to validate the values. The journal was saved without posting and a temporary number was created. The error in this case (when we clicked on SHOW LOG) was only a warning that the journal date was a valid format, but the date referred to a different year than the posting date. At this point, we can open the journal to review it or edit the line items, but we cannot correct the date, so we would have to correct the spreadsheet and re-upload it. Had the error been an incorrect tax code or G/L account, we could have corrected it online and posted it, or updated the spreadsheet to keep the source in line with the final posting (and in this case used it as a template for a future journal).

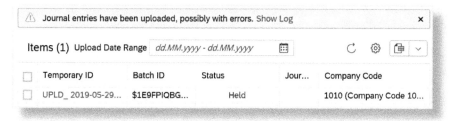

Figure 5.17: App F2548—journal entry upload validation error

When the journal upload is successful, a green ☑ success message appears (see Figure 5.18), but still with the TEMPORARY ID. We can now review the journal by drilling down into it and then posting it, or we can directly select it and click the POST button.

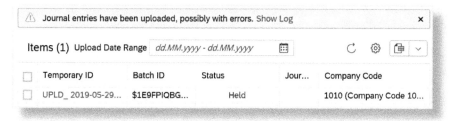

Figure 5.18: App F2548—successful journal upload awaiting posting

Once the entry is posted, the TEMPORARY ID is replaced with the final JOURNAL ENTRY number, see Figure 5.19, which you can drill down on if you wish to double-check the journal.

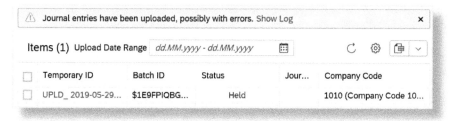

Figure 5.19: App F2548—journal upload successfully posted

If you go back into the upload journal app and enter a date range, you will see previously uploaded journals and their statuses. In the later cloud versions, if you drill down into a journal entry, you will see a new T-ACCOUNT VIEW button.

5.2.6   Journal entry T-account view

This is a new app currently only in SAP S/4HANA Cloud, which displays one or more journal entries in the accounting *T-account format*. See an example of a simple provision posted between a balance sheet account and a P&L account in Figure 5.20. The app is F3664 DISPLAY JOURNAL ENTRIES IN T-ACCOUNT VIEW.

Figure 5.20: App F3664—journal entry between balance sheet and profit and loss

There are a number of different fields that you can add to the display, see Figure 5.21. If you have a number of journals, you can color-code them to make it easier to follow complicated trails. In later cloud releases, there is a button called T-ACCOUNT VIEW, in app F0717 MANAGE JOURNAL ENTRIES, so you can directly jump to view a journal in T-account format. A related app, currently only in the cloud is F3665, DISPLAY DOCUMENT FLOW which links related documents together.

T-account

A T-ACCOUNT, used by accountants, is shaped like a T, with debit postings on the left and credit postings on the right and is very useful when following the debits and credits of a transaction flow.

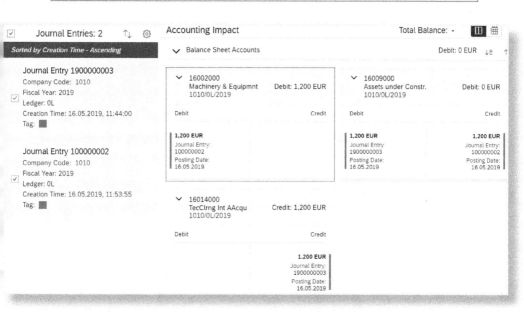

Figure 5.21: App F3664—two journals in T-account format

5.3 Clearing, resetting, and reversing

5.3.1 Clearing

Clearing means matching a debit with a credit. This allows you to see only the unmatched or *open* items when you are working on an account.

Each time you perform matching or clearing, a clearing document is created. Additional lines may be added to the clearing document if there is a foreign exchange difference, discount, rounding, or other write-off which creates a financial posting. Even if the original documents are posted in the local currency, you may still see a foreign exchange difference posting of zero if there is a difference in the group currency.

Only G/L accounts set as *open-item management* can be cleared. It can be tricky to switch open-item management on and off once postings have been made to the account, so it is important to ensure that you have the correct setting in the master data before you post anything.

Examples of G/L accounts that need regular clearing and reconciling are the goods received versus invoices received (GR/IR) account, the bank control accounts, manual accruals, provisions, and payroll control accounts. Clearing can be done automatically if you are able to set specific criteria to use for clearing.

Ledger-specific clearing

 If you have more than one ledger, for example, local GAAP and IFRS, and you want to clear a transaction such as a manual accrual or provision in one ledger, you need to select the relevant account group in the G/L account master data so that the field CLEARING SPECIFIC TO LEDGER GROUPS is active and can be selected in the company code section of the chart of accounts.

Manual clearing

For G/L accounts, you can use app F1579 CLEAR G/L ACCOUNTS MANUAL CLEARING. The first screen will show all the open item accounts with postings for you to select the relevant accounts. At the top left of the screen, you can select WITH LEDGER GROUPS or WITHOUT LEDGER GROUPS, see Figure 5.22.

Company Code	G/L Account	Number of Open It...	Open Debit Amount	Open Credit Amount	Balance	
1010	11001010	2	0.00 EUR	2,040.00 EUR	-2,040.00 EUR	>
1010	11001020	1	200.00 EUR	0.00 EUR	200.00 EUR	>
1010	24090000	1	0.00 EUR	500.00 EUR	-500.00 EUR	>

Figure 5.22: App F1579—selection of G/L accounts for clearing

You can select an account by clicking on the arrow on the right of the line for that account. At the top left of the next screen, you can choose which clearing currency to display. The top part of the screen contains the header data, such as dates, journal entry type, and any text that you want to enter. At the bottom left are the available items which you can select by clicking CLEAR to move them to the right of the screen, which shows the list of what has been allocated. You can partially allocate something by changing the amount in the ALLOCATED AMOUNT field. You can also click SELECT MORE and pull in additional accounts from the same company or from another company, if you want to make a cross-company code allocation. Everywhere you see the ⚙ button, you can add more columns to the layout. See Figure 5.23.

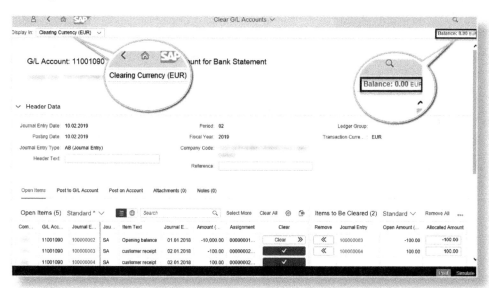

Figure 5.23: App F1579—clearing a G/L account

When you are happy with your selection and the total of allocated items comes back to zero, you can SIMULATE or POST directly, using the buttons at the bottom right of the screen.

Automatic clearing

Typically, the ASSIGNMENT FIELD and AMOUNT are used for clearing. You should ensure that the assignment field is filled with the relevant data by entering the correct sort key in the related G/L account master data.

Sort key

 The SORT KEY, found in the G/L account master data, as well as customer and supplier master data, contains a dropdown of options for the default sort key in line item reports. The selected item is also repeated in the assignment field used for automatic clearing.

Typically, the GR/IR account would have *014 (Purchase Order)* as the SORT KEY, so that the purchase order information is copied to the assignment field. This allows the automatic clearing program to match the invoices and goods receipts relating to the same purchase order.

There are a number of similar apps, CLEAR OPEN ITEMS AUTOMATICALLY (based on GUI transaction F.13), CLEAR OPEN ITEMS AUTOMATICALLY—FOR LEDGER GROUP (F.13L), and CLEAR OPEN ITEMS—AUTOMATIC CLEARING (F.13E), which behave in a similar way and can be used to clear G/L accounts, customer accounts, or supplier accounts. You can enter a tolerance to write off small rounding amounts. You can also run the clearing in test mode. Figure 5.24 gives examples of two documents that can be automatically cleared. Selecting GR/IR ACCOUNT SPECIAL PROGRESS is only necessary for complicated clearing, if you are using delivery schedules, for example.

```
Company Code      1010
Account Type      S
Account number    21120000
G/L Account       21120000


Doc. No.   Itm Clearing   Clrng doc. SG Crcy  Amount              Assignment

4800000000 001 11.04.2019             EUR                10.00- 450000000300010
5000000001 002 11.04.2019             EUR                40.00- 450000000300010
5100000001 002 11.04.2019             EUR                50.00  450000000300010
∗              11.04.2019             EUR                 0.00  450000000300010

5100000003 002 11.04.2019             EUR                20.53- 450000000500010
5000000002 002 11.04.2019             EUR               102.64- 450000000500010
5100000002 002 11.04.2019             EUR               123.17  450000000500010
∗              11.04.2019             EUR                 0.00  450000000500010
```

Figure 5.24: Transaction F.13E—clear open items, automatic clearing

82

Documents that cannot be cleared

After clearing items that can be matched, you can then select DOCUMENTS THAT CANNOT BE CLRD, to quickly see which items are still outstanding (and by how much) to investigate further.

5.3.2 Resetting

Reversing and resetting are linked because if you wish to reverse a document, say you have matched an invoice with the wrong credit or payment, you also have to undo or reset any clearing. Even if you only want to reset a clearing item, it may nevertheless be necessary to post a reversing entry if the original clearing included, for example, a foreign exchange difference, rounding, or any other posting.

The new app is F2223 RESET CLEARED ITEMS. The initial screen is an overview where you can search for items to reset. See Figure 5.25. The old app was based on GUI transaction FBRA and you needed to know the clearing document number in advance, whereas in the new app you can see all, or a range of, cleared items on the first screen.

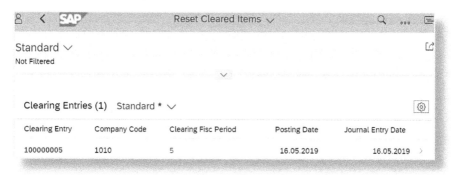

Figure 5.25: App F2223 reset cleared items—initial screen

Once you select an item to reset, you can review it to ensure that you have the correct item. Then choose RESET or RESET AND REVERSE using the buttons (bottom right), as shown in Figure 5.26.

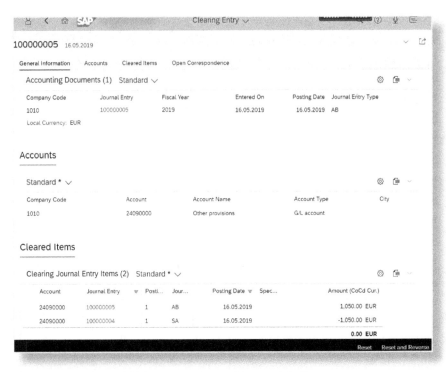

Figure 5.26: App F2223—reset cleared items detail screen

5.3.3 Reversals

You can reverse journals in app F0717 MANAGE JOURNAL ENTRIES.

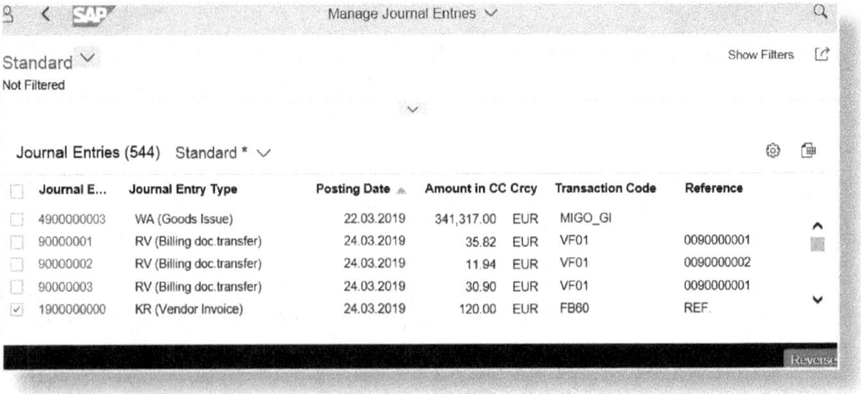

Figure 5.27: App F0717—manage journal entries, reverse journals

You can reverse one or more journals from the overview screen, as shown in Figure 5.27, or you can drill down into a journal to check it individually before reversing. See Figure 5.28.

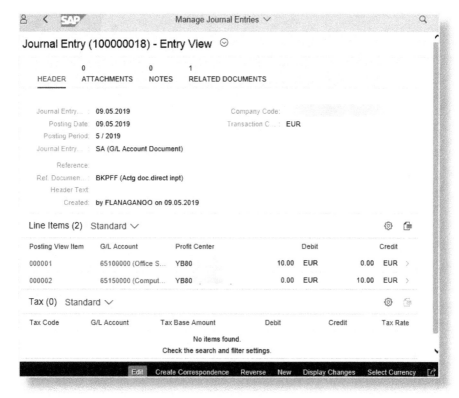

Figure 5.28: App F0717—manage journal entries, reverse one journal

When you click on the REVERSE button, a pop-up appears for you to fill in the reversal reason. Options may vary in different systems, but usually the first option is 01 WRONG POSTING which performs an identical posting in reverse with the same date as the original. Another option, 02 WRONG PERIOD allows you to enter the posting date, if the original was posted in a period that is now closed.

> **Change ledger view of journal**
>
> Clicking on the ⊙ to the right of the word ENTRY VIEW at the top of the page allows you to switch to a specific ledger, so ENTRY VIEW will then be replaced by, for example, LEDGER 0L or LEDGER 2L instead of ENTRY VIEW. See Figure 5.29.

85

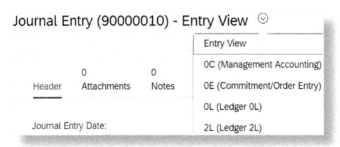

Figure 5.29: App F0717—manage journal entries

5.3.4 Recurring journals

Recurring journals can be used where identical postings are made every period, such as standing orders, or a charge for a year in advance, where the invoice is posted to prepayments and one twelfth of the amount is transferred to expenses every month.

The app is F1598 MANAGE RECURRING JOURNAL ENTRIES and you can list, create, edit, display, delete, post, and export to a spreadsheet. The initial screen is shown in Figure 5.30. A separate number range is used for the initial creation of the recurring journal, but a normal number range is used to assign a number each time the recurring journal is posted.

Figure 5.30: App F1598—manage recurring journal entries overview

The first step is to create the recurring journal template and recurrence rule by clicking on CREATE NEW RECURRING JOURNAL ENTRY. The journal itself is similar to a normal journal with header and line items and the relevant tax codes and cost objects, but there is an additional section for the RECURRENCE RULE. You can choose between monthly, weekly, period, or another pattern which you have to set up separately. See Figure 5.31.

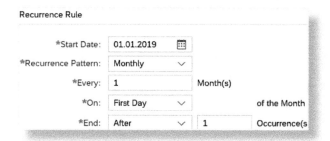

Figure 5.31: App F1598—manage recurring journal, recurrence rule

In the GUI, the recurring journal functionality was not very user-friendly, you had to use a number of transactions before you could post anything and it was awkward to make amendments. This discouraged many people from using it, especially if their organization had a custom upload journal entry available. In the SAP S/4HANA Fiori app, recurring journal entries can all be done simply in one app. Once you have created the initial journal template, go to the MANAGE RECURRING JOURNAL ENTRIES overview screen and select the journals that you want to post and click POST. Or, you can go into each journal and post from there. Inside the journal, you can see a header (not shown), LINE ITEMS, RECURRENCE RULE, and the POSTINGS sections. See Figure 5.32. The header shows who created it, document type, and so on, and you can add attachments to the journal.

The POSTINGS section shows the number of journals that are due to be posted based on the recurrence rule, so, for example, if you selected END AFTER 7 OCCURRENCES there would be 7 lines. In the example in Figure 5.32, we originally posted a recurring journal entry of €1,000 and after two months changed it to €1,200.

If you go to app F0717 MANAGE JOURNAL ENTRIES and select the posted journal entry, in the RELATED DOCUMENTS tab, you see the original recurring journal template, and any other related documents, such as controlling documents or reversals.

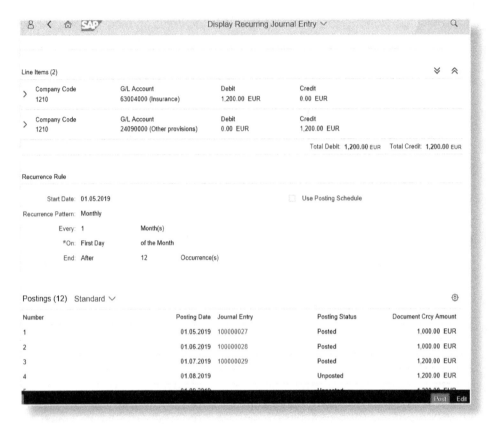

Figure 5.32: App F1598—recurring journal detail screen

5.4 Petty cash or cash journal

This is covered in the best practices scope item 1GO CASH JOURNAL. Petty cash is held in order to pay out or receive small payments where the full process of raising sales or purchase orders, or posting goods movements, invoices, and making bank payments is not practical. There can be more than one *petty cash journal* per company code, for example, in different branches of the company, and they can be in different currencies, for example, where small amounts of foreign cash might be required for employees travel expenses.

The POST CASH JOURNAL ENTRIES app is based on GUI transaction code FBCJ and works on the *Imprest* system, meaning that whenever the petty cash is low and needs to be replenished from the bank, the replenishment amount takes it back to a fixed sum each time. For example, if the fixed sum, or float, is 100 and you have 60 receipts and 80 paid out, you would top up by 40 to bring it back to 100.

The app screen is laid out with the time period at the top left and the opening balance, total receipts, and payments and closing balance at the top right of the screen. See Figure 5.33. The bottom part of the screen is where you enter the amounts.

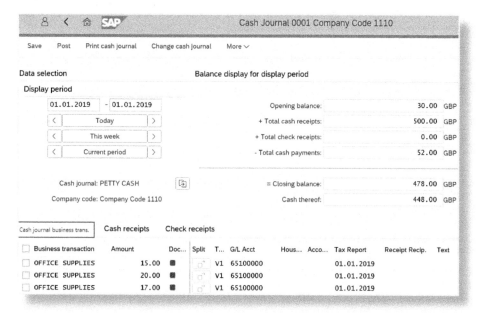

Figure 5.33: Transaction FBCJ—example of petty cash posting

With the app, you can post incoming cash receipts and payments to a G/L account or you can post directly to customer and supplier accounts if required. The main difference between the cash journal and an ordinary journal entry is that instead of looking up the relevant account in the app, the user can select a BUSINESS TRANSACTION from a smaller list with an easier or more relevant description, such as those in Figure 5.34.

It is possible to include tax or VAT, but as the amount to be recovered is usually very small compared to the work involved in getting a VAT receipt and splitting the amount correctly (especially if supplier details are required for the VAT register), many organizations post the whole amount to an expense account.

To enter a petty cash journal, you first choose the company code and cash journal number. Next, you enter the business transaction type that describes the type of receipt or payment, some examples are shown in Figure 5.34. The very first transaction will need to be a cash receipt because you cannot pay out what is not there.

Business transaction	≜ Tran...	CoCd	T...	G/L Acct
CUSTOMER	5	1010	D	
OFFICE SUPPLIES	1	1010	E	65100000
TRANSFER BANK TO JOURNAL	2	1010	C	11001010
TRANSFER JOURNAL TO BANK	3	1010	B	11001080
VENDOR	4	1010	K	

Figure 5.34: Post a cash journal—business transaction dropdown

There is also a DISPLAY CASH JOURNAL app based on GUI transaction S_ P6B_12000118, which lists the transactions that you have posted.

5.5   Intercompany journals

Intercompany (also called cross-company) journals can take place whenever a single posting is made covering two company codes. This may occur when a payment in one company is cleared against an invoice in another, or an invoice is posted in one company, but all or part of it refers to another company, or a journal entry is simply posted across two company codes.

Assuming intercompany G/L accounts have been set up correctly, the system will automatically add adjustment lines to ensure a double entry in both company codes. For example, a supplier invoice credits a supplier in company A and debits an expense in company B. The system will add a debit to the intercompany account in A and a credit to the intercompany account in B, producing one document number in each system as well as an overall intercompany document containing all four postings. Both entries will be reversed if there is an error.

App DISPLAY JOURNAL ENTRIES—CROSS-COMPANY CODE, based on GUI transaction FBU3 (not shown), allows you to see both postings (one in each company) of a cross-company or intercompany posting, or you can see each journal individually with the normal apps.

5.6   Display general ledger information

5.6.1   General ledger overview

App F2445 GENERAL LEDGER OVERVIEW, (see Figure 5.35), is a collection of cards that you can rearrange however you want. This is covered in best practices scope item BGC—SAP FIORI ANALYTICAL APPS FOR G/L ACCOUNTING IN FINANCE.

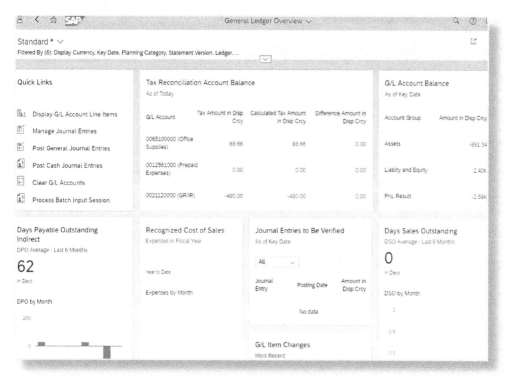

Figure 5.35: App F2445—general ledger overview app

The overview apps are quite new, only available from 1809 on-premise and in SAP S/4HANA Cloud and there are similar apps for accounts payables and receivables. There are quick links to transactions and some of the cards already show some information or charts that you can drill down on the card itself. You can filter the information shown by company code, date, ledger, etc.

5.6.2 FAGLL03H line item browser

The transaction FAGLL03H, the G/L ACCOUNT LINE ITEM BROWSER is a new transaction available in the GUI which is worth mentioning as it is slightly more flexible in some ways than the standard FAGLL03 transaction. See Figure 5.36. On the right-hand side, you have an impressive number of columns that you can add (726 in this particular 1809 on-premise release). You can export both the list of columns and the report to Microsoft Excel.

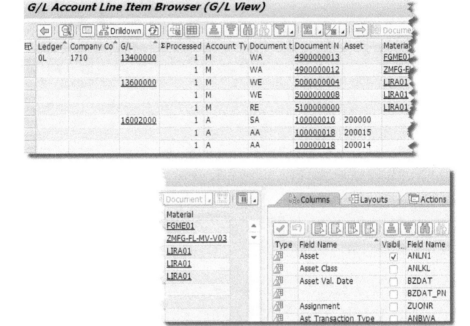

Figure 5.36: Transaction FAGLL03H—line item browser

Most of the other general ledger reports are similar to the accounts payable and receivable reports. They are shown together in section 10.2.

6 Accounts payable

This chapter is all about the accounts payable processes and the re-lated SAP Fiori apps. We cover the two different types of invoice post-ing and the different ways payments can be made. We explain what is meant by three-way matching and how to ensure the automatic accruals account, or GR/IR, is kept under control, and then we cover reporting and some closing tasks.

6.1 Purchase-to-pay process

Accounts payable is the term for the subledger for the management of sup-plier accounts. It includes invoices, payments, sending out balance con-firmations, reporting, and so on and is covered in the best practices scope item J60 ACCOUNTS PAYABLE. The end-to-end process is sometimes called the *purchase (or procure) to pay flow*, (or *P2P*). See Figure 6.1.

Figure 6.1 : Purchase to pay or accounts payable flow

Ideally, a purchase should be approved before the goods or service are ordered and before the invoices are received, in order to avoid maverick spending and ensure that the best prices and service are obtained from preferred sellers. The purchase should also be confirmed in writing to the supplier to ensure that everybody is in agreement about the exact item, quantity, price, and delivery details of what is being ordered and so that the seller has a reference to quote when sending the goods and invoice.

The process can start with a *purchase requisition* (PR), which is an internal request to buy something. Requisitions may be made by end users not in a position to identify the exact details and sent to a central purchasing depart-ment to complete. Requisitions may take many forms and may be created in SAP S/4HANA or *SAP Ariba* (SAP's full procurement and spend manage-ment solution) or a third-party system interfaced with SAP S/4HANA. In the case of manufacturing companies, the PR may be created automatically by the system, for example, in response to a *material requirement planning (MRP)* run.

The requisition is then turned into a *purchase order* (PO) and once approved, is usually sent to the supplier. This can be by postal service, fax, email, electronically, etc., or the order can be placed by phone and stating the PO number.

Stock items are booked into stock with a *goods receipt* (GR), but for non-stock items, a GR may or may not be required. It may not be practical for everybody to have access to the system and to post a GR every time minor stationery items are received. Particularly with services, repairs, and maintenance, the duration and any additional spare parts that are required will not be known at the time the PO is created, so it will be difficult to post an accurate GR. Some companies may decide that certain types of purchases or those beneath a certain amount can be assumed to be immaterial and no GR needs to be posted for those purchases.

6.1.1   Logistics invoice verification

Ideally, purchases should be authorized before the goods are ordered, but you don't want to approve the purchase and then have to re-approve the invoice, and you don't want to have too much delay before the invoice is paid as you may lose any early payment discounts, or even incur interest if outside the payment terms. The term *logistic invoice verification* is when you enter an invoice against a related PO in order for the system to carry out an automatic check.

The most efficient process is *three-way matching*, (see Figure 6.2) which is when the invoice price is checked against the PO price and the invoice quantity is checked against the GR quantity. If there is a discrepancy of more than the agreed tolerances, the invoice will be automatically blocked for payment, otherwise, the invoice will be selected automatically in the next automatic payment run for invoices with that due date.

Two-way matching is similar to three-way matching, but where the PO has been set up to have no GR, matching only takes place between the PO and the invoice.

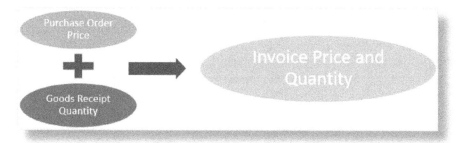

Figure 6.2: Three-way matching of invoice against PO and GR

Invoices may be physically received and posted manually against a PO, received electronically, or scanned using intelligent software that can be set to recognize the key fields for each supplier, such as the PO number, amounts, VAT, and so on. Invoices can also be created on supplier networks when a PO is *flipped*, i.e., when the buyer confirms that the invoice can be automatically created based on the PO and GR details shown.

Invoice numbering

 When a logistics invoice is posted against a PO, a material document and a financial document will be produced. As material numbers are global and financial numbering is company-code specific, the numbers may be different, so make sure you note the correct one if you are following up on a posting.

When a posting is made to a supplier account in the subledger, it will also simultaneously update the control or reconciliation account in the general ledger. There may be different supplier reconciliation accounts for domestic, foreign, and intercompany or they may be split out by other types of supplier.

Supplier/vendor terminology

 We will use the term supplier in most cases rather than vendor, but as SAP S/4HANA still uses both terms in different transactions, we may also use the term vendor interchangeably.

You can enter an invoice or a credit note against one or more POs using the SAP Fiori app F0859 CREATE SUPPLIER INVOICE, by completing the header details, such as transaction (invoice or credit), posting date, tax invoice date, company code currency, supplier's invoice number and amount, and then entering the PO number. The invoice will then propose the amount and quantity based on the PO and, where relevant, the GR. See Figure 6.3. This is similar in concept to GUI transaction MIRO.

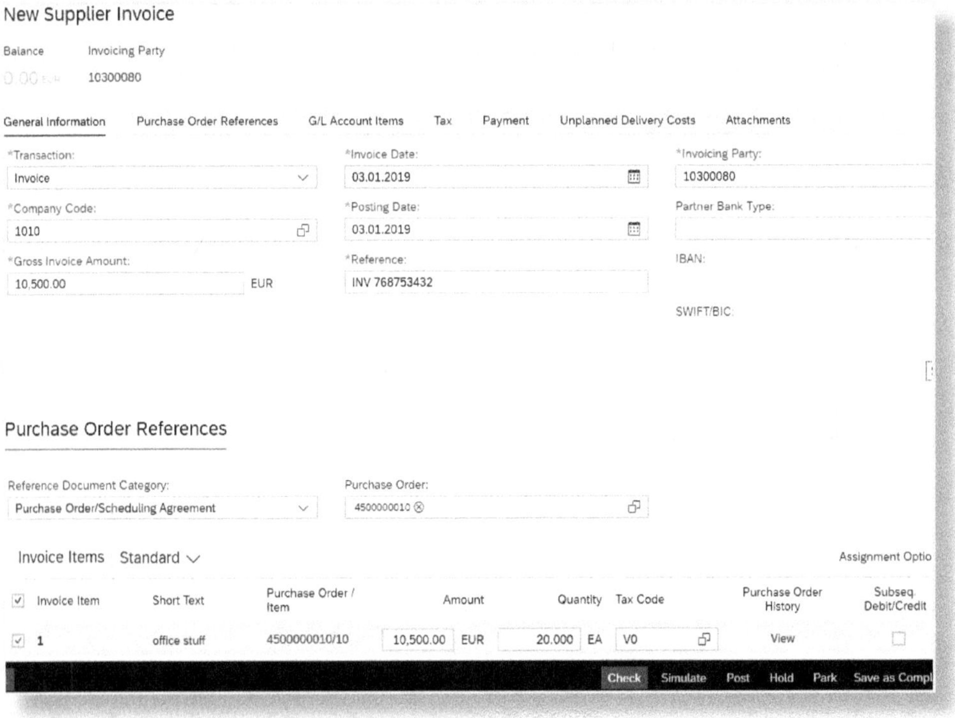

New Supplier Invoice

Balance   Invoicing Party

0.00 EUR   10300080

General Information	Purchase Order References	G/L Account Items	Tax	Payment	Unplanned Delivery Costs	Attachments

*Transaction:	*Invoice Date:	*Invoicing Party:
Invoice	03.01.2019	10300080
*Company Code:	*Posting Date:	Partner Bank Type:
1010	03.01.2019	
*Gross Invoice Amount:	*Reference:	IBAN:
10.500.00 EUR	INV 768753432	
		SWIFT/BIC:

Purchase Order References

Reference Document Category:	Purchase Order:
Purchase Order/Scheduling Agreement	4500000010 ⊗

Invoice Items Standard ∨   Assignment Optio

✓	Invoice Item	Short Text	Purchase Order / Item	Amount		Quantity	Tax Code		Purchase Order History	Subseq. Debit/Credit
✓	1	office stuff	4500000010/10	10,500.00	EUR	20.000 EA	V0		View	☐

Check Simulate Post Hold Park Save as Compl

Figure 6.3: App F0859—create supplier invoice

If you click on the VIEW button in the PURCHASE ORDER HISTORY column you can see the quantities and amounts already allocated. You can see a different example in Figure 6.4.

If the amount or quantity on the invoice is different to what is proposed, you amend the proposed amount and quantity to match the physical invoice. If the price is too high, there is a pop-up and yellow warning on the bottom left of the screen to signal that the invoice can be posted but it will not be paid. Although the balance of the posting is normally green if zero, it may be another color if the invoice is not 100% correct. This is also shown in Figure 6.3.

New Supplier Invoice

Balance	Invoicing Party
0.00 EUR	12300007

General Information   Purchase Order References   G/L Account Items   Tax   Payment   Unplanned Delivery Costs   Attachments

Purchase Order References

Reference Document Categor   Purchase Order History

Purchase Order/Scheduling

Invoice Items   Standar

			Quantity Ordered	Quantity Received	Quantity Invoiced	Amount Invoiced	Open Quantity	Net Price	Net PO Value
☑	Invoice Item	S	50,000.000 PC	50,000.000 PC	49,990.000 PC	8,998.20 EUR	10.000 PC	0.18 EUR / PC	9,000.00 EUR
☑	1	RAW15,PD	4500000002/10	1.80	EUR	10.000	PC	V0	View >

Figure 6.4: App F0859—purchase order history in create invoice screen

You can CHECK or SIMULATE the invoice (see Figure 6.5), prior to posting. You can HOLD or PARK it and return to it later, or POST it.

Item	Account type	G/L Account	Supplier	Amount	Tax Code	Company Code	Cost Center
1	K	21100000	10300080	-10,500.00 EUR	V0	1010	
2	S	21120000		10,000.00 EUR	V0	1010	10101601
3	S	65100000		500.00 EUR	V0	1010	10101601

Figure 6.5: App F0859—create supplier invoice, invoice simulation

If additional costs were omitted from the PO, but appear in the invoice, for example, delivery charges, you could amend the PO, or you could add the charges when posting the invoice. You can add a line to the invoice in the section under the PO line items headed G/L ACCOUNT ITEMS, in which case you need to supply the relevant details, such as G/L account number, tax code, cost object, and so on. Alternatively, if you want to increase the expense by the missing amount, you can enter the amount in the UNPLANNED DELIVERY COSTS field further down the screen. If there is more than one item in the PO, the additional cost will be split proportionately between the accounts used by each item.

App F2691 DISPLAY PROCESS FLOW—ACCOUNTS PAYABLE is useful to see the flow of transactions from the PO to the clearing of the invoice. See Figure 6.6 where a GR and two invoices have been posted against a PO. If you click on either document, you will see a pop-up with more information. In the JOURNAL ENTRY, or finance posting, the information includes, for example, the total invoice amount and the payment block reason. Clicking on the PO shows the approved price for the purchase.

In Figure 6.6, the words BLOCKED FOR PAYMENT will appear in red, because the invoice price was too high, but FREE FOR PAYMENT will be in green, where it has been paid. If there were any returns, credit notes, or related documents, they would also be shown.

You can jump to the process flow app from other apps (such as supplier line items) or go directly into the app and select any of the documents. You can restart the flow, export to spreadsheet, or show as a chart where you can add more fields.

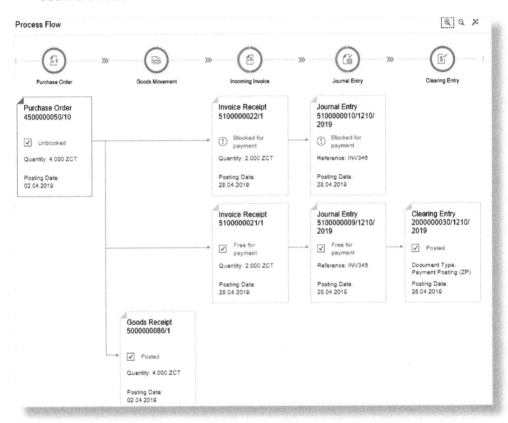

Figure 6.6: App F2691—display process flow, accounts payable app

Figure 6.7 shows the same PO flow, but using the older app based on GUI transaction ME23N to display the PURCHASE ORDER HISTORY tab.

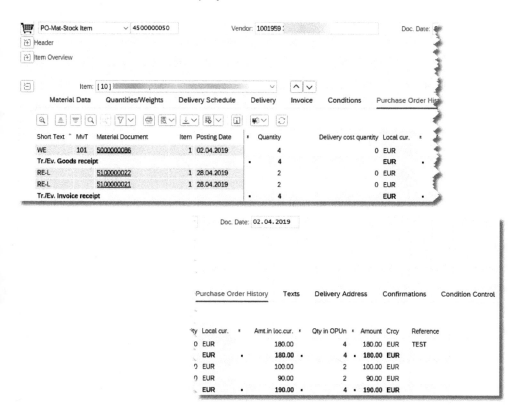

Figure 6.7: Transaction ME23N—purchase order history

6.1.2 Parked and held invoices

With both parked and held invoices, invoices are put aside for whatever reason to return to later, but the documents do not necessarily have to have all fields completed. Only parked documents appear in the PURCHASE ORDER HISTORY tab and AP process flow (see Figure 6.8). If the amount is filled in, a financial document number will be assigned and a parked financial document produced, which means that it can be seen in some reports.

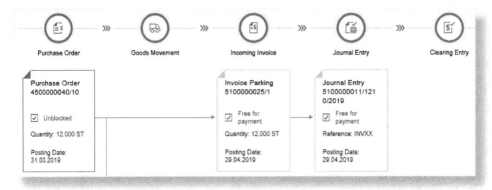

Figure 6.8: App F2691—AP process flow showing parked document

Figure 6.9 shows the supplier line item report with the parked items marked with a yellow triangle. In order to include parked items, you have to select the correct item type (see the dropdown in Figure 6.9), as the default is normal items.

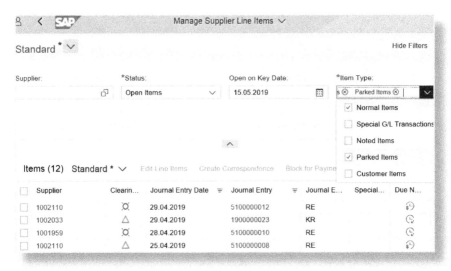

Figure 6.9: App F0712—manage supplier line items, parked/posted items

With app F1060 SUPPLIER INVOICES LIST, you can see both parked and held documents, as shown in Figure 6.10. You can also select a parked or held invoice from the app to complete and post it.

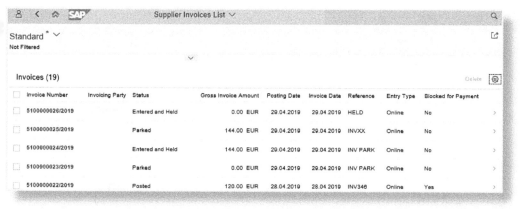

	Invoice Number	Invoicing Party	Status	Gross Invoice Amount	Posting Date	Invoice Date	Reference	Entry Type	Blocked for Payment	
☐	5100000026/2019		Entered and Held	0.00 EUR	29.04.2019	29.04.2019	HELD	Online	No	>
☐	5100000025/2019		Parked	144.00 EUR	29.04.2019	29.04.2019	INVXX	Online	No	>
☐	5100000024/2019		Entered and Held	144.00 EUR	29.04.2019	29.04.2019	INV PARK	Online	No	>
☐	5100000023/2019		Parked	0.00 EUR	29.04.2019	29.04.2019	INV PARK	Online	No	>
☐	5100000022/2019		Posted	120.00 EUR	28.04.2019	28.04.2019	INV346	Online	Yes	>

Figure 6.10: App F1060—supplier invoices list, parked/held documents

> ## Deleting parked documents
>
> Parked documents can be deleted, but the used document numbers cannot be reassigned. Instead, the document header is kept with the status deleted and the line items are removed.

6.1.3   Foreign currency invoices

The currency in the PO comes from the supplier master data and is proposed in the invoice. If the exchange rate is not fixed in the PO, the posting date rate will be used in the invoice. In app F0859 CREATE SUPPLIER INVOICE, click on SEE MORE (after completing the header) to check. For example, in Figure 6.11 the posting date rate is 1.11111.

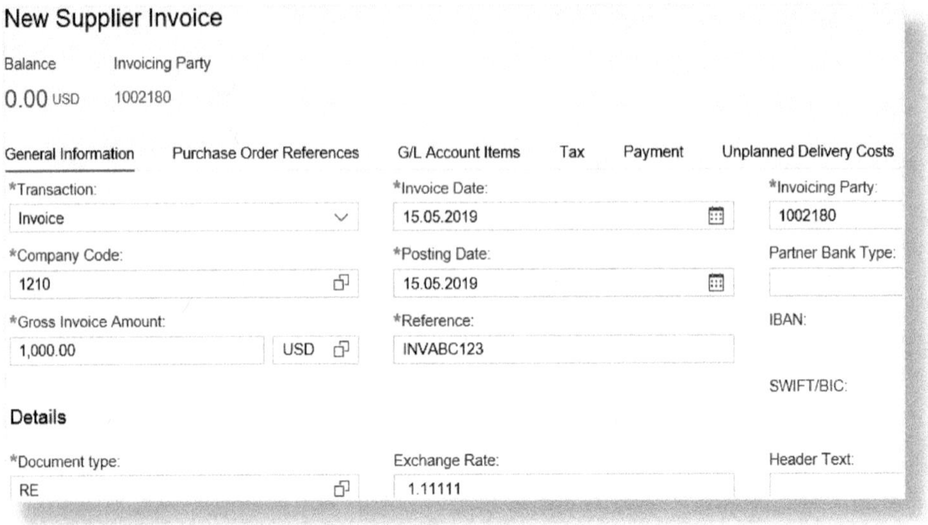

New Supplier Invoice

Balance Invoicing Party

0.00 USD 1002180

General Information	Purchase Order References	G/L Account Items	Tax	Payment	Unplanned Delivery Costs

*Transaction:

Invoice ⌄

*Company Code:

1210 ⊡

*Gross Invoice Amount:

1,000.00 USD ⊡

*Invoice Date:

15.05.2019 ⊞

*Posting Date:

15.05.2019 ⊞

*Reference:

INVABC123

*Invoicing Party:

1002180

Partner Bank Type:

IBAN:

SWIFT/BIC:

Details

*Document type:

RE ⊡

Exchange Rate:

1.11111

Header Text:

Figure 6.11: App F0859—create supplier invoice, foreign exchange rate

6.1.4   Goods/invoices received account (GR/IR)

GR postings typically debit an expense or stock account and credit the *GR/IR account*. Invoices credit the supplier account and debit the GR/IR account and debit taxes where applicable. Therefore, assuming GR's are posted on a timely basis, the balance on the GR/IR account will represent the accrual for goods that have been received, but not yet invoiced.

The GR will normally be posted at either standard cost (if the material has a price control equal to standard) or at the PO price if the invoice has not yet been received. If you are using GR-based invoice verification, you cannot post the invoice until the GR has been posted. If you are not using GR-based invoice verification and the invoice is posted before the GR, then the GR will use the price on the invoice rather than that of the PO.

If the quantity of both the invoice and goods receipt posting match, the account will be cleared, and if an expense, the difference will be posted to the expense account. If it refers to stock at moving average price, the difference will go to stock if there is sufficient stock to cover it, if not, and for stock at standard cost, the difference goes to the variance account.

Price difference on invoice for expenses

 A PO is for 5 (non-stock) items @ $10. A GR of quantity 5 is posted, debiting expenses with $50 and crediting the GR/IR account with $50. An invoice is received for 5 items @$11, i.e., a total of $55. Because the quantity matches, the GR/IR account will be cleared and so $50 is debited to the GR/IR account and $5 to the same expense account used before, with the remaining $55 crediting the supplier (assuming no tax applicable). Depending on the tolerance, this may result in the invoice being blocked for payment.

Service receipts

 A receipt of a service can be confirmed in the same way as a goods receipt, if it can easily be quantified, but frequently the exact quantity is unknown until the service is completed. There may be spare parts involved in the case of a repair, or the quantity may be in fractions. An alternative is using *service entry sheets* to confirm the service (best practices scope item 22Z—Procurement of Services), which is more flexible if you need to enter fractions or timesheets, however, the invoice posting process is similar.

The bulk of the items outstanding at period end should be timing differences, but various other types of errors may occur, for example, the supplier may have made an error on the invoice or in the delivery, and a credit note may be necessary; or the person entering the goods receipt or invoice may have made a mistake. Either way, it is necessary to reconcile the account on a regular basis in order to make timely corrections and avoid unexplained amounts on the account at the end of the year.

Repost GR/IR clearing

At the period end, an invoice might be posted to the GR/IR account, prior to the GR being entered. This might be due simply to delays in posting the goods receipt or because of a query currently under investigation. If immaterial, these items may simply be included in the total when reporting the accrual, or they can be automatically reposted to another account to be

103

reported in a separate area of the balance sheet. The app you can use is REPOST GR/IR CLEARING, based on GUI transaction F.19.

Clearing the GR/IR account

Normally, you can run automatic clearing (see section 5.3.1) on the GR/IR account based on the PO number, line item, and amount. The system will find all the invoices and goods receipts relating to that PO and if they net to zero, they can be cleared; small rounding differences can be written off automatically.

Maintaining the GR/IR account

App MAINTAIN GR/IR CLEARING, based on GUI transaction MR11, allows you to write off items that can no longer be matched or corrected, for example, where a goods receipt that caused a stock discrepancy can no longer be reversed after a stock-take, as it would make the stock incorrect, or would make the moving average price of a product negative and block postings to it.

GR/IR account reconciliation overview

In SAP S/4HANA Cloud and from 1809 on-premise, there is a new app, the F3303 MONITOR GR/IR ACCOUNT RECONCILIATION, shown in Figure 6.12 and Figure 6.13, to assist with the reconciliation of the GR/IR account. The app creates a worklist of outstanding (open) items by purchasing document; where there are missing or different quantities and amounts in the GR and invoice receipt.

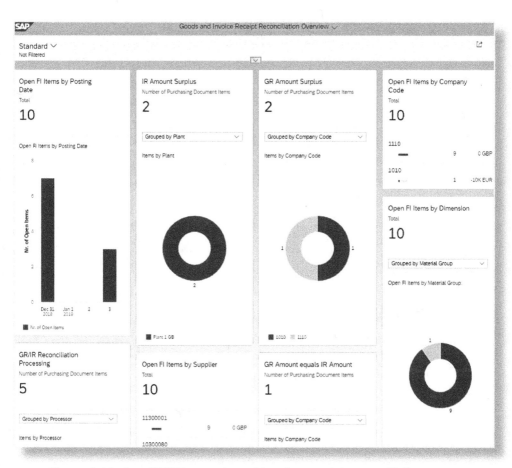

Figure 6.12: App F3303—goods and invoice receipt reconciliation

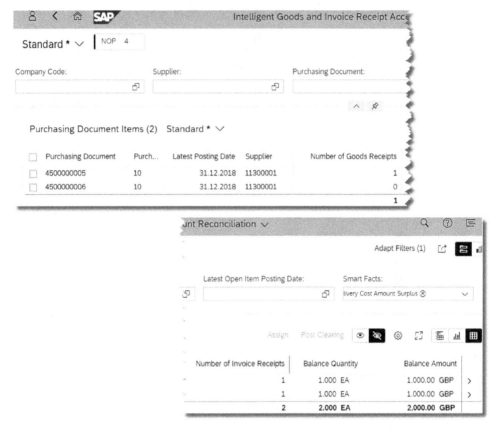

Figure 6.13: Intelligent goods/invoice receipt account reconciliation

6.1.5 Credit notes

If an invoice is posted against a PO and then subsequently a credit note is received, the credit can be posted using the same app as the original invoice, such as F0859 CREATE SUPPLIER INVOICE by changing the TRANSACTION type. See the dropdown list in Figure 6.14. If the credit note refers to a quantity difference, you must use the CREDIT MEMO option because this will update the GR/IR account. If it refers to a price correction, you can use the SUBSEQUENT CREDIT option as this will not update the GR/IR account. If there is an upward adjustment in price, you can use the SUBSEQUENT DEBIT option.

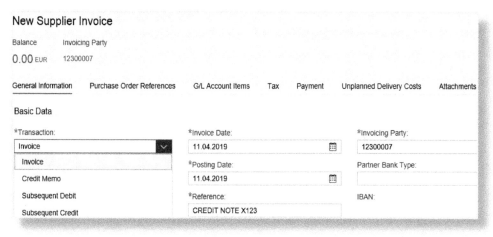

Figure 6.14: App F0859—create supplier invoice, credit note header

> **Credit notes**
>
> Care must be taken to use the correct TRANSACTION type when posting a credit note. The GR/IR account works on quantity, so if the credit involves quantity, then the document type credit memo should be used, otherwise the GR/IR will not be updated. If the document does not touch the quantity and only adjusts the price, then a subsequent credit should be used.

Returns

With a credit note for returned or damaged goods, you also need to ensure that the stock is updated, so you may need to create a return PO and post a return delivery goods issue to post the credit note against.

Cancellations

You would normally only cancel or reverse an invoice when it has been posted incorrectly or against the wrong item, as opposed to when the goods are returned to the supplier when you would expect to post a credit note against a return delivery.

With items that have a moving average price, you need to be careful when reversing an invoice if there is insufficient stock to absorb the correction, as the system will post the credit to price differences, even if the original invoice was posted to stock.

You can only reverse an item that has not been cleared by a payment and you have to reverse the whole document; you cannot reverse one item. If you posted the original document using a transaction which creates a material document, such as app F0859 CREATE SUPPLIER INVOICE, or the GUI transaction MIRO, you need to use a similar transaction (such as F1060A SUPPLIER INVOICE LIST) to do the reversal, and not reverse it only in finance. You could not, for example, post an invoice against a PO and then use app REVERSE JOURNAL ENTRIES based on GUI transaction FB08 to reverse the invoice, as FB08 is a finance-only transaction and would not reverse the material document.

6.1.6 Managing payment blocks

Payment blocks will always block the whole invoice against payment even if the block is only relevant to a single line item. There are different types of blocks, for example, *stochastic blocks* can be set for random checks, or *amount blocks* for invoices with and without POs over a certain amount, even if, in the case of an invoice with PO and GR, the price and quantity matches. There are also different ways to unblock invoices.

Automatic payment blocks

Using app RELEASE BLOCKED INVOICES, based on GUI transaction MRBR, you can automatically unblock invoices that have had the original blocking reason corrected. On the selection screen, enter the normal criteria (company code, range of dates, documents, etc.) and choose RELEASE AUTOMATICALLY, with BLOCKED DUE TO VARIANCES, MRBR effectively refreshes the three-way matching. See Figure 6.15 and Figure 6.16. If the invoice was higher than the PO price or goods receipt quantity, and either a credit note has been received, an additional GR has been posted, or the PO has been increased and re-approved, and the invoice now matches the PO and GR, the payment block will automatically be removed.

Automatic release

 Sometimes users are concerned about incorrectly releasing something, when RELEASE AUTOMATICALLY is selected. However, this transaction is quite safe because MRBR will never release anything that should not be released; it will only release items where the invoice now passes the three-way match.

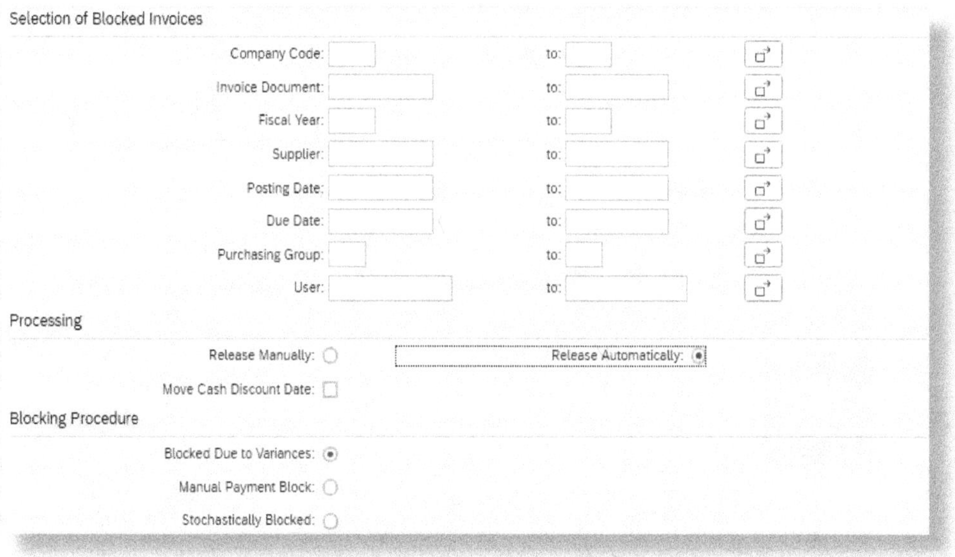

Selection of Blocked Invoices

Company Code:	to:	□
Invoice Document:	to:	□
Fiscal Year:	to:	□
Supplier:	to:	□
Posting Date:	to:	□
Due Date:	to:	□
Purchasing Group:	to:	□
User:	to:	□

Processing

Release Manually: ○   Release Automatically: ◉

Move Cash Discount Date: ☐

Blocking Procedure

Blocked Due to Variances: ◉

Manual Payment Block: ○

Stochastically Blocked: ○

Figure 6.15: Extract of MRBR, release blocked invoices

You can use the MRBR app RELEASE BLOCKED INVOICES in order to release invoices manually, but it doesn't solve the original issue.

Doc. No.	T...	Posting Date	Inv. Pty	Amount	Purch.doc.	Ite
5100000001	RE	31.12.2018	11300001	12,000.00	4500000003	1
5100000002	RE	31.12.2018	11300001	7,000.00	4500000004	1
5100000004	RE	31.12.2018	11300001	1,000.00	4500000006	1

Release Blocked Invoices

Item	Plant	PGr	Quantity	Diff. Qty	Diff. Value	Qty	Prc
10	1110	001	10.000	0	2,000.00		✕
10	1110	001	6.000	0	1,000.00		✕
10	1110	001	1.000	1	0.00	✕	

Figure 6.16: MRBR release blocked invoices

Releasing blocked invoices

 Invoices that are automatically blocked using invoice verification should be investigated and corrected rather than blindly released for payment. If, for example, a goods receipt for stock is entered with the incorrect quantity, then not correcting the goods receipt will leave a balance on the GR/IR account and the stocks incorrect. Where there is a price difference, not correcting the price at the source means the next PO may be raised for the wrong amount.

Manual payment blocks

Using app F0593 MANAGE PAYMENT BLOCK, you can also manually block or unblock accounts and line items for a supplier and enter a brief note of explanation if required. Figure 6.17 shows that the first supplier has the whole account blocked and the second has two invoices blocked, one manually (A-BLOCKED FOR PAYMENT), and one automatically (R-INVOICE VERIFICATION).

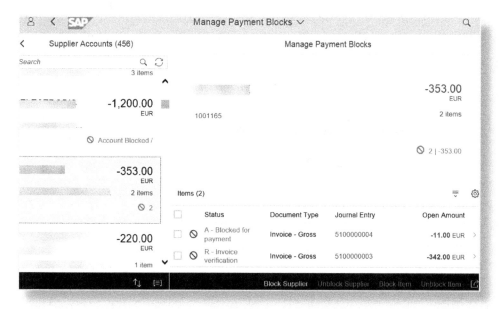

Figure 6.17: App F0593—manage payment blocks

To see why the automatic payment block is in place, you can use ⚙ to add the PO number to the display and then click on it to jump to DISPLAY PROCESS FLOW—ACCOUNTS PAYABLE to investigate the discrepancies. You can click on the invoice number and do the same thing. Jumping from the invoice document rather than the PO means that you may have to click on the PURCHASE ORDER in the process flow, and then in the pop-up, click on RESTART PROCESS FLOW FROM THIS OBJECT in order to pull in earlier objects, such as the GR.

6.2 Invoices without purchase orders

Ideally, all purchases should be made via a PO for better control, to analyze spend, and ensure purchases are approved in advance. In practice, some companies choose to post items where the exact amount is not known prior to the invoice receipt, such as utilities, directly in finance without a PO.

An invoice document has a header and line items, similar to a journal entry, with an invoice date (taken from the physical supplier invoice), a posting date (dictating which period it refers to), and a reference, which is usually the supplier invoice number. The supplier information is entered separately at the top of the page. In the line item, at a minimum, you need to enter a G/L account, cost object, amount, and tax code, and depending on the country, information such as the tax jurisdiction.

There are several ways to enter an invoice without a PO. You can use app CREATE INCOMING INVOICES (FB60), based on the GUI transaction, or app F0859 CREATE SUPPLIER INVOICE (or MANAGE SUPPLIER INVOICE after a recent name change), by entering G/L account details instead of the PO information. See Figure 6.18.

Figure 6.18: App F0859—create/manage supplier invoice

6.3 Credit note without PO

Posting a credit note without a PO is very similar to posting an invoice. You can use the same app that you used to create the invoice, i.e., either CREATE INCOMING INVOICES (FB60), based on GUI transaction, or F0859 CREATE SUPPLIER INVOICE (see Figure 6.19), but you need to change the transaction type. Both apps have a dropdown to choose the transaction, but remember to change it back to invoice afterwards!

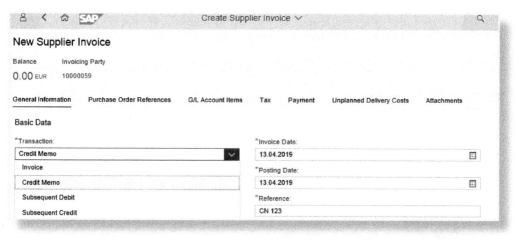

Figure 6.19: App F0859—credit memo transaction type

You can link the credit note to the invoice by entering the original SAP doc-ument number and year in the field INVOICE REFERENCE near the payment details (see Figure 6.20).This field is validated, so you must use an existing document number.

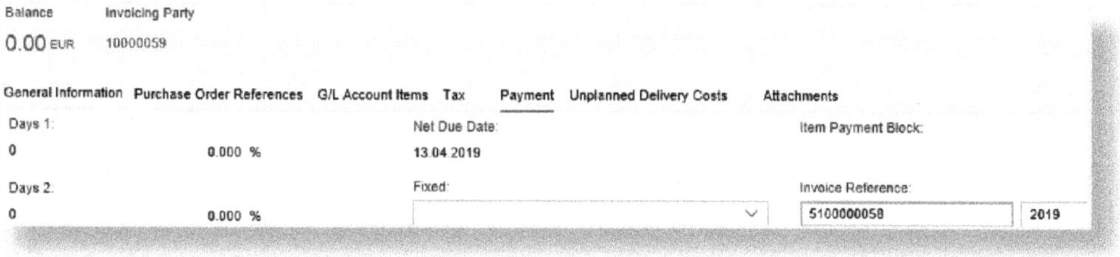

Figure 6.20: App F0859—create credit note for invoice without PO

6.4 One-time vendor functionality

Most companies prefer to have all purchases posted to individual supplier accounts, often vetted by the purchasing department to ensure their relia-bility, or to agree to prices beforehand. However, on occasion, it may not be worth creating a supplier account for small one-off purchases; a miscel-laneous, *one-time vendor,* account can be created for this purpose. Where this is permitted by the organization, the account is set up using a special CPD account group without bank details or address, and when that specific supplier number is selected during a transaction, such as an invoice, a pop-up will appear (see Figure 6.21) so that a new address and bank details can be entered for each purchase.

The account should be monitored to prevent misuse and if a supplier appears more than once, it should have its own account set up. The app we used to demonstrate the one-time vendor functionality is CREATE INCOMING INVOICE based on GUI transaction FB60. The same functionality is also available for one-time customers.

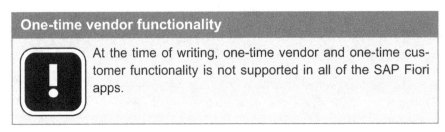

> **One-time vendor functionality**
>
> At the time of writing, one-time vendor and one-time customer functionality is not supported in all of the SAP Fiori apps.

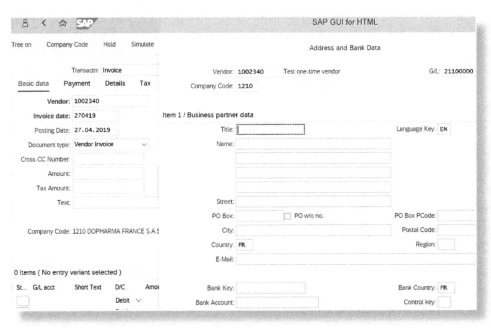

Figure 6.21: Transaction FB60 posting a one-time vendor invoice

6.5 Payments

6.5.1 Cash discounts

Most discounts are based on what you buy, whereas a cash discount is based on when you pay, regardless of what you have bought. Discount payment terms have at least two parts, one relating to the terms you get without discount and the others with different discounts for paying within a different number of days. For example, payment terms of 5% discount if you pay within 10 days, or the full amount within 30 days net. App F1735 CASH DISCOUNT FORECAST, allows you to see available and expired discounts, see Figure 6.22. You can analyze the discounts by company code, supplier or payment terms, and payment blocks.

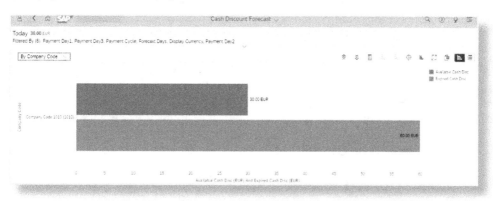

Figure 6.22: App F1735—cash discount forecast by company code

The bulk of payments to suppliers and payments collected by direct debit from customers should be made using the *automatic payment program*. Different payment methods can be selected for local payments (such as BACS in the UK and SEPA in the Eurozone), international transfers, urgent payments, checks, direct debits, and so on, but the payment method must either be assigned in the business partner master data or in the relevant documents. The payment program can also be used to pay employee travel expenses, but not for payroll-related items.

If the payment terms are set up correctly, the system can also identify early payment discounts, pay the invoice in time to get the discount, and auto-matically deduct the discount.

Some organizations also allow limited manual payments to be processed, which will be covered after the automatic payment program.

6.5.2 Automatic payment program

The typical sequence for the automatic payment run is as follows:

► Enter RUN DATE, ID, and PARAMETERS

► Schedule PROPOSAL RUN

► REVIEW and EDIT PROPOSAL

► Schedule PAYMENT RUN

► Create PAYMENT MEDIA (remittance, bank file/check)

There will normally be several approval steps, depending on how the banking process is set up.

The GUI transaction, F110 AUTOMATIC PAYMENTS, has similar steps and fields to complete as app F0770 MANAGE AUTOMATIC PAYMENTS, but is laid out somewhat differently and the app has some new functionality. We will mainly use the SAP Fiori app to illustrate the process, but Figure 6.23 illustrates the layout in tabs of the GUI transaction F110.

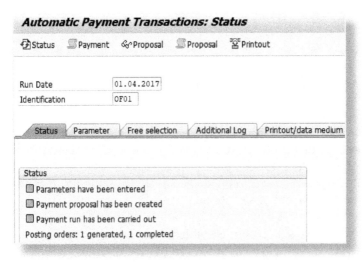

Figure 6.23: Transaction F110—status screen

Run date and identification (ID)

The two together form the unique identification for each payment run. In the SAP Fiori app, you can filter and sort by company code, payment method, creator, etc., but in the GUI transaction with the global list, you have to use the ID.

The *run date* is generally the current date, and you enter the 5-digit alpha-numeric *ID* of your choice. The ID only needs to be unique for that date and can be an abbreviation of something, the initials of the creator, or simply a sequence number.

Run date and ID example

 One option is to use the first two letters for the country, the third for the payment method, and the rest as a sequential number. If there are two U.S. check runs on the first day, you can use the ID *USC01* and the ID *USC02*. On sub-sequent days, you can re-use *USC01* and *USC02* as the run dates will be different and it is the combination of the two that must be unique.

Maintain parameters

First enter the *parameters* such as the company code, date range, and range of suppliers or customers to be paid. Having the posting date equal the payment date will help reconciliation later. You can also use the FREE SELECTION options to filter further, for example, to only include or exclude specific document numbers or document types.

Selecting a range

 To insert a range of suppliers or customers in the pa-rameters, click on the supplier or customer dropdown, select DEFINE CONDITIONS, and then choose *between*. See Figure 6.24.

Figure 6.24: Selecting a range of suppliers or customers to pay

Additional log

Ensure that you always select *YES* for ADDITIONAL LOG (Figure 6.25), as this gives additional information if payments are rejected for any reason.

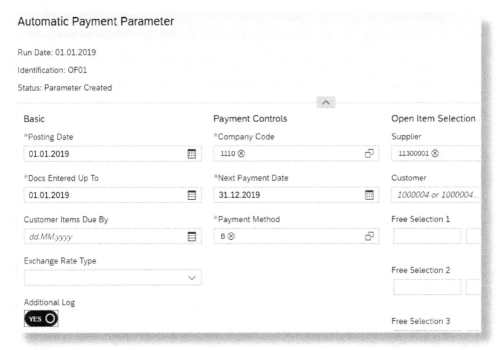

Figure 6.25: App F0770—manage automatic payments, parameters

Additional log in the GUI transaction

Entering the range of suppliers or customers in the Additional Log tab in the GUI and selecting the boxes shown in Figure 6.26, will give a more detailed explanation in the log in the event of an error.

Required logging type

☑ Due Date Check

☐ Payment Method Selection in All Cases

☑ Pmnt Method Selection If Not Successful

☑ Line Items of the Payment Documents

Accounts required

Vendors (from/to)		Customers (from/to)	
220001	229999		

Figure 6.26: Transaction F110—additional log tab

Run proposal

When the parameters are completed and saved, you can schedule the *proposal run* to run when you want. As the name implies, a proposed list of payments is produced, which you can then review and amend, if necessary. Figure 6.27 shows how you can revise the proposal in app F0770 Manage Automatic Payments, by clicking the Revise column, which then takes you to app F0771 Revise Payment Proposals (which shows the number of payment proposals in process on the face of the app).

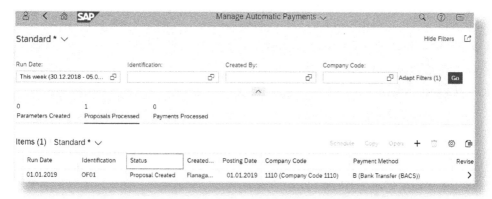

Figure 6.27: App F0770—manage automatic payments, proposal

Scheduling the proposal run

Take care not to schedule the payment run instead of the proposal, as they are very close on the screen. The payment run will update the ledgers (and may create payment media in the GUI), and is awkward to reverse. You should always review the proposal prior to scheduling the payment run.

The proposal run performs a number of checks in order to determine what items will be included. It selects the items due according to the specified parameters and checks whether the relevant bank and payment details are valid for the country, currency, time period, and so on.

Depending on the bank and payment method, additional checks may be required for the SWIFT or BIC (both bank identifier codes) and IBAN (international bank account number), any minimum or maximum payment restrictions, whether the customer has an authorized direct debit mandate, and so on.

Once the proposal is complete, it can be reviewed by drilling down on the proposal line in the SAP Fiori app or by clicking on the relevant button in the GUI transaction. In the GUI transaction, you can also see more detailed information by going to EDIT • PROPOSAL • PROPOSAL LIST from the top menu. Depending on the variant chosen, this list will show the rejected items at the top and the paid items at the bottom.

If anything is missing or incorrect, related items will be rejected and identified in the exception report, along with any items which are blocked for payment.

Exceptions

It is important to review the items that have been rejected as well as the items that are being paid, to avoid incurring interest charges or missing out on discounts if invoices are not paid on time.

Edit proposal

A decision may be made to hold back payment on some invoices because of cash flow or queries, or to investigate something. If you do not want to pay an invoice, you can block the invoice in the proposal for that payment run only. You can amend some of the bank details, change the cash discount, and so on, but if an item is omitted from the proposal due to incorrect or missing master data, once you correct the master data, you cannot refresh the proposal. Instead, you have to delete the existing proposal and run a new proposal to pick them up.

However, if you delete and rerun the proposal, it doesn't keep blocks from the previous proposal and you will have to re-enter them. You can also block an invoice directly in the invoice document (or manage payment blocks app), in which case it will stay permanently blocked until you go back in and unblock it.

To edit a proposal, click on the arrow to the right in the REVISE column. The EXCEPTIONS tab will identify if there is a problem with any payment and group the errors by number. See Figure 6.28.

0 8								
Payments	Exceptions	Summary						
Exceptions (8) Standard * ∨							Unblock Re	
☐ Supplier	Document No.	Blocked	Reference ID	Posting Date	Document Type...	Debit or Credit	Amount in Loca...	
∨ Error ID(Description): 003(Item is blocked for payment)								
☐ 0011300001	5100000001	⊘ Invoice ver...	PO INV1	31.12.2018	Invoice - Gross	Credit	-14,400.00	GBP
☐ 0011300001	5100000002	⊘ Invoice ver...	PO INV2	31.12.2018	Invoice - Gross	Credit	-8,400.00	GBP
☐ 0011300001	5100000004	⊘ Invoice ver...	PO INV4	31.12.2018	Invoice - Gross	Credit	-1,200.00	GBP
☐ 0011300090	1900000001	⊘ Manual pa...	ABC	31.10.2018	Vendor Invoice	Credit	-300.00	GBP
							-24,300.00	**GBP**
∨ Error ID(Description): 006(No valid payment method found)								
☐ 0011300001	5100000003		POINV3	31.12.2018	Invoice - Gross	Credit	-9,600.00	GBP
∨ Error ID(Description): 016(Pmnt methods for this run are not specified in master record or in item)								
☐ 0011300007	1900000002		9765	31.10.2018	Vendor Invoice	Credit	-270.00	GBP
☐ 0011300007	1900000003		123	31.12.2018	Vendor Invoice	Credit	-1,500.00	GBP
☐ 0011300090	1900000000		XYZ	31.12.2018	Vendor Invoice	Credit	-12,657.80	GBP
							-14,427.80	**GBP**
							-48,327.80	**GBP**

Figure 6.28: App F0770—manage automatic payment program exceptions

Error types 006 and 016 are quite common, but not always very clear. It usually means there is a mismatch between the payment method specified in the payment run and the details in the supplier master data or the invoice. For example, the payment method may be missing or different, the currency incorrect for that payment method, or the details of an alternative payee may be incorrect.

See the payment proposal in Figure 6.29. You can click on ⚙ to add columns, or to add the LOG button column for more information. Or, to go to app F1487 APPLICATION LOGS for additional detail, you can select the application log from the OPEN button.

Figure 6.29: App F0770—payment proposal processed with log

Figure 6.30 shows the log from the proposal and Figure 6.31 shows the log from F1487 APPLICATION LOGS.

The information in both logs is similar, but in app F1487 APPLICATION LOGS, you can add columns, filter, export the information to Microsoft Excel, or drill down further for more detail. In the case shown in Figure 6.31, there was some configuration missing in a test system.

Log Details
Search
> Document 5100000001 line item 001 via EUR 242.00-
> Terms of payment: 28.03.2019 30 0.000 % 0 0.000 % 0
> 00 days grace period is being considered
> Payment must take place before 27.04.2019; next payment on 31.12.2019
> Item is due with 0.000 % cash discount

Figure 6.30: App F0770—payment log opened from proposal

Log Details Standard ∨	
Severity	Description
ⓘ Information	> Bank details are being checked
ⓘ Information	> Customer/vendor bank details are being read
ⓘ Information	> Country GB / Bank key 404031 / Account 10000015 ...
ⓘ Information	> Customer/vendor bank details are being checked
ⓘ Information	> System reads house banks and checks if they are allowed
ⓘ Information	> Our bank BANK1 is being checked
⚠ Error	> In company code 1110 the house bank data BANK1 / account BANK1 is missing

Figure 6.31: App F0770—application log showing payment error

Once you have fixed any exceptions, you will need to delete the payment proposal and rerun it to pick up any missing items. In the pop-up, select KEEP PARAMETERS only if you are going to rerun the proposal with the corrected data. You can then reschedule the payment proposal.

Payment run

Once the proposal is correct, the *payment run* can be carried out or scheduled. This posts the payments to the supplier account (and relevant bank clearing account), clears the outstanding invoices included in the proposal, and produces the payment media. The *payment media* may include a printed or electronic remittance letter and a bank transfer file or a check, depending on the payment method in the supplier's master record (unless it has been overridden in the document, for example, changed to an urgent payment method).

Printing remittances

If you drill down to the supplier payment and select the OUTPUT ITEMS tab, you can print or send remittance letters.

Payment run reports

When you have created a payment proposal, you can click on REVISE to see a list of suppliers being paid and their bank details. You can export this list to Microsoft Excel by clicking on the EXPORT TO EXCEL button, ⊞, or you can drill down into a supplier payment and export that to Microsoft Excel in the same way.

Once the payment run has been processed, you can also export both the list of supplier payments and the individual list of invoices being paid for one supplier to Microsoft Excel. You can also click on the EXPORT TO PDF button, ⤓, to get a list, as shown in Figure 6.32.

Payment Li

Run On: May 1, 2019
Identification: OF01
Paying co. code:

Supplier / Customer	Payment No.	House Bank	Acct ID	Payt Meth	Amount Paid in Frgn Crcy	Company Code
1001862	2000000031	SGF1	EUR1	T	-100.00	1210
1001959	2000000032	SGF1	EUR1	T	-300.00	1210
1002076	2000000033	SGF1	EUR1	T	-100.00	1210
1002266	2000000034	SGF1	EUR1	T	-2,000.00	1210

Payment List

gn	Company Code	Document No.	Gross Amount in Frgn Crcy	Tot. Ded. in Frgn Crcy	Net Amount in Frgn Crcy	Frgn Crcy
	1210	1900000027	-100.00	0.00	-100.00	EUR
	1210	1900000024	-100.00	0.00	-100.00	EUR
		1900000025	-100.00	0.00	-100.00	
		1900000026	-100.00	0.00	-100.00	
	1210	1900000028	-100.00	0.00	-100.00	EUR
	1210	1900000021	-2,000.00	0.00	-2,000.00	EUR

Figure 6.32: App F0770—manage automatic payments, payment list

Payments can be made to customers and the automatic payment program can be used to collect direct debits from customers. See section 7.4.1.

Automatic payments

The automatic payment program can only be used to pay items such as invoices or down payment requests that have been physically posted to the supplier account and that are free for payment, in other words, no payment block exists.

Supplier and customer clearing

Supplier and customer items can be cleared against each other by selecting the boxes CLEARING WITH VENDOR and CLEARING WITH CUSTOMER in the relevant business partner roles. If the vendor and customer have different numbers, then the vendor number has to be inserted in the customer master and the customer number in the vendor master to link them together.

Alternative payees

In some cases, payment is not made directly to the supplier who provided the goods, for example, payment could be made to a financing company. In this case, you enter an ALTERNATIVE PAYEE in the business partner master data at either the global level under the tab VENDOR: GENERAL DATA, or the company code level in the VENDOR: PAYMENT TRANSACTIONS tab.

Head office and branches

You can enter the account number for the HEAD OFFICE account in the business partner master data under the financial accounting role on the VENDOR: ACCOUNT MANAGEMENT tab.

6.5.3 Manual outgoing payments

You can run the automatic payment program and produce payment media automatically to send to the bank. Or, you can make the payment at the bank manually and use the automatic payment program to clear the supplier account. This section deals with payments that you don't want to clear with the automatic payment program. It could be that there are separate processes or people that deal with urgent payments, or you may want to pay part of an invoice, or perhaps it is easier to clear, for example, outgoing direct debits this way.

Most companies will try to avoid manual payments where possible and manual payments should be the exception rather than the rule. The most important thing is to implement the appropriate controls and authorizations if manual payments are allowed.

The first option we will cover is using two steps, one to post the payment, the second to post the clearing. The supplier payment is posted to the bank clearing account (or to the supplier as well), in one step by one department, for example, from the bank statement, and accounts payable clears the payment against the relevant documents in a separate step, not necessarily in that order. This app works in a similar way to the G/L clearing app. The relevant SAP Fiori app for this is F1367 CLEAR OUTGOING PAYMENTS.

On the first screen, you see all the unallocated payments and the supplier they refer to. See Figure 6.33. You can select the payment that you want to allocate, and on the second screen you match that payment against the relevant invoices.

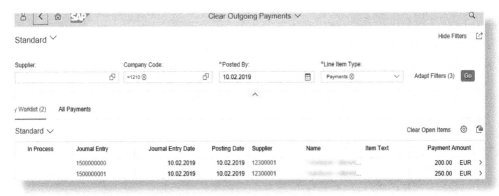

Figure 6.33: App F1367—clear outgoing payments—initial screen

Or, you can click on CLEAR OPEN ITEMS and on the next screen you will see all open items, including all the payments and invoices, and you can allocate more than one at a time. See Figure 6.34. When ready, you can simulate the posting, or post directly.

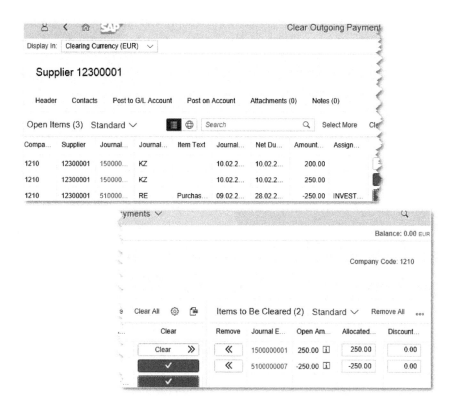

Figure 6.34: App F1367—clear outgoing payments—multiple items

The second flow is one step, using app F1612 POST OUTGOING PAYMENT, where you can clear a supplier account and post the balance to bank clearing in the same posting. This app is almost identical to app F1345 POST INCOMING PAYMENTS which is described in detail in section 7.4 (apart from defaulting to the account and document type of the customer rather than supplier), so we will not cover it in this section.

6.5.4 Down payments

A *down payment* can be required, for example, where a large expenditure needs to be made upfront for the purchase of a large fixed asset, such as a plant or building, or a marketing campaign. In such cases, the supplier may request a percentage of the total expected value of the invoice upfront, or in several stages. It can also occur where you simply send a payment in advance, for example, for a membership or magazine subscription, and only afterwards receive the tax invoice.

127

The down payment process consists of posting a *down payment request* (effectively a dummy or statistical invoice) to the supplier account so that the automatic payment program has a document to pay against. The down payment request is posted as a one-sided journal entry to the supplier account with app F1688 MANAGE SUPPLIER DOWN PAYMENT REQUESTS (MANAGE DOWN PAYMENT REQUEST FOR SUPPLIER in some releases) and does not show up in the trial balance or in the general ledger account balances, only in the supplier line items if you select *Noted Items* as the ITEM TYPE.

Once the payment is made, it will show up in the general ledger as well as the supplier account. Instead of showing up as a reduction of the supplier payables, it will be linked to a different G/L account (for example, in the receivables section of the balance sheet).

Items that are linked to a different account in this way will have a different posting key and a *special G/L indicator*, so in some reports (such as app F0712 MANAGE SUPPLIER LINE ITEMS) you will have to select *Special G/L Transactions* as well as *Normal Items* in the ITEM TYPE field.

When the final invoice is received, the down payment is then cleared against it and, if necessary, a payment made for the balance of the invoice.

6.5.5 Payment comparison

With app F1749 SUPPLIER PAYMENT ANALYSIS (AUTOMATIC AND MANUAL PAYMENTS), you can run by user, company code, supplier, or currency. You can choose the time period and the currency to display in, or filter on a specific supplier, user, company code, etc. See Figure 6.35.

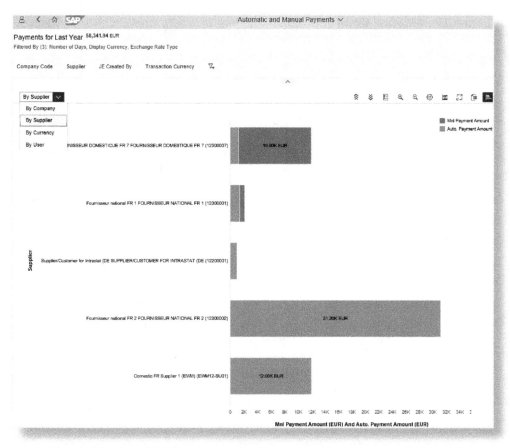

Figure 6.35: App F1749—comparison of automatic and manual payments

6.6 Accounts payable closing tasks

Many of the closing tasks are similar for accounts payable and receivable, and even the general ledger, for example, the foreign currency revaluation (shown in section 11.2.2), so we will only show a few examples in each section.

6.6.1   Balance confirmations

In order to ensure that the amount reported in the books as owing to or from suppliers and customers is correct, auditors will carry out various checks. The organization being audited will typically send out balance confirmations to customers and suppliers using their own corporate letterhead, requesting their cooperation on behalf of the auditors.

The balance confirmation usually consists of a statement of the amounts outstanding between the organization and the related customer or supplier. Accompanying this will be a polite request that confirmation of the balance is sent directly to the organization's auditors, or if the balance is not correct, then they should send the outstanding figure. The document is known as a balance confirmation and is usually prepared around the end of the year, but could also occur ad hoc.

The balance confirmation program in SAP S/4HANA produces a form automatically, containing the letter plus the amount outstanding and usually a confirmation sheet to be returned to the auditor. SAP Fiori app F2959 MA-NAGE SUPPLIER BALANCE CONFIRMATIONS is available in SAP S/4HANA Cloud, which gives you an overview of the existing confirmations. You can create new confirmations using app F2257 SCHEDULE ACCOUNTS PAYABLE JOBS, as shown in Figure 6.36. As usual, with the scheduler apps, you can select a date range to see items that have already been run or you can click + in order to schedule a new run.

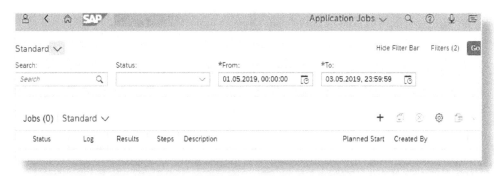

Figure 6.36: App F2257—schedule accounts payable jobs

To schedule the new run, select the correct JOB TEMPLATE, in this case SUP-PLIER BALANCE CONFIRMATION, and give a JOB NAME; see Figure 6.37. Depending on the job template you choose, you will see different parameters appear in the lower section of the screen. START IMMEDIATELY and SINGLE RUN are usually selected as default or you can set a time or recurrence pattern.

Supplier Balance Confirmation

GENERAL INFORMATION   SCHEDULING OPTIONS   PARAMETERS

Parameter Section

General Selections

			Further Selections	
*Company Code:			*Reconciliation Key Date:	dd.MM.yyyy
Supplier:			Special G/L Indicator:	
			Noted Items: ☐	

Output Control

*Description:	
*Date of Issue:	dd.MM.yyyy
No Reply:	☐
Date for Reply:	dd.MM.yyyy
Reply To:	
Confirmation Procedure:	
Use Print Bundling:	☐ ▾

Figure 6.37: App F2257—schedule balance confirmation parameters

Once you have selected SCHEDULE, the job status will show in process, and when you refresh, the status will change to finish, and you can click on the LOG to check the details. See Figure 6.38.

				Application Jobs ⌄		

Standard ⌄   Show Filter

Jobs (2) Standard * ⌄   + ⎘

Status	Log	Results	Steps	Description	Planned Start	Created By	
Finished	ⓘ		1	Supplier Balance Confirmation	16.05.2019, 13:29	OonaFlanagan	>
Finished	ⓘ		1	Supplier Balance Confirmation	16.05.2019, 13:25	OonaFlanagan	>

Figure 6.38: App F2257—schedule balance confirmation

It will then appear in F2959 MANAGE BALANCE CONFIRMATIONS FOR SUPPLIERS, as shown in Figure 6.39.

Figure 6.39: App F2959—manage balance confirmations for suppliers

If you drill down into the required run, you see a list of the documents produced and you can open the PDF next to each item to display it. In Figure 6.40, the first item is a checklist of all the confirmations that have been produced in that run and the second is the letter itself.

Output Details

	Item ID	Status	Output Type	Recipient	Channel	Form Template	Changed On	Display		
						Send Output Duplicate Retry Set to Completed Show Application Log ⚙				
☐	1	Completed (4)	CHECKLIST		PRINT	FIN_FO_BLNC _CNFRM_CHK LST	16.05.2019	🗋		Output Details
☐	2	Completed (4)	LETTER	(10300002)	PRINT	FIN_FO_BLNC _CNFRM_LTTR	16.05.2019	🗋		Output Details

Figure 6.40: App F2959—supplier confirmation PDFs and checklist

If you don't have the new apps, the following apps are based on GUI transactions

▶ CREATE BALANCE CONFIRMATIONS—FOR SUPPLIERS (F.18) CREATE BALANCE CONFIRMATIONS AS PDF—FOR SUPPLIERS (F18P).

6.6.2 Reclassifications

Suppliers with a debit balance, for example, for returned goods or an overpayment, may need to be reclassified under receivables. The supplier account stays the same, but adjustment accounts are used to transfer the balance to the appropriate place in the balance sheet. The equivalent adjustment occurs on the customer side.

Some countries require a split between outstanding items, for example, under 1 year, 1-5 years, and over 5 years, or need to move fixed asset purchases to a separate line in the balance sheet for capital expenditure (capex) suppliers. Again, adjustment accounts are required as the adjustment cannot be posted directly to the supplier or the supplier reconciliation account.

The current app is based on GUI transaction FAGLF101. You enter the company code, sort method, and valuation area (country or accounting principle such as IFRS) in the header. See Figure 6.41.

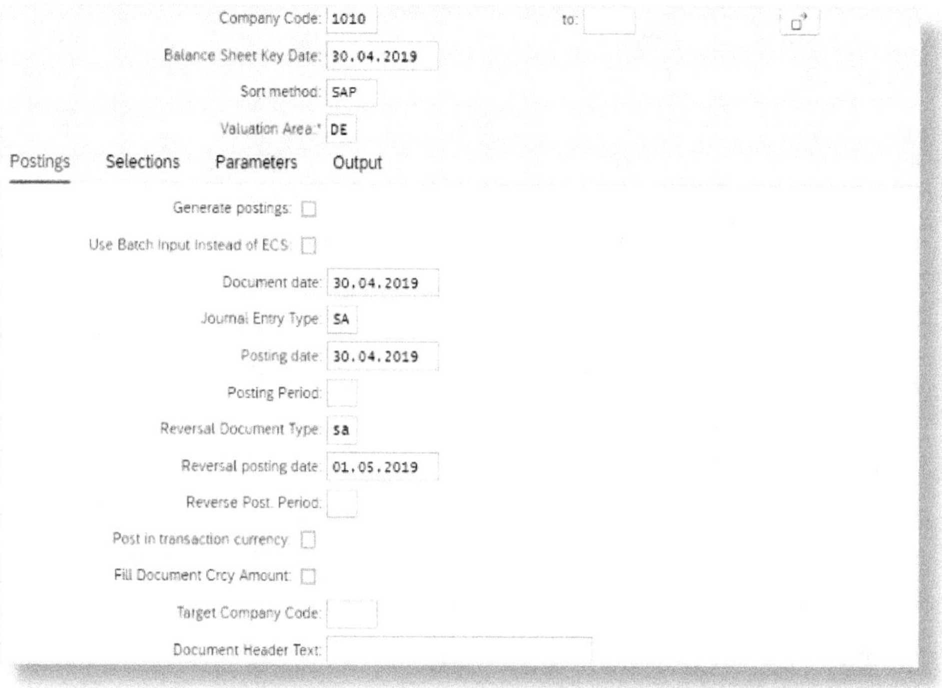

Figure 6.41: Transaction FAGLF101—regroup payables/receivables

In POSTINGS, you select the document types and dates. In SELECTIONS, you enter the range of accounts that you want to regroup and complete the remaining tabs as appropriate. If you are regrouping investments, you need to select the DISPLAY INVESTMENTS field on the PARAMETERS tab and on the OUTPUT tab, you can elect to save a log of the proposed and posted items. When you select EXECUTE, you see a list of the documents chosen and you can click on MESSAGES at the top of the resulting screen to check any error or POSTINGS to see what documents will be posted.

6.7   Viewing supplier information

As many G/L, supplier, and customer reports are quite similar, they will be covered in the general reporting section in Chapter 10. However, some display transactions are covered below.

6.7.1   Overview

Figure 6.42 shows app F2917 ACCOUNTS PAYABLE OVERVIEW, which is available from 1809 on-premise and Cloud releases. It consists of large tiles called *cards* with quite a bit of information and KPIs directly on the cards themselves.

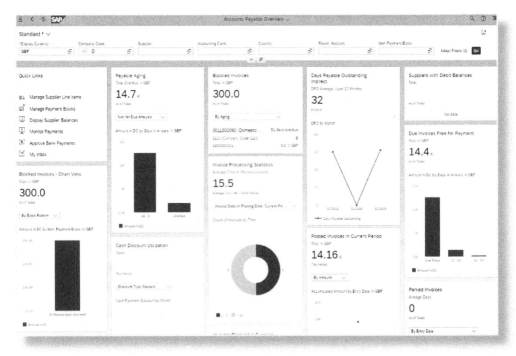

Figure 6.42: App F2917—accounts payable overview page

You can choose which cards to display where, change filters, and choose other options on the card in the small dropdowns.

6.7.2 Supplier factsheet

App F0354 SUPPLIER FACTSHEET, shown in Figure 6.43, shows a 360-degree view of the supplier, including master data and some transactional data, such as invoices and POs. You can jump to the factsheet from other apps, such as app F1861 DISPLAY SUPPLIER LIST, by clicking on the supplier number, then in the pop-up, selecting the supplier number again instead of a link.

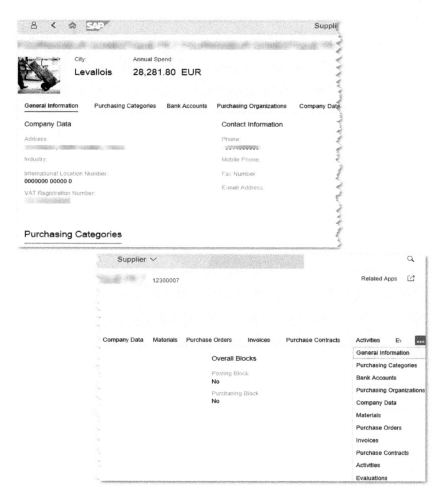

Figure 6.43: Supplier factsheet

135

6.7.3 Display supplier balances

The following three figures are all from app F0701 DISPLAY SUPPLIER BALANCES, which shows the debit, credit, and total balances by period. You can select one supplier or a range of suppliers and drill down to further detail.

> **Drilldown**
>
> Ensure that you select the exact amount you want a breakdown of. If you select, for example, the amount of 19,451.01 euros, see Figure 6.44, you will only see all the debits for period one. If you want to see everything for a period, you need to click on the BALANCE column for that period or click on the total at the bottom for the whole year.

BALANCES	SPECIAL G/L	COMPARE					
Currency: EUR							
Period	Debit	Credit	Balance	Cumulative Balan...		Purchases	Imputed Interest
Opening Balance				-33,219.94			
01	19,451.01	22,676.13	-3,225.12	-36,445.06		-22,676.13	-5.03
02	14,105.96	33,780.00	-19,674.04	-56,119.10		-33,750.00	-7.55
03	75,352.62	41,302.62	34,050.00	-22,069.10		-31,834.00	-4.93

Figure 6.44: App F0701—display supplier balances

You can compare purchases in one year with purchases in another, see Figure 6.45, and you can see special G/L indicators, such as down payments, shown in Figure 6.46.

BALANCES	SPECIAL G/L	COMPARE			
Currency: EUR	Compare with	2018			
Period	Purchases 2019	Purchases 2018	Absolute Difference	Difference in %	
Opening Balance					
01	-22,676.13	-20,000.00	-2,676.13	13.38%	
02	-33,750.00	-10,000.00	-23,750.00	237.5%	
03	-31,834.00	-9,159.10	-22,674.90	247.57%	

Figure 6.45: App F0701—compare supplier balances by year

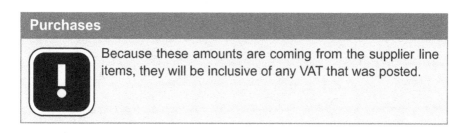

Figure 6.46: App F0701—supplier down payment balances

6.7.4 Line items

App F0712 MANAGE SUPPLIER LINE ITEMS, see Figure 6.47, lists line items. You can add columns, and sort and filter as required, for example, to add in related customer items in the filter.

	Supplier	Clearin...	Reference	Journal Entry Date	Journal Entry	Journ...	Amount (CoCd Cur.)	
	Items (68) Standard * ∨			Edit Line Items	Create Correspondence	Block for Payment	Unblock	
>	Supplier: 1001862 -						0.00	EUR
∨	Supplier: 1001865 -							
☑	1001865	☐		08.04.2019	2000000020	ZP	1,000.00	EUR
☐	1001865	☐	EUR	08.04.2019	1900000017	KR	-1,000.00	EUR
	1001865						**0.00**	**EUR**
∨	Supplier: 1001955 -							
☐	1001955	⚙	REF3	20.03.2019	1900000009	KR	-133.33	EUR
☐	1001955	⚙	REF	20.03.2019	1900000001	KR	-133.33	EUR
	1001955						**-266.66**	**EUR**

Figure 6.47: App F0712—manage supplier line items grouped by supplier

To group by supplier, go to ⚙, choose the GROUP tab, and select SUPPLIER. You can also use the dropdown on the SUPPLIER column to add a group.

7 Accounts receivable

This chapter is all about the accounts receivable processes and the related SAP Fiori apps. We explain the different types of sales invoices and how the incoming payments can be processed. In this section, we explain financial supply chain management (FSCM) and cover credit and dispute management and debt collection.

7.1 The order-to-cash process

Accounts receivable is the term for the subledger dealing with everything related to customer accounts, but excluding the actual sales processes, and is covered in the best practices scope item J59 ACCOUNTS RECEIVABLE.

The end-to-end process is known either as the *order-to-cash* flow *(O2C)* or as *quotation-to-cash (Q2C)*. A summarized O2C flow is shown in Figure 7.1. We will run briefly through the whole sales process in order to gain a better understanding of what will happen in finance.

Figure 7.1: Simplified accounts receivable flow/order to cash

The sales process usually starts with an inquiry, and perhaps a quote, or sales order. If the customer is new, they will usually need to be assessed before they can be given goods or services on credit. If they have an existing account, there will normally be a credit limit placed on the amount of goods or services they can have outstanding at any one time. Control of the credit is usually within finance, either as part of accounts receivable or as a separate credit control department, depending on the size of the organization.

If the sales order is within the credit limit, it can be processed and the goods sent to the customer. If not, then the order may be blocked and sent for review to the credit control department who can decide whether to release it or wait for a payment to be received.

Picking, packing, printing, shipment, or delivery notes may occur before the goods leave the warehouse and the goods issue is posted. The service industry may have a time confirmation or time recording process instead of the physical goods issue process.

Sales may be initiated in the sales module of SAP S/4HANA itself or in an external system and sometimes sales of non-trading items (fixed asset sales or the recharge of services) may be posted without a sales order, directly in finance.

7.2   Invoice with sales order (billing)

Once the goods or services are deemed to be either on their way or with the customer, the next step is *billing.* Billing consists of creating a sales invoice or billing document and triggering the posting to the general ledger. In some cases, this is seamless and the billing document and accounting document share the same number, but not always. Inside SAP S/4HANA, they are two distinct objects. On (hopefully) rare occasions, a billing document may be produced and posted without the accounting document due to an error in the accounting information, and needs to be investigated.

There are other permutations, for example, direct deliveries, where the organization takes the order and bills the customer, but goods are sent direct from the manufacturer without passing through the organization's own warehouse.

Once the goods have been delivered, billing can take place. This creates a billing document and a physical tax invoice to be sent to the customer, as well as a financial document that updates the customer account and the general ledger. Depending on the organization, billing may occur each time goods are loaded for delivery, or scheduled to run overnight. The invoices may be physically printed and posted or sent electronically. Figure 7.2 shows APP F2692 DISPLAY PROCESS FLOW—ACCOUNTS RECEIVABLE. This shows the accounts receivable flow from quotation to payment.

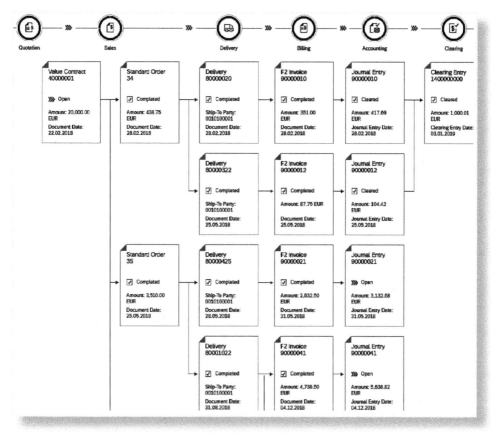

Figure 7.2: App F2692—display process flow, accounts receivable

7.3 Invoice without sales order

For certain types of sales, organizations may prefer to post a manual sales invoice directly in finance, without going through the whole sales order process. This could be for things like miscellaneous sales, services, fixed asset sales, or recharges. App CREATE OUTGOING INVOICE, shown in Figure 7.3, based on GUI transaction FB70, can be used, which is fairly similar to the accounts payable CREATE INCOMING INVOICE app, based on FB60 GUI transaction. You enter the company code, date, reference, and amount in the header items and details of what is being sold in the line items along with the G/L account number and either a cost or profit center (possibly additional information for a profit segment in CO-PA) depending on the type of account. You can simulate before posting, if required.

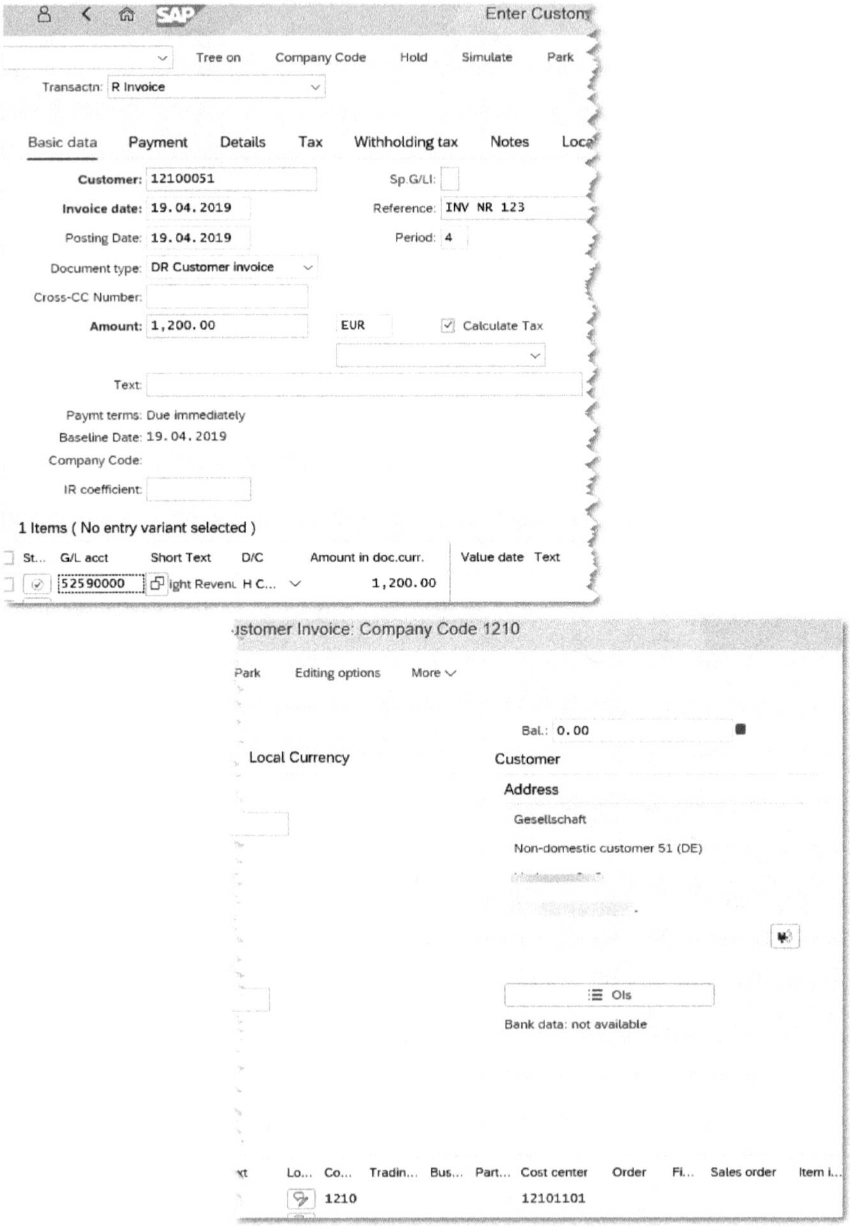

Figure 7.3: Transaction FB70—create outgoing invoice

Because the invoice is posted directly in finance, there is no automatic customer invoice document produced, but you can create a document using the correspondence function if required and configured. Some organizations may use Microsoft Excel or Microsoft Word for this type of sale, especially if it is very rare and requires specialized wording. Asset sales are covered in section 9.6, under retirements with customer.

7.4 Incoming payments

Based on the agreed payment terms, when the invoice is due for payment, the customer can make payment in several ways. In Europe, this is typically by bank transfer, which is initiated by the customer sending the payment, or by direct debit, which is initiated by the company receiving the payment. In some countries, physical checks are still used. Sometimes, cash discounts are offered to encourage early payment. For example, the payment term may be 30 days, but if the customer pays within, say, 10 days, he can deduct 2% from the payment.

7.4.1 Direct debits

This process is similar to the automatic payment process in that a payment proposal is produced and reviewed, then posted to the accounts, producing a payment file which is sent to the bank. However, payment is collected from the customer rather than being paid out to the supplier. In addition, some companies may also send out a direct debit prenotification to inform the customer of the exact amount and date of the upcoming payment. Direct debits are covered in the best practices scope item 19M DIRECT DEBIT. In most countries, you have to have direct debit mandates signed prior to being able to collect money from a customer's account. SAP S/4HANA has various apps based on GUI transactions to enter details of the mandates into the system and to block the payment collection if the mandates are not entered or invalid. The master data script for creating a SEPA mandate is BNV CREATE SEPA MANDATE.

The main apps are: FSEPA_M1 (CREATE), FSEPA_M2 (AMEND), FSEPA_M3 (DISPLAY), and FSEPA_M4 (LIST). You also have a collection authorization indicator in the bank payment section of the customer master, which can be used to confirm whether the correct mandate has been completed correctly and is held on file, if you are not using SEPA mandates. See Figure 7.4.

New Bank Account

General Data

ID:	Account Number:

Bank Country:	Reference Details:

Bank Key:	Account Holder:

Control Key:	Account Name:

IBAN:	Bank Valid From:
	dd.MM.yyyy

IBAN Valid From:	Bank Valid To:
dd.MM.yyyy	dd.MM.yyyy

Collection Authorization Indicator:
☐

Figure 7.4: App F0850A—customer collection authorization Indicator

7.4.2 Checks received

Checks may be physically received at the customer's premises, recorded, and taken to the bank. The customer accounts can be updated with the payment as soon as the check is received, but it may be several days before the check physically clears through the banking system and appears on the bank statement.

7.4.3 Bank transfers received

Most companies will have some sort of automation whereby the bank statement is uploaded to the system. Where customers supply sufficient detail with their payment, companies are able to transfer the payment automatically to the customer account, and in many cases, automatically clear the related invoices at the same time.

7.4.4   Matching payments against invoices

One of the areas which can be time-consuming is matching payments against the correct invoices. In some countries, for example in Finland, it is mandatory to enter specific references when sending the payment file. These references appear in the bank statement file, which means a high percentage of payments can be matched automatically. Even where an invoice cannot be immediately matched from the electronic bank statement, it will show as an unmatched item (on either the bank clearing or the customer account) and can be matched later as part of the post-processing of the bank statement or transferred to the customer account to be investigated.

With improving technology, more and more information can be captured automatically from the bank statement files and SAP has also introduced machine learning to help automate the matching of payments against invoices. However, many companies are still obliged to post some, if not all, payments to the customer account and clear the related invoices manually. App F1345 Post Incoming Payments can be used to post the payment amount against the bank clearing account and clear invoices on the customer account in one transaction. You enter the company and bank details, dates, amounts, and customer number in the header, then you select the items that are being paid by clicking on Clear in the bottom left-hand section of the screen. The items then appear in the bottom right-hand section, see Figure 7.5. If you receive a payment that refers to more than one customer account or deducts amounts owing on the supplier, you can go to Select More and add additional accounts or items.

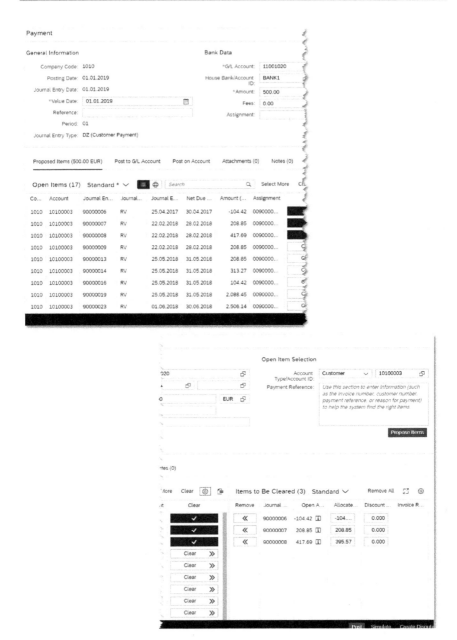

Figure 7.5: App F1345—post incoming payments, manual with clearing

In the example shown in Figure 7.5, the payment did not exactly match the invoices, so two invoices were fully paid and cleared and the third invoice was only partially paid. Similar to accounts payable, when a payment is smaller than the invoice, there are several options. If the difference refers to a cash discount that you are going to allow, you can enter it in the discount field. If it is a small amount that is under the tolerance, you can write it off automatically. If you want to show that the invoice is only partially paid, you can enter it as a partial payment or as a residual amount. A *residual amount* will clear the invoice and replace it with a new document containing only the residual amount, but you may need to adjust the due date. A *partial payment* will leave both the invoice and the payment showing on the account. Both options are available in the bottom right part of the screen, shown on its own in Figure 7.6, although you may need to add columns or scroll across to the right to find them. In the classic GUI they are in separate tabs.

You can also add a reason code for the payment difference, especially if a future credit note is likely to be issued. Examples of reason codes could be discounts, bank charges, invoice error, price query, wrong quantity, late or short delivery, and so on. This field can also be added to the displayed columns if not shown by default.

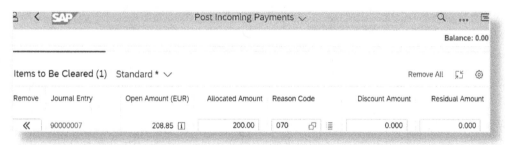

Figure 7.6: App F1345—incoming payments, items to be cleared

You can also create a dispute case from this screen. See section 7.6.2 for further information on dispute cases.

7.4.5   Customer down payments

These are similar to down payments in accounts payable, however they are posted to the customer account and cleared by an incoming payment from the customer. App F1689 MANAGE CUSTOMER DOWN PAYMENT REQUESTS allows you to manage and create customer down payment requests. See Figure 7.7 and Figure 7.8.

Figure 7.7: App F1689—create down payment request

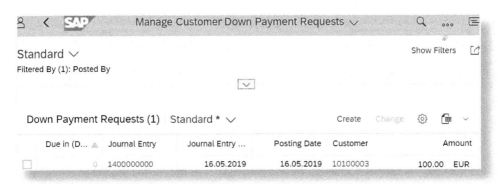

Figure 7.8: App F1689—manage down payment requests overview

When payment is received for the down payment, you can use app F1345 POST INCOMING PAYMENTS as if you were clearing an invoice. You may need to go to SELECT MORE and select the option LINE ITEM TYPE for SPECIAL G/L TRANSACTIONS, if it is not selected by default.

7.5 Credit management

The scope items for credit management are BD6 BASIC CREDIT MANAGEMENT and 1QM ADVANCED CREDIT MANAGEMENT (which needs an additional license). You may hear the term *FSCM*, which stands for *SAP Financial Supply Chain Management* and includes banking, cash management, credit management, dispute management, and collections management. SAP FSCM credit management is often used to differentiate between the original credit management in SAP and the SAP FSCM version introduced in 2004 which was the first area to use business partner functionality. SAP FSCM is the only credit management available in SAP S/4HANA and the one we will cover in this section, followed by dispute management, and then collections management.

Credit management starts when a new customer wishes to open an account and you have to decide how creditworthy they are. Not all companies may be subject to background checks, for example, you are unlikely to carry out checks on other companies in the group, and perhaps governmental departments or tax offices. You may also take into account whether you already buy a lot from them as a supplier, as this would reduce the risk, (you may be able to deduct any overdue amounts from what you owe them).

With a new customer, most companies will review a customer's background and credit history with other companies and credit agencies prior to assigning an appropriate credit limit and then review that credit limit along with their payment history and sales record on a regular basis.

If the customer orders goods or services which do not exceed the credit limit, the order can be processed. If the sales order plus any outstanding items, such as opening sales orders, open deliveries, or unpaid invoices, is over the credit limit, the order will be initially blocked and sent for review to the credit control department who can choose to release or reject it, or keep it blocked until payment is received. Another criterion which may block a sales order is if the customer is within his credit limit, but his account is substantially overdue for payment.

SAP S/4HANA has a number of tools relating to credit management. For example, you can link to credit agencies and you can use formulas to enter credit scores to automate the calculation of the credit limit. If a sales order fails the credit check, a credit case is automatically created, and can be assigned to the relevant credit analyst to review and resolve any issues, as well as document the status, action, and final decision on whether or not to release the order. You can also factor into the credit limit and risk whether you are able to get insurance to cover a customer if he doesn't pay and whether there is any collateral.

7.5.1 Credit master data

To use SAP FSCM, you create a separate credit role (UKM000 SAP CREDIT MANAGEMENT) in the customer master record (business partner transaction). Some of the customer's credit information is contained in the BUSINESS PARTNER (GEN) role in the CREDIT PROFILE (see Figure 7.9) and CREDITWORTHINESS DATA tabs and some in the CREDIT SEGMENT DATA in the credit management role.

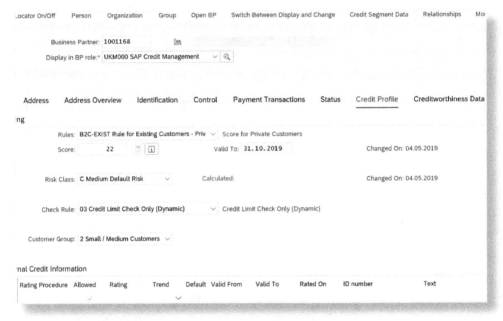

Figure 7.9: Business partner—credit profile data

In the CREDIT PROFILE tab, you can choose to have a standard rule with no automatic calculation, which means that you can decide on the credit limit yourself. If you choose a rule, then clicking on the ⛃ button to the right of the SCORE field will calculate a score and clicking on the ⓘ button next to it will explain how the score was calculated. You may have different rules for existing, new, private, or business customers.

You can choose a RISK CLASS, depending on whether you think that particular customer represents a low, medium, high, or very high risk. Some customers may be no risk at all, such as affiliated companies or governments.

In the CHECK RULE field, you can choose the type of check, for example CREDIT LIMIT CHECK ONLY (DYNAMIC), CREDIT LIMIT CHECK ONLY (STATISTICAL), or ALL CHECKS ACTIVE. ALL CHECKS ACTIVE might include maximum amount, items overdue over 180 days, and other checks. Statistical and dynamic rules are similar with the main difference being that dynamic includes a specific time horizon, taking into account only orders that are due in that specific time period.

If you select the CREDIT SEGMENT DATA button at the top of the screen, you will have additional tabs below for CREDIT LIMIT AND CONTROL (see Figure 7.10), as well as PAYMENT BEHAVIOR KEY FIGURES, and KPI PAYMENT BEHAVIOR. Note that the RULES are assigned in the CREDIT PROFILE tab and only displayed in the CREDIT SEGMENT tab. When you enter the credit limit, you can also enter a validity check. If an order is placed outside of the credit limit validity date, the order will be blocked with reason CREDIT LIMIT INVALID.

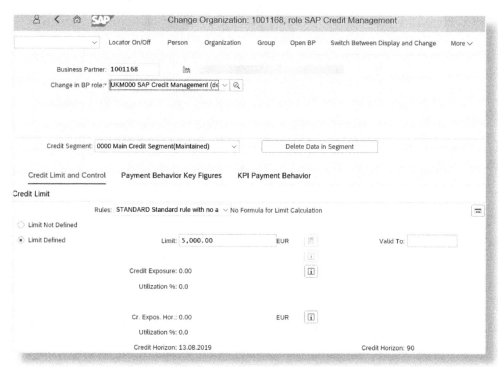

Figure 7.10: Business partner credit segment data

Credit profile and creditworthiness data tabs

 These tabs appear when you are still in the general data area and only when you have the credit management role assigned. For the CREDIT LIMIT AND CONTROL tabs and the two behavior tabs you have to actually switch to the CREDIT SEGMENT data to see them.

An organization may split their credit management into *credit segments*, which could, for example, be related to sales division, retail/wholesale, company code, region, or business area. Each customer must be assigned to a main credit segment, but can also be assigned to additional segments, and each of the additional segments may have different credit information in the master data.

In the credit segment, you can also block a customer manually and give a block reason (for example, no insurance available, fraud possible, credit limit to be approved, score invalid, etc.).

App DISPLAY CREDIT MASTER, based on GUI transaction UKM_BP_DISPLAY, is useful because you first see an overview page (see Figure 7.11), and you can then click on BUSINESS PARTNER MASTER RECORD to jump to the customer's credit data if you need more information.

Partner	Cr.Segment	Credit Limit	B...	Valid To	Changed On	Submission	Calculated Sp....	Zero	Reasn	Limit Requested	C.. Requested	Requested On
1000265	1000	8,000.00			25.03.2019		0.00			0.00		
1000266	1000	5.00	X	31.12.2019	25.03.2019		0.00		02	0.00		
1000268	1000	5.00		31.12.2019	25.03.2019		0.00			0.00		

Figure 7.11: Display credit master—master data list

You can also click on LIABILITY TOTALS (sometimes a button and sometimes found under MORE depending on screen size) to see the credit exposure details, such as those shown in Figure 7.12. You can sort; filter; add columns; total columns; subtotal columns; download to a local file; and so on.

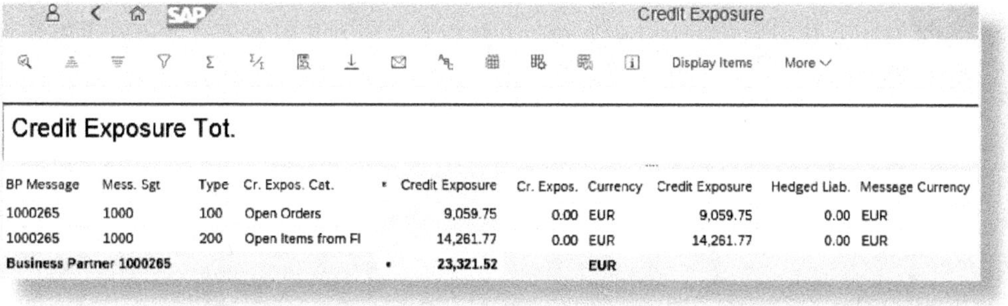

BP Message	Mess. Sgt	Type	Cr. Expos. Cat.	• Credit Exposure	Cr. Expos.	Currency	Credit Exposure	Hedged Liab.	Message Currency
1000265	1000	100	Open Orders	9,059.75	0.00	EUR	9,059.75	0.00	EUR
1000265	1000	200	Open Items from FI	14,261.77	0.00	EUR	14,261.77	0.00	EUR
Business Partner 1000265				• 23,321.52		EUR			

Figure 7.12: Display credit master—credit exposure

Note that instead of using ⚙ to add columns like in the true SAP Fiori apps, GUI-based transactions have a button a bit like a Rubik's cube ⊞ that you can click on. In the pop-up you will see the existing columns on the left-hand side and all other available columns on the right. You can select an item and use the arrow keys to add or remove it from what is displayed on the main screen. To total something, you can select the column and click on the sigma button, Σ, and once you have totaled a column a new button will appear for further subtotals, $\frac{\Sigma}{1}$. Filter (once you have selected a column) is ∇ and sort ascending and descending are ≞ ≝.

7.5.2 Credit case

App MANAGE CREDIT CASES is based on GUI transaction UKM_CASE. A credit case or *documented credit decision* is created automatically when a sales order is blocked by credit management. It is used to manage and record correspondence and conversations with the customer and other actions taken. You can assign statuses and escalate to different departments and so on. See Figure 7.13.

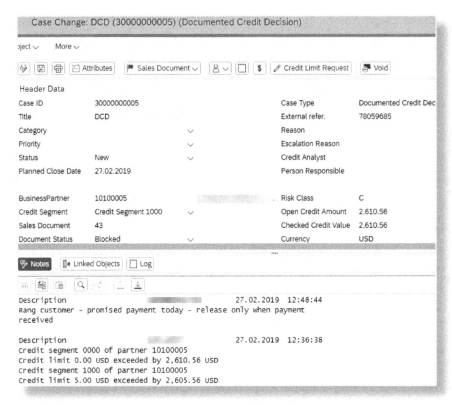

Figure 7.13: Documented credit decision case and decision notes

7.5.3 Displaying credit data reports

The following are some additional credit management apps (with GUI-related transactions where relevant).

- ▶ DISPLAY CREDIT DATA CREDIT PROFILE—UKM_MASS_DSP1

- ▶ DISPLAY CREDIT DATA SEGMENT—UKM_MASS_DSP2

- ▶ F2162 DISPLAY CREDIT MANAGEMENT LOG

- ▶ DISPLAY CREDIT LIMIT UTILIZATION—UKM_MALUS_DSP

- ▶ DISPLAY CREDIT MASTER DATA—UKM_BP_DISPLAY

7.6 Dispute management

Where there are a lot of queries on invoices, for example, delivery- or qual-ity-related issues, dispute management is a useful tool to monitor and follow up the queried items and to ensure they are dealt with in a timely fashion. Disputes may be raised in different ways, either immediately if the customer gets in contact beforehand, or later when payment is withheld and has to be chased. Sometimes the dispute may come to light when the disputed item is deducted from a payment. Resolving disputes is a fairly manual process as each dispute may be different and sometimes subjective and a goodwill credit may need to be raised if there is no clear-cut procedure.

Dispute cases can be created where you see a CREATE DISPUTE button, for example, in the customer line items, while posting payments or working on collections.

7.6.1 Process receivables

App F0106 PROCESS RECEIVABLES is used to review the customer's out-standing invoices in order to create *promises to pay* and *dispute cases* if required, or to send correspondence. You need to have configured *SAP Dispute Management* and *SAP Collections Management* for the app to run properly.

The first screen is an overview list of customers. Once you select the cus-tomer, you will see the contact details at the top, and tabs for invoices, payments, disputes, promises, and resubmissions, for you to review. The customer history is shown on the right-hand side. Figure 7.14 shows the body of the report and the INVOICES tab.

| 16 | 0 | 1 | 1 | 0 |
| INVOICES | CLEARED ITEMS | DISPUTES | PROMISES | RESUBMISSIONS |

Invoices Standard * ∨   Create Dispute   Create Promise   Resend Billing Document   Create Correspondence

	Document No.		Document Date	Days in Arrears	Posting K...	Outstanding		State of Promise	Promised For	Dispute Reason	Due Date
☐	90000004	⌂	25.04.2017	611	Credit me...	-313.25	EUR	Not Promised		Not Disputed	30.04.2017
☐	90000010	⌂	28.02.2018	307	Invoice	417.68	EUR	Open	03.01.2019	Not Disputed	28.02.2018
☐	90000011	⌂	28.02.2018	307	Invoice	417.68	EUR	Not Promised		Price Difference	28.02.2018
☐	90000012	⌂	25.05.2018	215	Invoice	104.42	EUR	Not Promised		Not Disputed	31.05.2018
☐	90000015	⌂	25.05.2018	215	Invoice	208.84	EUR	Not Promised		Not Disputed	31.05.2018

Figure 7.14: App F0106—process receivables

7.6.2 Dispute cases

The dispute case may be updated manually or automatically by certain actions, for example, clearing the invoice with a credit note or payment. Dispute cases are frequently created during payment allocation when it is noticed that an invoice or part of an invoice has been omitted from the payment, perhaps with a note that it is disputed, and the dispute case serves as a reminder to follow it up. A dispute case can be created from other apps, such as the PROCESS RECEIVABLES app by clicking on the CREATE DISPUTE CASE button, and can be managed by app F0702 MANAGE DISPUTE CASES, as shown in Figure 7.15, and you can also send emails from the dispute case.

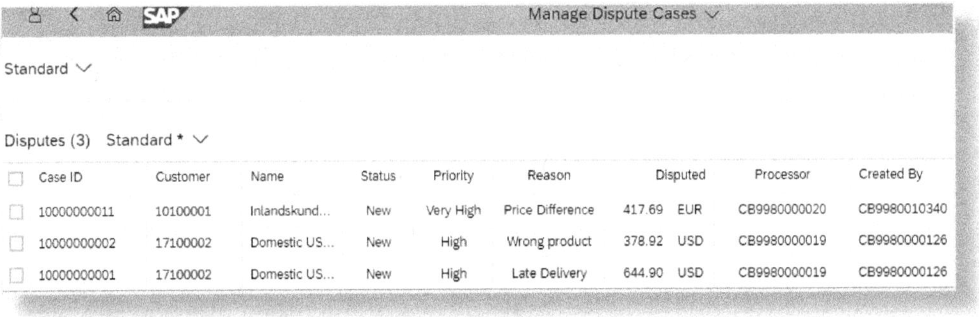
Manage Dispute Cases
Standard
Disputes (3) Standard *
Case ID | Customer | Name | Status | Priority | Reason | Disputed | Processor | Created By
10000000011 | 10100001 | Inlandskund... | New | Very High | Price Difference | 417.69 EUR | CB9980000020 | CB9980010340
10000000002 | 17100002 | Domestic US... | New | High | Wrong product | 378.92 USD | CB9980000019 | CB9980000126
10000000001 | 17100002 | Domestic US... | New | High | Late Delivery | 644.90 USD | CB9980000019 | CB9980000126

Figure 7.15: App F0702—manage dispute cases

7.7 Collections management

Collections management is a tool to help controllers better manage their department by assigning customer lists to the processors (or accounts receivable/credit control clerks) who then follow up or chase payments from the customers.

A COLLECTIONS MANAGEMENT role can be assigned in the business partner customer master record, allowing you to enter collection data on the COLLECTION PROFILE tab, such as a collection profile and collection segment to group the customer, as shown in Figure 7.16.

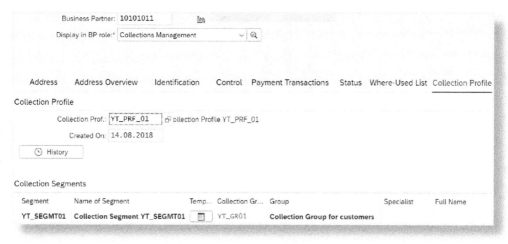

Figure 7.16: Business partner collection profile

You decide on a *collection strategy* for each company and set up rules, such as including overdue items over a certain amount, overdue more than a certain number of days, broken promises to pay, or at a certain dunning level. You can then create worklists, (see Figure 7.17), prioritize customers, define time intervals, and so on. You can also assign substitute processors. In the work list, you can see information from credit management and dispute management.

Figure 7.17: App F0380—process collections worklist

App F2375 SUPERVISE COLLECTIONS WORKLIST, shown in Figure 7.18, allows supervisors to have an overview of the progress of their department in collecting cash. The supervisor can prioritize the most urgent customers to chase or change the assignment of collection specialists to customers.

Figure 7.18: App F2375—supervise collections

7.8 Customer communications

7.8.1 Dunning letters

Dunning is used for sending reminder letters to customers who have outstanding invoices that are overdue for payment. The dunning program analyzes which invoices are relevant and proposes a list to be included in the reminder letter. You can set up several different letters to be triggered at a set date, for example, the first letter to be sent ten days after the invoice becomes overdue for payment, then a subsequent letter two weeks after that, and so on. The first letter is normally quite polite and subsequent letters get progressively stronger, perhaps putting the account on stop, and eventually threatening legal action with the last letter. Each letter would be a separate *dunning level.* You may have different letters for different groups of customers, for example, polite letters for important customers and stricter for smaller customers who don't have a good credit rating, and you may add dunning charges depending on the dunning level. The groups or letters and rules form a *dunning procedure.* You can set a minimum amount for dunning, below which the customer is ignored. If suppliers owe you money for a rebate or credit note, you can also include those suppliers in the dunning run.

It is important, as usual, to get the master data correct. You need to enter the correct dunning procedure in the company code correspondence tab of the customer master record (business partner). After dunning has been carried out, you can see when the customer was last dunned and what the dunning level (last letter) was. You can block the customer account from being dunned with a dunning block reason, if you have already discussed the account with the customer and are aware of reasons why an invoice has been withheld from payment. Examples of dunning reasons could be: disputed, promise given to pay, to be clarified with sales department or legal department, and so on.

Where you have a linked head office and branches, usually the head office receives one dunning notice with all items due from a branch unless decentralized processing is selected in the branch accounts.

There are separate fields in the customer master record for dunning and accounting clerks, but the setup is the same, so in the dropdown you will see the same set of clerks. A customer can have the same accounting clerk and dunning clerk, or they can have different ones.

The dunning procedure is split into steps and requires a dunning ID of your choice and a run date, similar in some ways to the automatic payment program. You may need to assign an accounting clerk. The steps are:

▶ Maintain parameters

▶ Dunning run

▶ Edit dunning proposal (optional)

▶ Print dunning letters

You can use app Create Dunning Notices, based on GUI transaction F150, to create these steps. (F150 is a GUI transaction and not an SAP Fiori number in this case). There is also app F2435 My Dunning Proposals, (in SAP S/4HANA Cloud and from 1709 on-premise).

In the parameters shown in Figure 7.19, the dunning date is the date that the letters will be issued, and is also used for the basis of calculating the days in arrears. Once the parameters are complete, you can click Schedule and create the dunning notices.

App F2328 Display Dunning History, allows you to see an overview of the customers who have been dunned, and to drill down to see the details of the dunning notices and the letters sent to them.

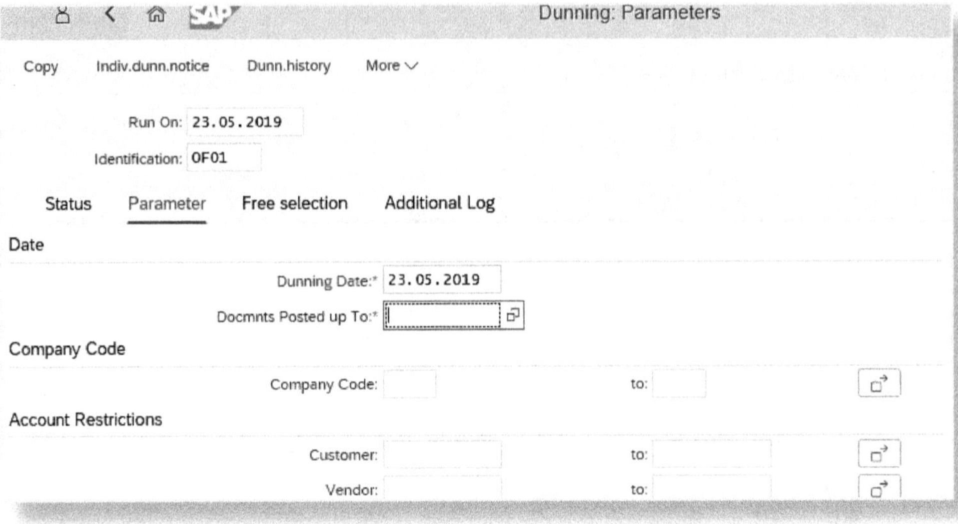

Figure 7.19: Transaction F150—create dunning notices

7.8.2 Correspondence

You can set up different forms for correspondence, for example, invoices, customer statements, open items, and so on. Correspondence can be triggered from different places, for example, from a document or app, such as process receivables, display customer (or supplier) balances, display customer (or supplier) line items; and dedicated apps, such as F0744 CREATE CORRESPONDENCE and F0744A CREATE CORRESPONDENCE (VERSION 2). Correspondence can be printed, emailed, or faxed. The first step is to create a request and the selection criteria will vary depending on the correspondence type. You can then preview the document prior to printing or sending. See Figure 7.20. Best practices scope item 1LQ OUTPUT MANAGEMENT covers forms, printing, and emailing.

7.8.3 Customer statements

In order to create a statement for a customer, you need to ensure that the relevant field in the customer master data is set for a weekly or monthly statement, however, customer statements can also be generated ad-hoc or as required.

Statement field in business partner

The statement frequency field is still called BANK STATEMENT in the business partner master data, although it definitely refers to the customer periodic statement and not the bank statement. It is under the COMPANY CODE DATA • CUSTOMER: CORRESPONDENCE tab.

You can use app CREATE PERIODIC ACCOUNT STATEMENTS, based on GUI transaction F-27, or you can use the correspondence functionality with apps F0744 and F0744A CREATE CORRESPONDENCE which allow you to print or email statements to customers. F0744A is the newer version available in SAP S/4HANA Cloud and from on-premise 1809 release and is shown in Figure 7.20. You can also display the history with app F2934 DISPLAY CORRESPONDENCE HISTORY.

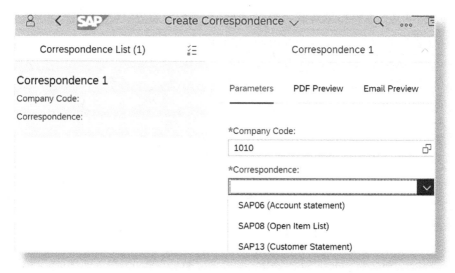

Figure 7.20: App F0744A—create correspondence

7.8.4 Balance confirmations

Balance confirmations for customers are almost identical to balance confirmations for suppliers as explained in section 6.6.1, so we won't repeat them here except to mention the two relevant apps are F2366 Schedule Accounts Receivable Jobs and F2834 Manage Balance Confirmations for Customers.

7.9 Display customer information

If you set up *accounting clerks* linked to a related user and assign the relevant customers to that accounting clerk, it makes it easier for each user to run reports for their own customers. The accounting clerk's name and telephone number can be included as a contact in certain forms, such as the customer statement. The app shown in Figure 7.21 is based on the GUI transaction in the IMG, but is almost identical to app F1009 Define Accounting Clerks, with the same four columns.

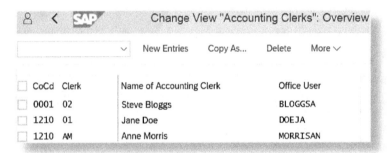

Figure 7.21: App F1009—define accounting clerks

7.9.1 Accounts receivable overview

Figure 7.22 shows app F3242 Accounts Receivable Overview. In the ME area, you have an additional setting, Manage Cards, which allows you to add or remove cards (the large tiles) and you can adapt the filters, save variants, or follow links to other apps. You can do some changes on the face of the card, such as change the AR Aging Analysis card to show by company code or accounting clerk instead of due date or the Days Sales Outstanding by company code, etc.

Figure 7.22: App F3242—accounts receivable overview app

7.9.2 Customer factsheet

The equivalent of the supplier factsheet is app F2187 CUSTOMER—360 DE-GREES VIEW, shown in Figure 7.23.

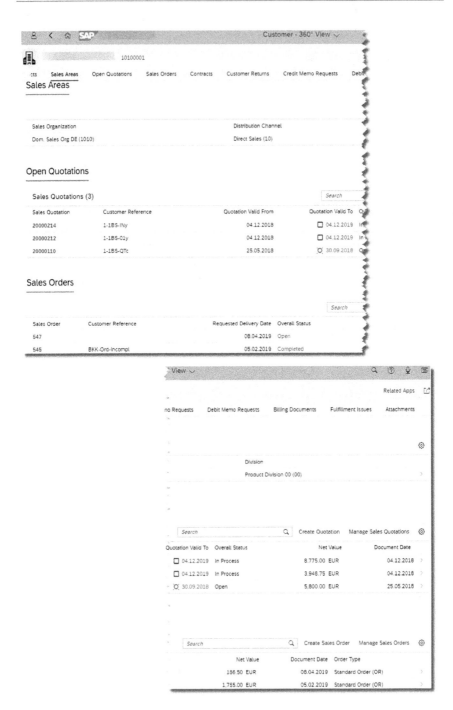

Figure 7.23: App F2187—customer factsheet

With some apps, you can get to the customer and supplier factsheets by drilling down to, or clicking on the customer or supplier number. The fact-sheet contains contracts, invoices, sales orders, POs, materials, etc., and allows you to create new sales orders, credit and debit memo requests, and searches, and to drill down into further detail in some areas.

7.9.3   Display customer balances

App F0703 DISPLAY CUSTOMER BALANCES is similar to app F0701 DISPLAY SUP-PLIER BALANCES in section 6.7.3.You can drill down to the detail for one, many, or all customers; in total, by period, or period debits or credits. Similar to the accounts payable side, the sales figures are tax- and interest-inclusive if applicable, as they must tie back to the amounts in the customer line items. You can compare sales over two years, (COMPARE tab), and see down payments and items with special G/L indicators (SPECIAL G/L tab).

7.9.4   Customer line items

App F0711 MANAGE CUSTOMER LINE ITEMS displays individual customer documents and allows drill down to the actual document by jumping to other apps. Figure 7.24 shows an example of line items from several different customers and company codes.

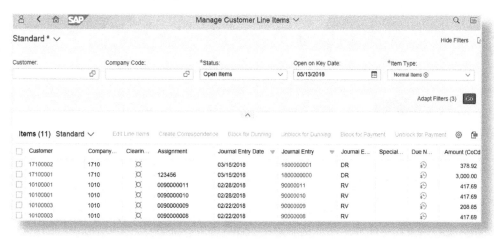

Figure 7.24: App F0711—customer line items

You can perform a number of tasks, such as EDIT LINE ITEM, CREATE CORRESPONDENCE, BLOCK FOR DUNNING, UNBLOCK FOR DUNNING, BLOCK FOR PAYMENT, and UNBLOCK FOR PAYMENT. You cannot change dates, amounts, and taxes, but Figure 7.25 shows some fields that can be edited with EDIT LINE ITEMS.

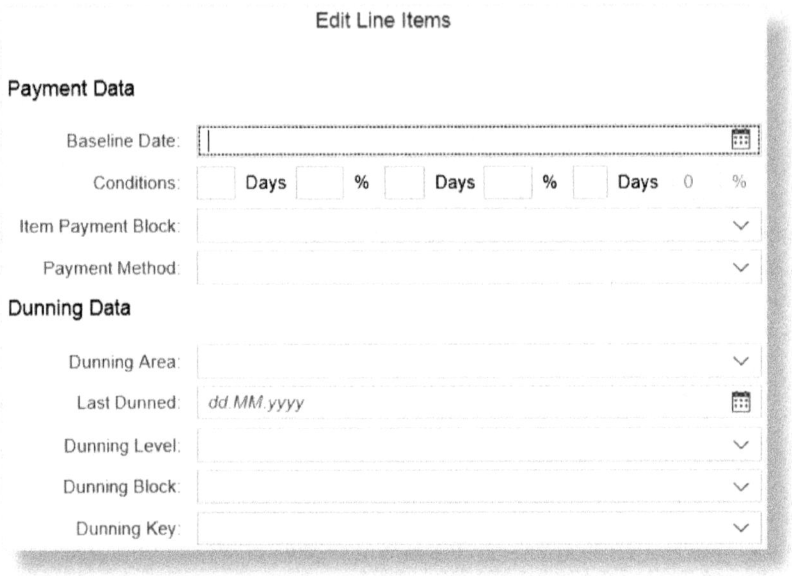

Figure 7.25: App F0711—manage customer line items, edit line items

There is a button for exporting to a spreadsheet ⊞ , on the right-hand side and the usual settings ⚙ button to change the layout of the columns. See Figure 7.26.

Figure 7.26: App F0711—line item settings, add or remove columns

8 Banking and cash management

Cash management covers the movement of cash in and out of the company and ensures sufficient funds are available, as well as preventing surplus cash from lying idle. SAP makes use of internal bank clearing accounts for the movement of cash. We explain how the different types of bank accounts are used and how to set them up. We talk about how to manage bank statements, balances, and bank reconciliations.

There are two types of bank and cash management and two related scope items for each. The first type is *basic*, (originally known as *light*), and the second is *advanced*. The two best practice scope items relating to the first are BFA BASIC BANK ACCOUNT MANAGEMENT and BFB BASIC CASH OPERATIONS, and relating to the second are J77 ADVANCED BANK ACCOUNT MANAGEMENT and J78 ADVANCED CASH OPERATIONS.

Basic scope items are included in the SAP S/4HANA license to allow you to access the standard banking and cash transactions. You will need special licenses for advanced transactions, such as hierarchies, contact persons, overdraft limits, cash pooling/concentration, foreign bank reports, workflows, etc.

8.1 Bank master data

8.1.1 Bank master records

The bank account numbers belonging to suppliers and customers are held in the business partner master data for that supplier or customer. The same bank may be used by many suppliers or customers, so rather than re-entering the bank details each time, each bank is created once in the system, with a unique bank number or *bank key* and linked to the bank account number in the business partner with that key.

The bank key is the *bank identifier code (BIC)* in banking terminology. The code and length vary from country to country. It can be numeric, like the UK sort code, but some countries use the alphanumeric *SWIFT* code instead. Depending on the country, the SWIFT code may also be required to transfer money or make a payment, so it is good practice to ensure the separate field specifically for the SWIFT code is always filled in when creating the bank, plus it can act as a double-check to ensure that you have the correct bank.

App F1574 Manage Banks Basic allows you to list or edit the existing bank accounts, export them to Microsoft Excel, and jump to other apps for the bank hierarchy, bank statements, and cash flow analyzer.

8.1.2 House bank master record

The organization's own bank to receive incoming payments and make outgoing payments is called a *house bank* and the related bank accounts are *house bank accounts*. You first have to set up the bank master data in app F1574 Manage Banks Basic and also the G/L accounts before you can create a house bank account. The steps involved are shown in Figure 8.1.

Figure 8.1: Setting up the company's house (own) bank accounts

Setting up the house bank itself used to be part of the configuration done by consultants or support departments, rather than users, however, in SAP S/4HANA, this became one of the first things that moved into the hands of business users. If you have the license for full bank account management, you can set up a workflow to review and approve new and changed banks and signatories. Bank accounts cannot be transported (the usual method of moving configuration between systems). Instead, new bank accounts are exported and imported between systems using the app in XML format. Once you have created the house bank, you can add a column in app F1574 Manage Banks to show which banks are house banks.

Each house bank has a unique ID and each related house bank account has an ID, often linked to the type or currency, so a house bank might be *HSBC1* and the accounts *GBP1, EUR1,* or *CURR1, DEP1* (current/deposit); whatever makes sense for your banks.

8.1.3 House bank accounts

The length and format of bank accounts varies, and some countries, such as France, include a check-digit based on an algorithm of the combination of bank number and bank account. An *international bank account number (IBAN)* is also mandatory for most of Europe. App F1366A Manage Bank Accounts, shown in Figure 8.2 and Figure 8.3, allows you to open, manage, and close the company's own bank accounts.

Figure 8.2: App F1366A—manage bank accounts

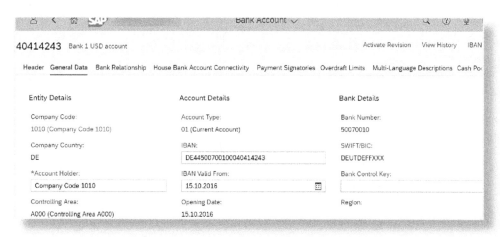

Figure 8.3: App F1366A—bank account master record

8.1.4 Bank account export and import

Bank accounts are moved from one system to another using import and export functionality that is available in the F1366A MANAGE BANK ACCOUNTS (see Figure 8.2). The format is *XML* so there are some additional steps.

First, you export the bank accounts and then you export the XML spreadsheet template (see Figure 8.4). You open the template in Microsoft Excel, go to the *developer* tab, and import the bank accounts. You will get the bank accounts in an XML format that you can read in Microsoft Excel (and, if required, amend or add to, if setting up). You can then go to the developer tab to export the bank account master to a new XML file to import to another system.

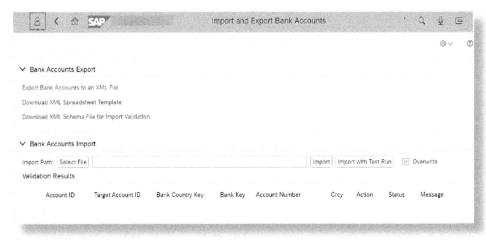

Figure 8.4: App F1366A—import and export bank accounts

8.1.5 Bank hierarchies

Bank hierarchies are an optional way to organize your bank accounts if you have a lot of them. Hierarchies can be created with app F1366 MANAGE BANK ACCOUNTS—BANK HIERARCHY VIEW, as shown in Figure 8.5 and the hierarchies can be used in some cash management reports. You create the nodes of the hierarchy on the right and then select and move the bank accounts from the left to the node that you wish to assign them to on the right.

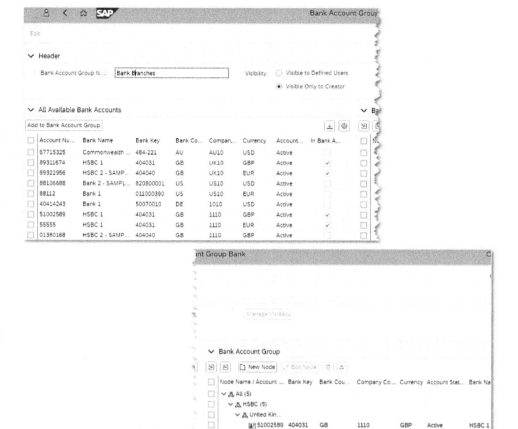

Figure 8.5: App F1366—setting up bank hierarchy groups

8.2   Cash management

Typically, the main cash movements in a company will be payments received from the sale of goods and services and payments made to suppliers, payroll, and the government. There may be bank fees and charges, as well as interest paid for overdrafts or interest received on certain types of accounts. There may also be pooling (where several accounts may be

171

combined into one account), and transfers between different house bank accounts.

Ideally, many of the processes will be automated, for example, bank statements can be automatically downloaded and imported into SAP S/4HANA overnight and you can see (on the face of the app) how many were successful and how many need reprocessing. Outgoing payments can be sent automatically to the bank once the correct approvals have taken place.

8.2.1　Banking process

The exact process will vary, some organizations still post bank statements manually, some upload electronic bank statements but do a lot of the clearing manually, and some manage to do a lot of the clearing automatically during the bank statement upload. A summarized flow is shown in Figure 8.6.

Figure 8.6: Banking process steps

Start by assuming there are some open invoices on the supplier and customer accounts. As you will see, customer and supplier payments are not posted directly to the actual bank account, but via a clearing account, as illustrated in Figure 8.7, with the numbered steps from the figure explained below:

1.　Opening invoices—this represents open items already posted to the supplier and customer some time previously

2.　Payment run—day 1, we pay the supplier. The automatic payment program debits the supplier with the payment and clears the invoice; the offsetting posting credits the bank clearing account.

3.　Statement—day 2, we post the bank statement for day 1, containing the payment to the suppliers, as well as some receipts from customers and bank charges. The bank account is debited and credited with each item and the offsetting account is either the relevant bank clearing account or the P&L bank charges account.

4. Payment receipt—if the statement file is accurate enough, the customer invoice can be automatically cleared during the posting of the bank statement. If not, the accounts receivable department will see from the statement that a payment has been received and clear the customer invoice manually.

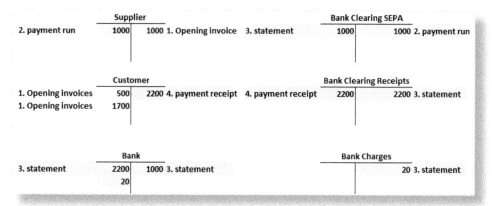

Figure 8.7: Bank clearing T-accounts

The main bank account must agree with the bank statement and should never be open-item managed. Clearing accounts must be open-item managed and cleared on a regular basis.

Although most of the postings on the clearing accounts happen automatically, the clearing often has to be manual. For example, a payment or direct debit run will create a separate document for each supplier and customer and clear invoices on the supplier and customer account, however, the physical payment to the bank often shows as a lump sum on the bank statement. If you can't clear them automatically using the payment media reference, it is usually easy to identify which items from the payment run match the statement by filtering by date, although sometimes payments are returned either due to faulty bank details or lack of funds.

Bank reconciliations take the balance at the bank (i.e., the main account as per the bank statement) and add or deduct the clearing accounts once all postings have been made. This gives the real bank balance because open items still on the clearing account should refer to timing differences, such as a check that has been sent to a supplier, but is still in transit.

In the example in Figure 8.7, we showed two bank clearing accounts. Each bank account has a main G/L account and one or more clearing accounts, sometimes called control accounts. If you have a lot of payments, you may want to use one account for each type of payment or one for incoming and one for outgoing. Some companies have one clearing account for all payments.

In the best practices scope item, some P&L items, such as bank charges or interest, are configured to post directly to a revenue or expense account, although some companies prefer to post everything to a clearing account first. APP F3001 MONITOR BANK FEES in Figure 8.8 gives an overview of the bank fees.

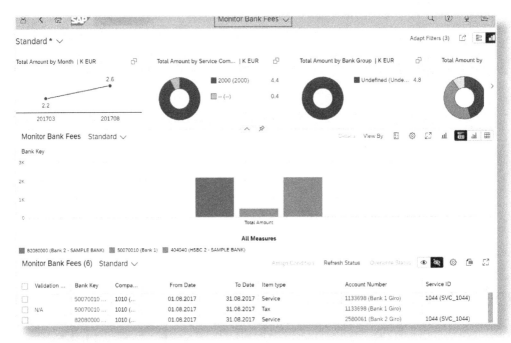

Figure 8.8: App F3001—monitor bank fees

8.2.2 Bank statements

Bank statements can be either imported automatically using *SAP Multi-Bank Connectivity (MBC)*, uploaded as an electronic file, or entered manually. Scope items 1EG—BANK INTEGRATION WITH FILE INTERFACE and 16R—BANK INTEGRATION WITH SAP MULTI-BANK CONNECTIVITY cover the import of the bank statements (as well as the transfer of files).

App F1564 MANAGE BANK STATEMENTS gives an overview and allows you to view, create, and edit manual bank statements. To post a manual statement using F1564 MANAGE BANK STATEMENTS, you use the + to add a statement, enter the header details, (bank account, amounts, statement number and date, opening and closing balances), then click on the + again to enter the new line items. See Figure 8.9.

Figure 8.9: App F1564—manage bank statement, create new

A statement line item will appear. If you don't see all the fields that you need, you can add columns or click on the arrow at the end of the line to see a separate statement line item screen, as shown in Figure 8.10. Here you can enter the MANUAL TRANSACTION code (for example, *F001* for an incoming customer payment, *F004* for an outgoing payment run), and the amount. If you are entering a customer receipt, you will need to enter the invoice number in the CUSTOMER REF NO: field, in order for the payment to clear the invoice automatically. The customer invoice number is held in the reference field when the invoice is posted, if you need to check.

Figure 8.10: App F1564—bank statement line item

If the item on the statement refers to an automatic payment run, you can enter the payment media reference number in the CUSTOMER REF NO: field, which will then allow it to clear the related entries on the bank clearing account from the automatic payment program posting. The payment media reference can be found in app F1868 MANAGE PAYMENT MEDIA, if it is not shown on the bank statement. After entering any other relevant data, click on APPLY at the bottom right of the statement line item screen to return to the main screen. When finished, assuming the total of the line items equals the difference between the opening and closing balances, you can click POST.

Depending on the transaction, this should post between the bank and either a clearing or expense/revenue account. If the information is there, it should also post to the subledger (in addition to the bank clearing account) and clear the relevant item, for example, the customer invoice, or in the case of an automatic payment run, it should clear the payment documents in the clearing account.

Figure 8.11 shows two manually posted statements (with only one entry on each statement). You can see from the SUBLEDGER POSTED = YES, that BANK STATEMENT NO. = 2 contained bank charges which were posted directly, crediting the bank and debiting the P&L bank fees expense account.

Figure 8.11: App F1564—manage bank statement, list of statements

Statement *1* (SUBLEDGER POSTED = NO) has only posted to the clearing account and needs to be post-processed, for example, with F1520 REPRO-CESS BANK STATEMENT ITEMS. This allows you to post the receipt to the customer account and match it against the appropriate invoices. In the example in Figure 8.12, only the customer number was entered when posting the statement, as the invoice numbers were not known. When the same statement item was opened in app F1520 REPROCESS BANK STATEMENT ITEMS, the screen opened automatically on that customer's account to allow you to choose the relevant invoices to clear.

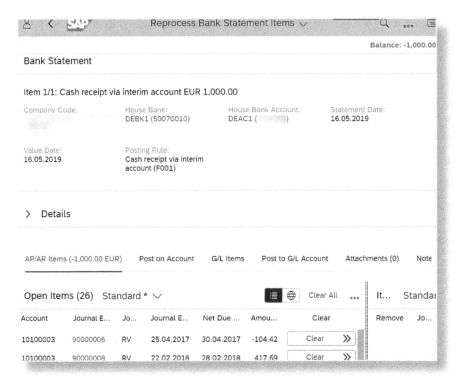

Figure 8.12: App F1520—re-process bank statements items

8.2.3 Bank-related reporting

Cash management and forecast

Apps DISPLAY CASH POSITION, based on GUI transaction FF7AN, and DISPLAY LIQUIDITY FORECAST, based on GUI transaction FF7BN are similar, but one has the field CASH POSITION preselected and the other has LIQUIDITY FORECAST preselected. Different variants can be displayed by selecting different options in GROUPING (on the selection screen) and you can toggle between currencies, accounts, and levels using the buttons at the top of the screen. Figure 8.13 uses the F77BN app.

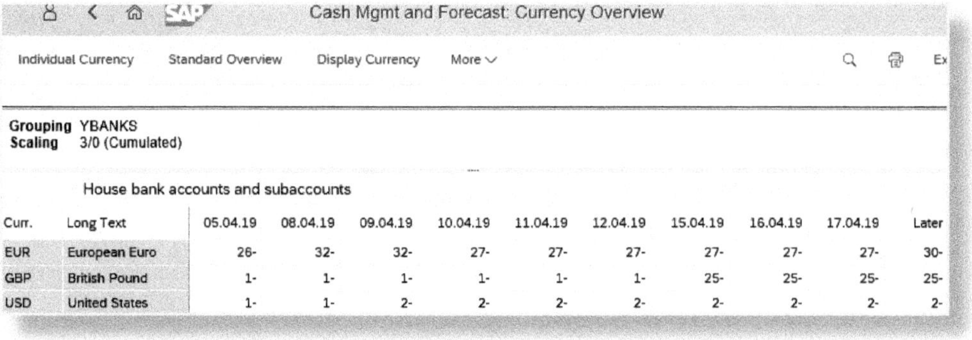

Figure 8.13: Transaction FF7BN—display liquidity forecast

Cash flow analyzer

APP F2332 CASH FLOW ANALYZER (scope item J78 ADVANCED CASH OPERATIONS), shown in Figure 8.14, gives an overview of the cash position over time periods, such as daily, period, quarter, or year. You can drill down by company code, then by bank account, and then by the different liquidity items, and you can create your own variant. You can also display the report by bank hierarchy, (or liquidity item hierarchy), or SWITCH VIEWS.

Figure 8.14: App F2332—cash flow analyzer shown by day

179

9 Asset accounting and reporting

In this chapter, we explain the key concepts of asset accounting in SAP, such as the chart of depreciation, depreciation areas, asset classes, and depreciation methods. We then talk about the daily transactions in asset accounting such as creating master data, posting acquisitions and retirements, and so on. Finally, we run through the periodic activities, reporting, and year-end closing.

9.1 Introduction to asset accounting

You may have heard of the term *new asset accounting.* This was introduced in the later versions of SAP ECC 6.0, but was revamped in SAP S/4HANA with better integration to the general ledger and real-time posting to all ledgers, (although the word new was dropped in later releases). The best practices scope items J62 ASSET ACCOUNTING and BFH ASSET UNDER CONSTRUCTION, contain most of the basics, but there are related items if you have additional ledgers or *assets under construction (AUC)* such as 1GB ASSET ACCOUNTING—GROUP LEDGER IFRS, BHF ASSET UNDER CONSTRUCTION, and 1GF ASSET UNDER CONSTRUCTION—GROUP LEDGER IFRS. Figure 9.1 shows new app F3096 ASSET ACCOUNTING OVERVIEW, (which is covered under scope item 2QY ANALYTICAL APPS FOR ASSET ACCOUNTING FINANCE).

Figure 9.1: App F3096—asset accounting overview app

9.1.1   Definition of an asset

A *tangible fixed asset* is usually a physical item of material value which is intended for long-term use by an organization in its normal course of business. The *acquisition and production costs (APC)* is the total initial cost of the asset, or gross book value. In order to match the cost of the asset with periods in which it is used, a proportion of the APC is charged to the P&L over the expected useful life of the asset. This is known as depreciation. The APC less the accumulated depreciation to date gives the *net book value (NBV)* of the asset.

An *intangible fixed asset* is also material and long-term, but not physical in nature. Examples of intangible assets include software, trademarks, copyrights, intellectual property, research and development, goodwill, and brand recognition.

In SAP S/4HANA, the different types of tangible and intangible assets are grouped into *asset classes*, such as land, buildings, plant and machinery, computers, motor vehicles, and so on. Typically, a computer might have an expected life of 3 or 4 years, whereas a factory building might have a life of over 40 years. The asset classes link to the account determinations which contain the mapping for each asset class to G/L accounts.

Most countries require organizations to record all transactions relating to a specific asset (acquisition, transfers, retirements, depreciation, revaluation, etc.) in some form of asset register and to be able to report fully on them.

9.1.2   Plant maintenance

Some fixed assets, usually plant and machinery, need regular maintenance which can be managed in the plant maintenance module. SAP S/4HANA asset accounting can be integrated with plant maintenance so that one asset can be created in asset accounting and the same asset master record can be used for plant maintenance.

In practice, the way assets are capitalized from a financial point of view may be quite different from the way they need to be organized from a maintenance point of view, so integration is not mandatory and often not fully used.

9.2 Structure and methodolgy

9.2.1 Chart of depreciation

In SAP S/4HANA, the underlying object which groups together the legal requirements and depreciation methods of a specific country is the *chart of depreciation*.

9.2.2 Depreciation areas

Each chart of depreciation contains *depreciation areas* which link to different accounting principles and tax requirements. They allow the same asset to have a number of different values and depreciation calculations so that the organization can report differently for local purposes, tax purposes, IFRS, group, or any other requirement.

For instance, something might be classified as an asset according to group accounting principles, but local regulations may require that item to be treated as a cost and not capitalized. An asset may be depreciated over 5 years using the straight-line depreciation method to fit in with local GAAP, but may be depreciated over 8 years, using declining (reducing) balance for group purposes, and possibly different again for tax.

The asset can be set up differently for each accounting principle by using depreciation areas. Each depreciation area in SAP S/4HANA is assigned to an accounting principle which is assigned to a ledger group in financial accounting. A depreciation area can be set to post in real time to financial accounting or not, or, for example, to post only depreciation depending on what is required for tax, controlling, or other purposes.

9.2.3 Depreciation keys

Depreciation keys contain all the depreciation calculations, such as whether depreciation is charged from the start of, middle of, or following month on a new asset, or on a daily basis, with additional options for disposals. You can have different depreciation keys for each depreciation area and you can set a default for each asset class.

The key also dictates the method of depreciation. The simplest depreciation methods are probably straight-line and declining balance. With the straight-line method, you would depreciate the same amount each year over the useful life of the asset. Where an asset loses most of its value early on in life, the declining balance method would charge a larger amount of depreciation in the first year and less in subsequent years.

In most countries, depreciation is calculated by asset, although some countries calculate on a group asset level by linking assets to a group asset for the depreciation calculation.

9.3 Different methods of asset acquisition

The first step in the process varies, depending on the purchasing process and type of organization.

9.3.1 Direct capitalization

If most assets are brought into use and capitalized immediately, the asset master record can be created at the point of ordering and entered directly either in the PR or in the PO (or directly in the integrated acquisition posting if there is no PO). When the GR and invoice are posted, they update the asset directly.

Alternatively, if the asset is not brought into use immediately, (perhaps it needs to be constructed from a number of different items), costs can be collected on an AUC and later settled to the final asset, when it is ready to be capitalized.

9.3.2 Investment management

A company with a lot of constructed assets may implement investment management to better control capital expenditure. *Investment orders* can be used to record simpler investments and where investments have more complicated constructions, *projects* and *WBS elements* are better suited to plan and gather the different costs such as labor, fees, and physical parts together.

Investment management covers the whole investment process from the capital requisition, through managing the budget, and so on, but is not covered in this book.

9.4 Asset master record

9.4.1 Creating an asset master record

The process to create an asset or AUC is the same, but using different asset classes. App CREATE ASSET MASTER RECORD, based on GUI transaction AS01, gives you the choice of using an existing asset as reference or creating one from scratch in the relevant asset class and company code. See Figure 9.2.

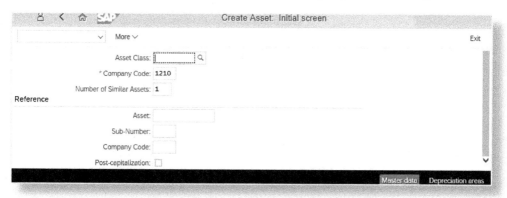

Figure 9.2: Transaction AS01—create asset master record

If you have related parts to an asset that you want to capitalize together and still be able to see the detail of the parts, you can create separate components with app CREATE ASSET SUBNUMBER based on GUI transaction AS11. The main asset will show with a suffix of 0, with the components sharing the main number, but with different suffixes.

Creating more than one asset at a time

 If you have purchased, say, 10 laptops, you can enter the quantity in the NUMBER OF SIMILAR ASSETS box. When you have completed the first asset, you will see a pop-up asking whether to create the other 9 the same or if you wish to change any fields first. If you select CREATE, 10 identical assets are created. With MAINTAIN, a table appears where you can change, for example, the cost center or inventory number. See Figure 9.3.

Maintain Fields that Should Be Different in Similar Assets

No	* Description	Inventory ...	* Cost center	Profit Ctr	Segment	Ev.1	Ev.2	Ev.3	Ev.4	Ev.Grp 5
1	Pump for Mach...		17101101	YB600	1000_C					
2	Pump for Mach...		17101201	YB600	1000_C					
3	Pump for Mach...		17101301	YB600	1000_C					
4	Pump for Mach...		17101101	YB600	1000_C					
5	Pump for Mach...		17101101	YB600	1000_C					
6	Pump for Mach...		17101101	YB600	1000_C					
7	Pump for Mach...		17101101	YB600	1000_C					
8	Pump for Mach...		17101101	YB600	1000_C					
9	Pump for Mach...		17101101	YB600	1000_C					
10	Pump for Mach...		17101101	YB600	1000_C					

Figure 9.3: Transaction AS01—creating multiple assets

General data

On the next screen, the description is mandatory, but other fields will depend on your organization. You may want to enter the machine or equipment serial number or another reference if the inventory number is not the SAP number. If you enter a quantity, you also need to enter the unit of measure, for example EA for each or PC for piece. See Figure 9.4.

The capitalization data is filled automatically when data is first posted to the asset on goods receipt, invoice receipt, or settlement, depending on the organization's process. To the right of the description there is a small 🖉 button, which allows you to add a lot more additional text if required, but this text will not appear in standard reports.

Group assets, which are required to calculate group depreciation in the U.S., have their own master record, but have other assets linked to them. The app to create a group asset is AS21 CREATE GROUP ASSET, with similar apps to amend, display, and delete.

Time-dependent tab

In the time-dependent section, you enter the relevant cost center which will be used for charging the depreciation. See Figure 9.5. The profit center and segment will default in automatically based on the cost center, assuming the master data is linked correctly. You can also enter other fields, as required.

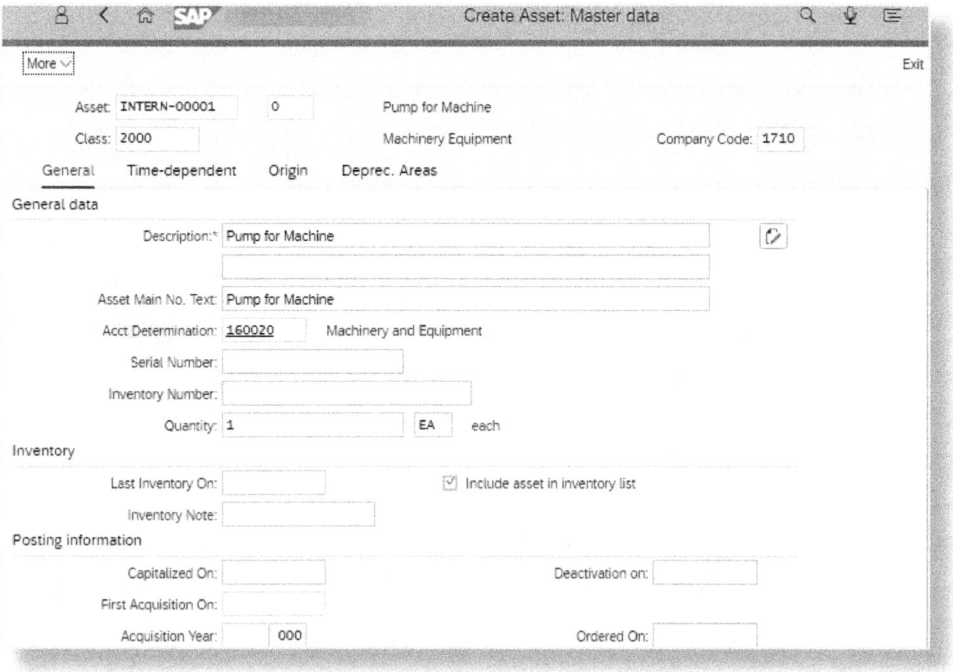

Figure 9.4: Transaction AS01—create asset master, general tab

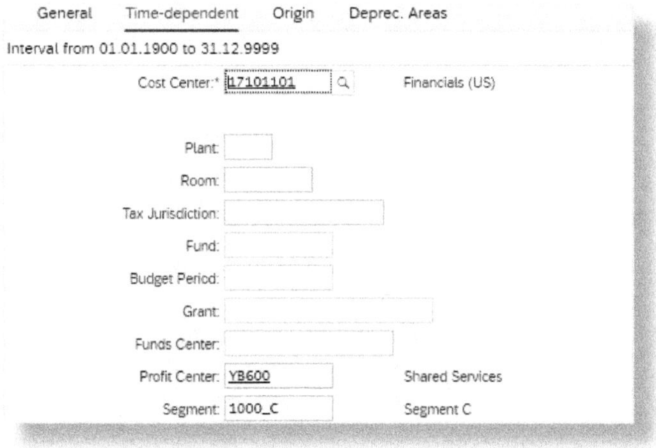

Figure 9.5: Transaction AS01—create asset master, time-dependent

187

> ### Changing the cost center, profit center, or segment
>
> If you enter a new cost or profit center linked to a different profit center or segment, you will get an error message. If they match, a retirement and acquisition may be posted to update the balance sheet with the new profit center or segment.

Because certain fields are time-dependent, you can have depreciation posting to one cost center for part of the year, then to another cost center for the rest of the year if the asset is then transferred to a different department.

Origin tab

The supplier number is usually filled automatically, but you can complete the other fields, if required. See Figure 9.6. The ORIGINAL ASSET field is autofilled if the asset has been transferred from another asset in the same system.

| General | Time-dependent | Origin | Deprec. Areas |

Origin

Supplier:

Manufacturer:

☐ Asset purch. new

☐ Purchased used

Trading Partner No.:

Country of Origin:

Type name:

Original Asset: Acq. On:

Orig. Acquis. Year:

Original Value: USD

In-House Prod. Perc.:

Figure 9.6: Transaction AS01—create asset master, origin tab

Depreciation areas tab

This screen can be filled automatically with a default depreciation key and useful life, set by asset class, or it can be left blank to be manually filled. The start date of depreciation is dependent on the date of capitalization and the configuration, but can also be changed if the asset is not brought into use immediately. For example, the depreciation key can be configured to start depreciation at the beginning or middle of the current or next month regardless of the actual day of capitalization. Figure 9.7 shows a number of depreciation areas with different depreciation keys and different useful lives.

General	Time-dependent	Origin	Deprec. Areas			
Valuation						
Deact	...	Depreciation area	DKey	UseLife	Prd	ODep Start
☐	01	Book Deprctn	YSL1	10		
	31	LocGAAPGrCry	YSL1	10	0	
☐	32	IFRS loc cur	YSL1	8		
	33	IFRS grp cur	YSL1	8	0	
☐	90	ACRS/MACRS	Y200	7		
☐	91	ALT MIN	Y150	7		
☐	92	ACE	Y150	7		
☐	93	E&P	YSL5	10		

Figure 9.7: Transaction AS01—create asset master, depreciation

Other asset master record apps that are available include AS02 CHANGE ASSET, AS03 DISPLAY ASSET, AS05 BLOCK ASSET, and AS06 DELETE ASSET. Depending on how the asset master has been configured, there may be additional tabs available in the individual fixed asset master data screens. Your organization may also be using *evaluation groups* which are existing fields that you can use for your own purposes, for example, to group the assets differently. New fields can also be added to the master record as required using app F1481 CUSTOM FIELDS AND LOGIC. See section 1.5. Unlike evaluation groups, with custom fields, you can choose the format of the field, such as a date, amount, or number.

9.4.2   Asset master worklist

In app F1592 DISPLAY ASSET MASTER WORKLIST, you can select various criteria such as company code, asset class, asset number, cost center, locations, etc. On selecting GO, you will see lists of those assets on different tabs, according to their status (see Figure 9.8). You can jump to other apps or drill down on the asset number into app F1684 MANAGE FIXED ASSETS to see details of the individual asset.

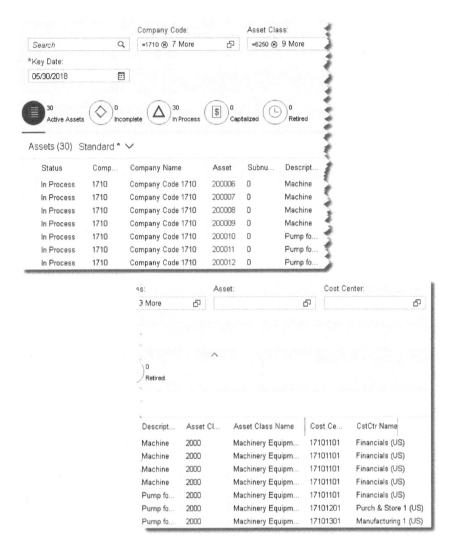

Figure 9.8: App F1592—asset master worklist

9.5 Asset acquisitions

As previously mentioned, assets may be capitalized in a number of different ways. An *integrated posting* means that the asset is debited and the other side of the posting is to a supplier, customer, or GR/IR account; and a *non-integrated posting* means the other side of the asset posting is direct to a standard G/L account.

9.5.1 Non-integrated transactions

This only occurs where no supplier, customer, or GR/IR account is involved in the actual asset posting, for example, the asset (or AUC) is posted to directly with a journal entry and the offsetting account is a normal G/L account. It may be that the invoice was posted via a clearing account or posted incorrectly to an expense account first, but in the document that updates the asset, there is no invoice or GR.

Figure 9.9 shows app POST ACQUISITION (NON-INTEGRATED) WITH AUTOMATIC OFFSETTING ENTRY, which is based on GUI transaction ABZOL. (App ACQUISITION FROM AFFILIATED COMPANY—ABZPL is almost identical, but defaults in a different transaction code which you can amend). When posted, this will contain only a debit to the asset and a credit to a clearing account. If you do not want it to post to the standard clearing account, you can change the offsetting account on the ADDITIONAL DETAILS tab.

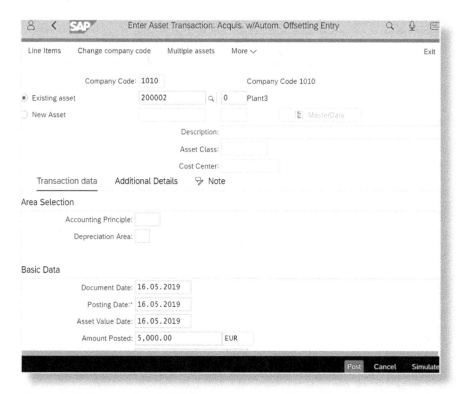

Figure 9.9: Transaction ABZOL—asset acquisition with automatic offsetting entry

Asset clearing accounts

There are two separate clearing accounts for assets. One is used as an offset in transactions such as ABZOL. The other, specifically named the TECHNICAL CLEARING ACCOUNT, is used for integrated transactions to allow different values for each accounting principle.

9.5.2 Integrated transactions

If a posting is made directly between a supplier and an asset, this is known as an integrated transaction. This would happen where a supplier invoice is posted directly to the asset from financial accounting, as shown in Figure 9.10, which is posted using app POST ACQUISITION (INTEGRATED AP) WITHOUT PURCHASE ORDER based on GUI transaction F-90.

		Enter Vendor Invoice: Display Overview
Choose	Display Currency	G/L item fast entry	Taxes	Asset Accounting	More ∨

Document Date:	23.04.2019	Type:	KR	Company Code:	1010
Posting Date:	23.04.2019	Period:	4	Currency:	EUR
Document Number:	INTERNAL	Fiscal Year:	2019	Translatn Date:	23.04.2019
Reference:	INV NR 12345			Cross-CC no.:	
Doc.Header Text:	asset 600000			Trading Part.BA:	

Items in document currency

PK	BusA	Acct		EUR Amount	Tax amnt
001	31	0010300001 Inlandslieferant DE		1,000.00-	**
002	70	0016014000 000000600000 0000		1,000.00	V0

Figure 9.10: Transaction F-90—posting an integrated acquisition

It can also be used where PO processing is used and a GR or invoice is posted directly against the asset. The flow in Figure 9.11 describes an asset acquisition through direct capitalization, meaning that the asset is entered in the PR or PO and when the GR is posted, it directly updates the asset. If the invoice does not exactly match the GR posting, any adjustment posting will update the asset.

Figure 9.11: Asset acquisition steps through direct capitalization

9.5.3 Technical clearing account

Where an organization has set up parallel ledgers, it is possible to make adjustment postings to one or more ledgers without updating the other ledgers. However, it is not allowed to make such *unilateral postings* (one ledger only) to supplier accounts, customer accounts, tax accounts, or the GR/IR account. Therefore, in order to be able to make integrated postings of different values to different ledgers from asset accounting, a technical clearing account is used.

For an integrated asset acquisition without a PO, the posting is split between an operational part and a valuating part. The operational part posts between the supplier and the technical clearing account and the valuating part posts between the technical clearing part and the asset. Figure 9.12 shows the integrated posting of the leading ledger documents with a third non-leading-ledger document added manually to the figure so that you can compare the three together.

Type	Period	Ledger Grp	AccP	TPBA	Ref. doc.	Doc. No.	Item	PK	BusA	Segment	Profit Ctr	G/L A/c	Short Text	Amount	Crcy
KR	4				1900000000	1900000000	1	31				21100000	Paybls Domestic	1,000.00-	EUR
KR	4						2	70		1000_C	YB600	16014000	000000600000 0000	1,000.00	EUR
						1900000000								0.00	EUR
KR	4	0L	DEAP			1900000001	1	70		1000_C	YB600	16007000	000000600000 0000	1,000.00	EUR
KR	4	0L	DEAP				2	75		1000_C	YB600	16014000	000000600000 0000	1,000.00-	EUR
						1900000001								0.00	EUR
KR	4	2L	IFRS			7000000000	1	70		1000_C	YB600	16007000	000000600000 0000	1,000.00	EUR
KR	4	2L	IFRS				2	75		1000_C	YB600	16014000	000000600000 0000	1,000.00-	EUR
						7000000000								0.00	EUR

Figure 9.12: Transaction F-90—integrated asset posting with supplier invoice

You will see that the first posting is to all ledgers and accounting principles and is between the supplier account and the technical clearing account. The second posting is for the leading ledger and accounting principle (in this case the local GAAP or DEAP) and is between the technical clearing account and the asset. The third posting (added manually to the figure) is for the parallel IFRS ledger and is also between the technical clearing account and the asset.

To see this screen, after posting the invoice, go to MORE • DOCUMENT • DISPLAY and select ASSET ACCOUNTING. You will see the first two documents posted to the leading ledger. To see the other documents, you have to go to A/P CURRENCY (A/P in this case means accounting principle) and choose the other ledgers and currencies.

For an integrated acquisition with PO, the operational part is between the GR/IR account and the technical clearing account. Figure 9.13 shows the posting to all ledger groups between the GR/IR and the technical clearing account and also lists the related documents.

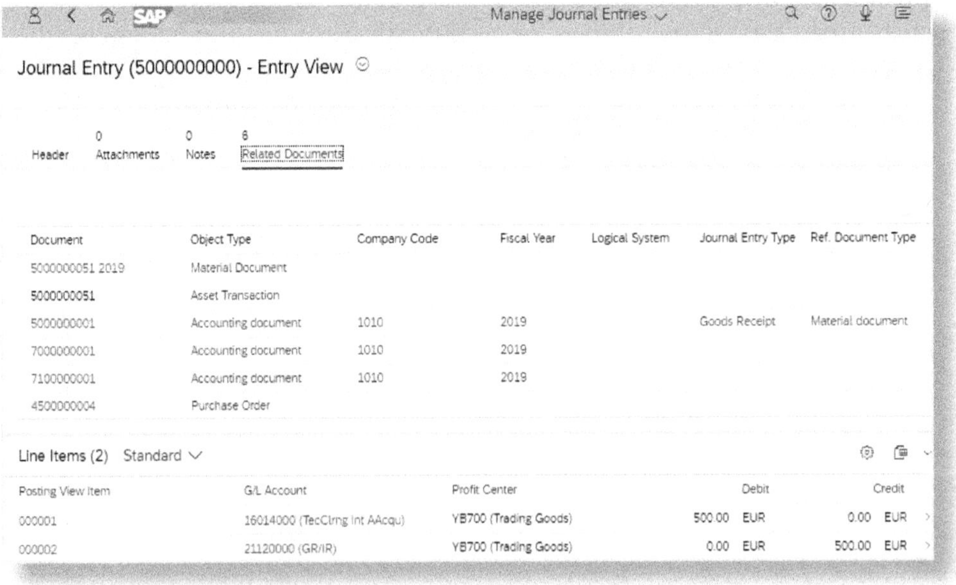

Figure 9.13: App F0717—journal for asset acquisition with PO

The postings between the technical clearing account and the asset are shown in Figure 9.14 and Figure 9.15.

Figure 9.14: Asset acquisition, leading ledger posting

Journal Entry (7100000001) - Entry View ⊗

	0	0	6	
Header	Attachments	Notes	Related Documents	

Journal Entry Date: 23.04.2019   Company Code: 1010 (Company Code 1010)   Reference:
Posting Date: 23.04.2019   Transaction Currency: EUR   Ref. Document Type: MKPF (Material document)
Posting Period: 4 / 2019   Header Text: of
Journal Entry Type: WE (Goods Receipt)   Created: by CB9980013135 on 23.04.2019
Jrnl. Entry Attrib.: L (Posting Not in Leading Ledger)

Show More

Line Items (2)   Standard ∨

Posting View Item	G/L Account	Profit Center	Debit		Credit	
000001	16006000 (Furniture & Fixtures)	YB700 (Trading Goods)	500.00	EUR	0.00	EUR
000002	16014000 (TecClrng Int AAcqu)	YB700 (Trading Goods)	0.00	EUR	500.00	EUR

Figure 9.15: Asset acquisition, parallel ledger posting

An integrated sale is similar, but with the customer instead of supplier, so the operating part posts between the customer and the technical clearing and the valuating part between the technical clearing and the asset. In some countries, the asset can't be capitalized until the invoice is received even if the asset is in use, so a non-valuated GR setting in the PO may be selected. This means that no value will be posted at the point of goods receipt, and the whole value will be posted when the invoice is received.

Asset personal value list

In some of the GUI-based apps when you search for an asset, you may see a reduced list of assets that you have used recently. If you click on the globe button ⊕, you will be able to display all the values. To turn off completely, in a GUI transaction or GUI-based app, go to HELP • SETTINGS at the top of the screen, or in a GUI-based app, go to MORE and then HELP • SETTINGS, and at the top of the [F4] Help tab you will see a box that you can select which says DO NOT DISPLAY PERS. VALUE LIST AUTOMATICALLY.

9.5.4   Assets under construction

AUCs are used to collect costs temporarily until the asset is brought into use and can be fully capitalized. They are especially useful for large construction projects, such as buildings or large plant and machinery, such as production lines. The steps are summarized in Figure 9.16.

Figure 9.16: Asset under construction steps

Create asset under construction

An AUC is created in a similar way to an ordinary fixed asset, but uses a special asset class, which has no depreciation. An AUC can be posted to directly by entering the AUC number in the supplier invoice or PO. It can also be settled to from an investment order or WBS element. Once the asset is ready, and is brought into use, the costs are settled from the AUC to the final asset.

Settlement of asset under construction

Settlement describes the process of automatically transferring costs from one object to another object, in this case from an asset under construction to a final asset. Using app DEFINE DISTRIBUTION RULES FOR AUC, based on GUI transaction AIAB, you can select the costs you want to allocate and allocate them differently to each accounting principle/depreciation area. See Figure 9.17.

	Status	Asset	Area	AccP	Ledger Group	Doc. No.	Document ...	TType	AssetValDate		Amount
☐	◉	400000	1	DEAP	0L	1900000003	23.04.2019	100	23.04.2019		600.00
☐	◉	400000	32	IFRS	2L	7000000002		100			600.00
☐	◉	400000	34	USGP	3L	7100000002		100			600.00
☐										•	**1,800.00**

Company code 1010
Asset 400000 AUC
Subnumber 0

Figure 9.17: Transaction AIAB—settlement of AUC costs to asset

You define rules to say which asset the costs should be settled to and you can post 100% of the costs to one asset (see Figure 9.18), or split by percentages or amounts to different assets. You can have different rules for different accounting principles, depreciation areas, and ledger groups. The STATUS will turn green when the rule is completed and saved.

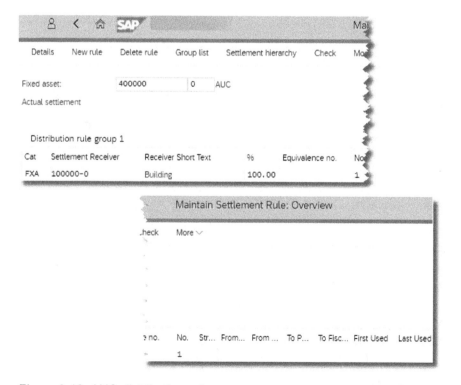

Figure 9.18: AUC distribution rules

You can use app EXECUTE SETTLEMENT FOR AUC based on GUI transaction AIBU. In this case, there is no necessity for the technical clearing account as the posting is between the asset and the AUC, however, a separate document for each accounting principle is still produced. See Figure 9.19 and Figure 9.20.

Figure 9.19: Settlement documents posted by accounting principle

Journal Entry (100000016) - Entry View ⌄

	0	0	4
Header	Attachments	Notes	Related Documents

Document	Object Type	Company Code	Fiscal Year	Logical System	Journal Entry Type	Ref. Document Type
000000000110102019	AIBU					
0000000001	Asset Transaction					
7000000003	Accounting document	1010	2019		Asset Posting	Assts und.const.set.
7100000003	Accounting document	1010	2019			

Line Items (2)   Standard ⌄

Posting View Item	G/L Account	Profit Center	Debit	Credit
000001	16009000 (Assets under Constr.)	YB110 (Product A)	0.00 EUR	600.00 EUR
000002	16001000 (Buildings)	YB600 (Shared Services)	600.00 EUR	0.00 EUR

Figure 9.20: Settlement posting to asset from AUC

Post-capitalization

If an asset should have been capitalized at an earlier date in the same fiscal year and therefore additional depreciation should be charged, you can simply amend the capitalization and depreciation start dates when you create the asset, and the system will adjust the current period depreciation accordingly. If the assets should have been capitalized in an earlier year, by selecting the *Post-capitalization* box on the initial create asset screen, the portion of the adjustment of depreciation referring to a previous fiscal year will be posted to reserves. The app where you enter (i.e., post) the post-capitalization is called POST POST-CAPITALIZATION, based on GUI transaction ABNAN. This can then be used in a similar way to the asset value adjustment transactions in section 9.7.

9.6 Retirements with customer

Retirements or disposals of assets can be made in several ways. In this section, we will describe an integrated posting with the customer using app POST RETIREMENT (INTEGRATED AR)—WITH CUSTOMER based on GUI transaction F-92. Retirement without customer will be covered later in this chapter.

An integrated sale with customer is when the posting to the customer account is made at the same time as the posting to remove the asset from the asset register. It involves the use of posting keys and because it is an integrated transaction, it will also post via the TECHNICAL CLEARING ACCOUNT. The first step is to complete the document header and then to enter the customer account number (see Figure 9.21). You need to enter the posting key (PSTKY) *01* so that the system knows the account number in the next field, ACCOUNT, refers to a customer account and not a G/L or supplier. The posting key and account together indicate what will appear on the next screen.

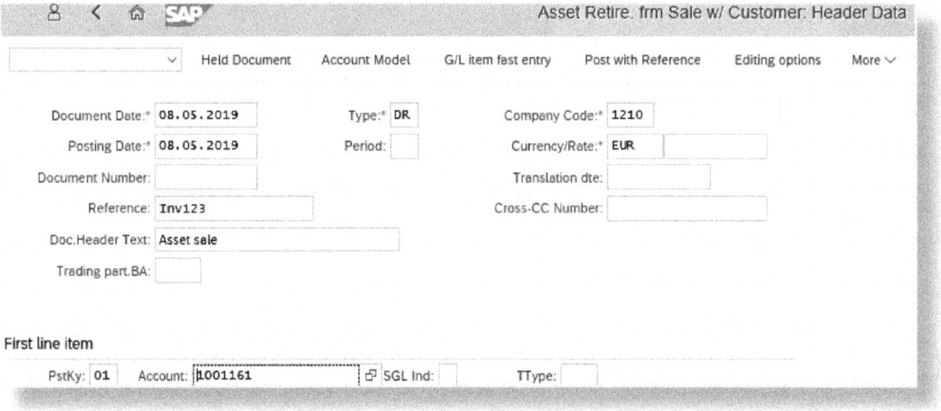

Figure 9.21: Transaction F-92—asset sale with customer header

You then enter the amount and text as required. Fields like the PAYT.TERMS and PAYT METHOD should be filled from the customer master. At the bottom of the screen, you enter the posting key for the second entry. This will be the G/L account where you want the revenue to go to, so you need to enter posting key *50* and the asset revenue account. See Figure 9.22. Although we are not including tax in this example, you can enter either the tax amount in this screen or click calculate tax if you want to include tax.

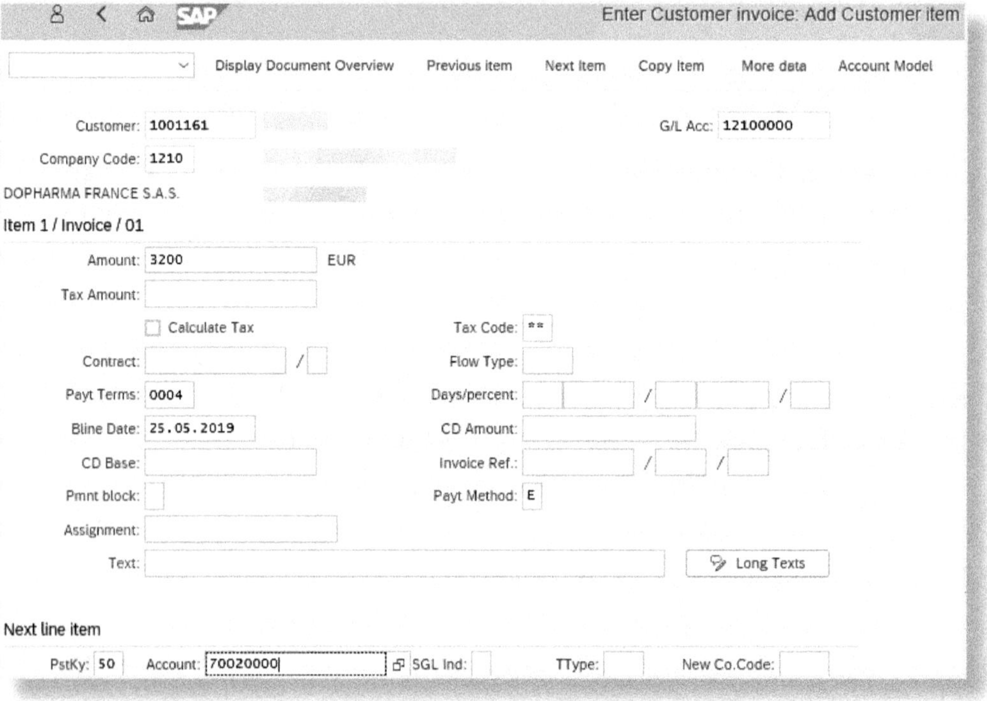

Figure 9.22: Transaction F-92—asset sale with customer first line

On the next screen, you can enter the amount for the revenue and the relevant tax code (not shown) and you will see a new button, ASST. RETIREMENT, which you need to select. See Figure 9.23. You will also need to enter a cost object, such as a cost center.

When you have selected the asset retirement indicator and pressed Enter, a new pop-up will appear for you to enter the asset details, such as asset number, value date, and amount. You can choose to select the COMPL.RETIREMNT box if you are selling the whole asset, or you can enter a partial amount or percentage if you are only selling part of the asset. (Note that the asset retirement indicator does not stay selected after you complete the asset details and return to the line item screen).

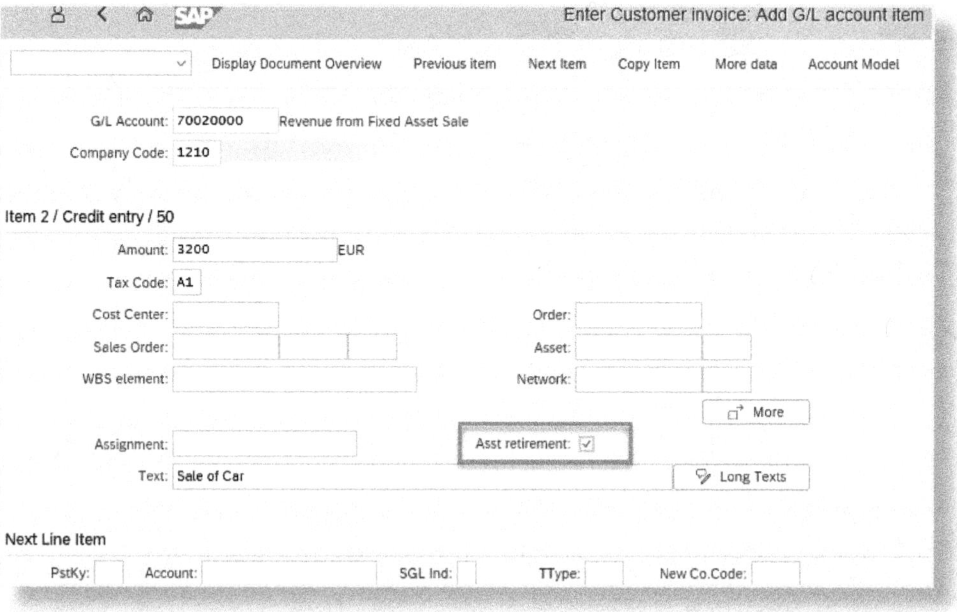

Figure 9.23 Transaction F-92—asset sale with customer second line

If you click DISPLAY DOCUMENT OVERVIEW at the top of the screen after pressing CONTINUE, this will take you to the two items you created, as shown in Figure 9.24.

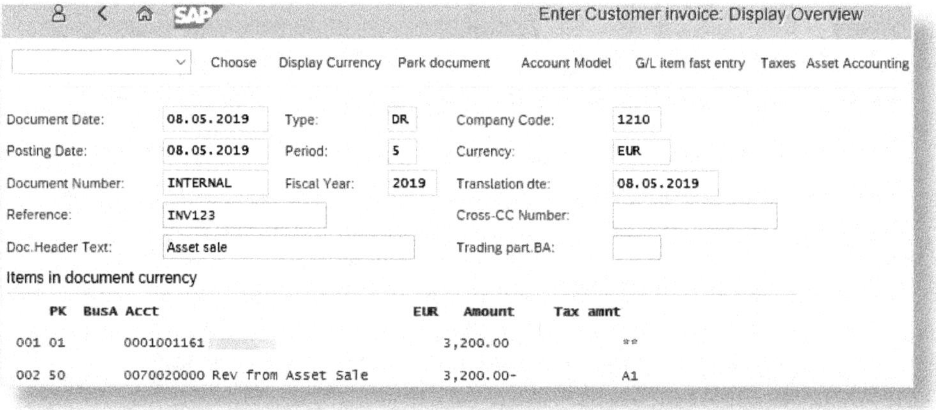

Figure 9.24: Transaction F-92—asset sale with customer overview

To see the full asset postings, click ASSET ACCOUNTING, as shown in Figure 9.25. Note that some countries have different rules about netting off the gain or loss on the sale of an asset and may use a slightly different combination of accounts for the revenue.

Figure 9.25: Transaction F-92—asset sale with customer simulation

9.7 Asset value adjustments

Many of the transactions to adjust the asset or depreciation value are quite similar and a lot are still based on GUI transactions. There is an initial pop-up where you enter the company code and asset number. The last field, TRANS TYPE, may have a default code in it, which will vary depending on the transaction, but can be changed. The dropdown list for the field will show similar codes relevant to the transaction. You will need to check that you have the correct code, for example, if adjusting an asset acquired in a previous year you will also need a prior-year transaction code, such as the *640* used in Figure 9.26, rather than a current year one and vice versa.

Most of the value adjustment transactions in this section will have an identical layout down (the screen) as far as the TEXT field and some will have a separate section at the bottom (not shown) specific to the transaction. We will go through the generic fields and then only explain what is different for each transaction.

These transactions differ from previous versions of SAP because they allow you to choose an accounting principle and depreciation area to post to, but otherwise the principle is the same. You are directly posting a one-off value, sometimes to the asset itself and sometimes to increase or decrease the depreciation posted to date. The document date and posting date are like the normal dates in a journal, but the asset value date is quite specific to the asset you are adjusting and should make sense, so for example you cannot dispose of an asset on the 25th of a month if the capitalization date was only at the end of the month.

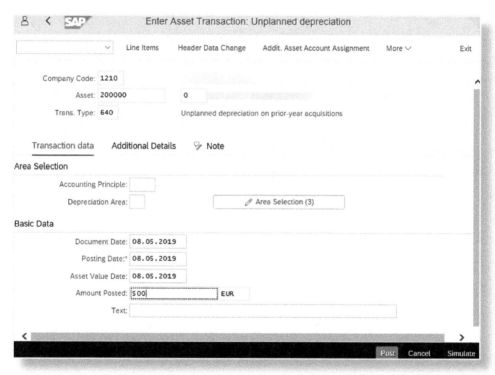

Figure 9.26: Transaction ABAAL—asset value adjustment

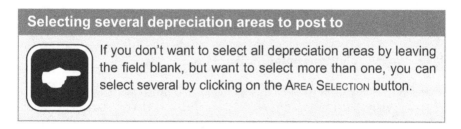

Selecting several depreciation areas to post to

If you don't want to select all depreciation areas by leaving the field blank, but want to select more than one, you can select several by clicking on the AREA SELECTION button.

Clicking on the Line Items button will display the amount to be posted to each depreciation area, and you can add additional columns by choosing Change Layout when you click on the arrow in the layout button . You can change cost centers, profit centers, internal orders, and WBS elements where relevant by clicking on Addit. Asset Account Assignment. Note that in the example in Figure 9.27, we changed the transaction type from *640* to *650* because the asset was a current year acquisition, not a prior year acquisition.

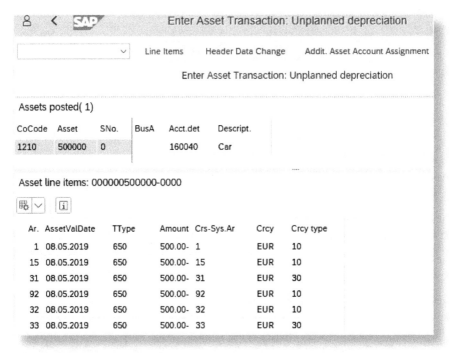

Figure 9.27: Transaction ABAAL—line Item, asset value adjustment

The following sections cover some adjustment transactions following a similar layout.

9.7.1   Depreciation adjustments

The SAP Fiori app is ABAAL Post Depreciation Manually—Unplanned and Planned, with GUI transactions ABAAL and ABAAN Unplanned Depreciation. The depreciation posted with this transaction does not immediately update the general ledger although it will show on the asset explorer transaction

AW01N or app Asset Values based on the same transaction (see Figure 9.28). The entry will only update when the depreciation run is posted.

Similar transactions in the classic GUI

In case you use or are more familiar with other similar transaction codes, the original GUI transaction here was ABAA, followed by ABAAN, (N=new), then ABAAL, (L=Ledger groups). In fact, all three transactions point to the same program and a similar naming scheme is followed in many other transactions. Sometimes the SAP Fiori app uses the transaction ending in N and sometimes the one ending in L in the app ID.

Asset:* 500000   0   Car

Fiscal year: < 2019 >

Planned values   Posted values   Comparisons   Parameters

Planned values Book Depreciation

Value	Fiscal year start	Change	Year-end	Crcy
APC transactions		3,000.00	3,000.00	EUR
Acquisition value		3,000.00	3,000.00	EUR
Ordinary deprec.		414.00-	414.00-	EUR
Unplanned dep.		20.00-	20.00-	EUR
Write-up				EUR
Value adjustment				EUR

Transactions

AssetValDate	Amount	TType	Transaction Type Name	Crcy
25.04.2019	1,000.00	100	External asset acquisition	EUR
25.04.2019	2,000.00	100	External asset acquisition	EUR
08.05.2019	20.00-	650	Unplanned depreciation on current-yr acquisition	EUR

Figure 9.28: Transaction AW01N—asset explorer, unplanned depreciation

In addition, app Post Write-up based on GUI transaction ABZU, has an additional section, shown in Figure 9.29, to adjust the depreciation in prior years.

205

Write-Up Specifications

Ordinary Dep. PY:		EUR
Cum. Special Dep.:		EUR
Unplnd.Dep.Prev.Year:	0.00	EUR
Reserves Transf. PY:	0.00	EUR

Figure 9.29: Transaction ABZU—post write-up

9.7.2 Non-integrated retirements

There are two types of non-integrated retirements. In both cases, if you have several assets to retire, once you have entered the company code, the MULTIPLE ASSETS button at the top of the screen allows you to enter a list of assets to be retired.

Retirement without customer

The difference between scrapping and sale without customer is that the sale without customer is usually a sale to a customer, but the customer posting is done in a different step, for example, following the sales order and billing flow.

The SAP Fiori app is POST RETIREMENT (NON-INTEGRATED)—WITHOUT CUSTO-MER, based on GUI transaction ABAON—ASSET SALE WITHOUT CUSTOMER. The transaction has some additional fields for MANUAL REVENUE and REV. FROM NBV, one of which needs to be selected. The reason for entering a manual revenue amount (even though the revenue amount is posted in a different transaction) is so that the system can work out if a gain or loss has been made on the sale and the balance gets posted accordingly, if you have separate G/L accounts for gains and losses. If you know the value because there is a separate customer invoice, you can enter it, or you can select the REV. FROM NBV, in which case you need to give a depreciation area for the system to take the NBV from.

Scrapping

Scrapping is generally used where an asset is disposed of without revenue, for example, thrown away, damaged, stolen, lost, etc., and simply needs to be removed from the asset register. The SAP Fiori app is POST RETIREment—By Scrapping, based on GUI transaction ABAVN (Asset retirement by scrapping).

9.7.3   Asset revaluations

The main app is Post Asset Revaluation, based on GUI transaction ABAWL. This posts a valuation adjustment to an individual asset and has an additional field Reval.O.Dep CY to adjust the related depreciation. The revaluation adjustments don't post to the general ledger immediately. Instead, they are posted as part of the depreciation run and you have to specifically select the accounting principles to be revalued.

There is a separate revaluation process, which is not covered in this book, to carry out a mass revaluation of a number of assets in one go (GUI transaction AR29N).

9.7.4   Corrections

Credit notes would normally follow the same process as the original invoice; however, you may need to post a credit directly, if it is not directly related to a supplier invoice. Credit memos can be posted in a similar way to value adjustments. The two SAP Fiori apps are Credit Memo Previous Year, based on GUI transaction ABGFL (strangely named Credit Memo in Year after Invoice), and Post Credit Memo—In Year of Invoice, based on GUI transaction ABGLL (Enter Credit Memo in Year of Invoice).

9.8   Reverse asset posting

If you need to cancel or reverse a posting that was initiated in the asset module, you need to post the reversal from the asset module as well. And depending on the point at which it is reversed, there may also be a subsequent depreciation correction. If the reversal involves a settlement, there is a reversal option in the settlement program.

App Reverse Journal Entry, shown in Figure 9.30, based on GUI transaction AB08, can be used to reverse a posting to an asset and a general ledger posting at the same time. You may need to take into account other factors, for example, if there is a PO, GR, and invoice involved, do you need to correct the GR or post a credit note from the supplier? If the transaction is correct, but, for example, the asset class was not, then it may be better to ignore the invoice and taxes and transfer the value from one asset to another.

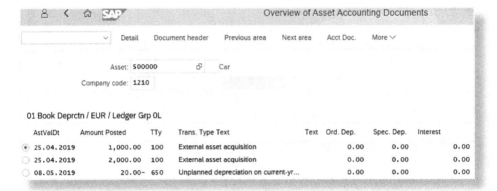

Figure 9.30: Transaction AB08—reverse asset journal entry

On the first screen, you need to enter the company code and asset. Next, you select which transaction you want to reverse. Finally, there will be a pop-up where you enter the posting date and the reversal reason. The reversal reasons are similar to the ones used when reversing an ordinary financial journal in the general ledger. The posting updates the asset and the general ledger, creating new documents.

9.9 Asset transfers

An existing asset can be transferred to another asset in an associated company in the same client, or to another asset within the same company. In both transactions, you have the choice of creating the asset master data first or creating it during the transaction.

Intracompany asset transfers

This is often used when an asset is set up in the wrong asset class and involves transferring the value from one asset to another within the same company code. App POST TRANSFER—WITHIN COMPANY CODE, is based on GUI transaction ABUMN.

If you want to transfer to an existing asset (or one created beforehand for this purpose), you need to select the EXISTING ASSET button and give the existing asset number. If you want to create a new asset during the transaction, you can click on the NEW ASSET button. Once you have selected NEW ASSET, the MASTERDATA button will no longer be grayed out, and you can choose whether to set up the asset with a minimum of the description, asset class, and cost center (available on the same screen) or whether you want to click on the MASTERDATA button. The MASTERDATA button produces a pop-up screen where you can enter additional detail such as an inventory number or location and any other fields available for that asset class. You can also reference the sending asset, in other words, copy data such as the description and cost center from the sending asset to the target asset. Figure 9.31 shows the initial screen of the app.

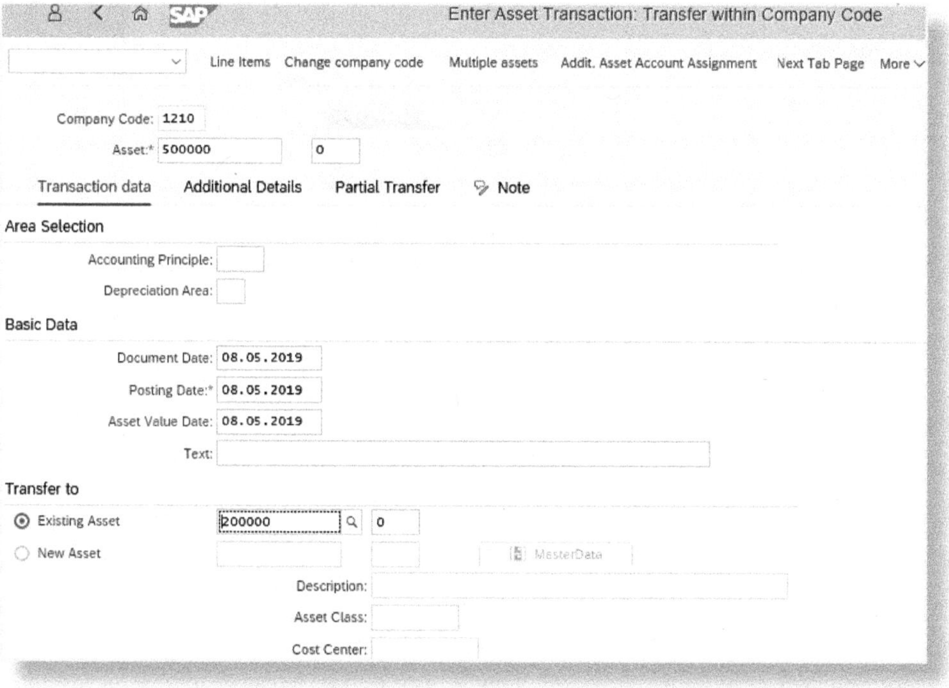

Figure 9.31: Transaction ABUMN—transfer within company code

The ADDITIONAL DETAILS tab allows you to change the document type, and how the amount is transferred (covered under the intercompany transfer example shown in Figure 9.32) or you can enter partial amounts or percentages on the PARTIAL TRANSFER tab.

Current/prior year acquisition

At the bottom of the partial transfer tab, there are radio buttons to toggle between a prior year acquisition and a current year acquisition, if the default one is not correct.

Intercompany asset transfers

SAP Fiori apps Post Transfer—Across Company Codes Within the Same Country, based on GUI transaction ABT1N, and Asset Transfer Intercompany, based on GUI transaction ABT1L, (on-premise only), seem identical and both transactions in the GUI are linked to the same program. Both apps enable you to do a disposal in one company code and an acquisition in another at the same time and you can choose whether it is at the same amount, at NBV, or for a revenue amount. However, you may not always be able to post the transfer automatically if there are too many inconsistencies in customizing between the two companies, regardless of their country.

Transferring between two companies

If the customizing is inconsistent, for example, the target company has a business area but the source company does not, or the companies have different charts of depreciation, you may have to manually post separate journals in each company.

The intercompany transactions are almost identical to the intracompany except that you have an additional field to complete for the target company code. Figure 9.32 shows the Transfer Variant dropdown on the Additional Details tab, which allows you to choose, for example, whether to transfer gross (i.e., including the depreciation separately) or net amounts.

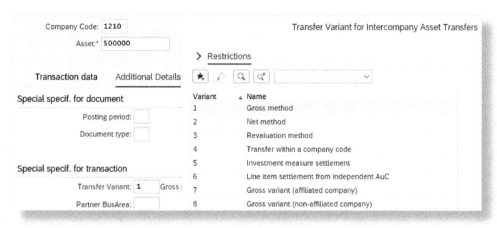

Figure 9.32: Transaction ABT1L intercompany transfer—transfer variants

9.10 Depreciation and closing tasks

The depreciation run takes the planned depreciation and posts it. The app to schedule the depreciation is F1914 SCHEDULE ASSET ACCOUNTING JOBS in the SAP Fiori app library, and is similar to most of the scheduling apps. The asset accounting jobs that can be run with this app are:

► DEPRECIATION POSTING RUN

► RECALCULATE DEPRECIATION

► FILL MASTER DATA FOR SEGMENT REPORTING

► YEAR-END CLOSING ASSET ACCOUNTING

► ASSET TRANSACTIONS REPORT

In app F1914 SCHEDULE ASSET ACCOUNTING JOBS, the first page is an overview of all the tasks and statuses. You click on NEW to schedule a new task and on the next screen (see Figure 9.33), select the JOB TEMPLATE, for example depreciation posting run. Next, enter the details related to that job template, in this case the company code, accounting principle (leave blank for all), and whether you want a test run and detailed log.

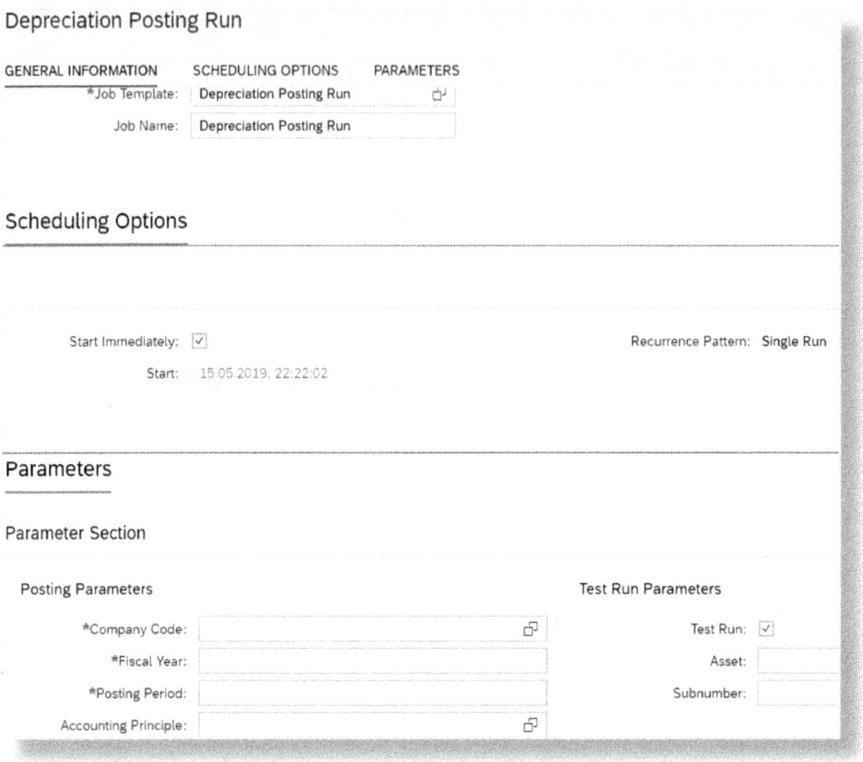

Depreciation Posting Run

GENERAL INFORMATION   SCHEDULING OPTIONS   PARAMETERS

*Job Template: Depreciation Posting Run

Job Name: Depreciation Posting Run

Scheduling Options

Start Immediately: ☑   Recurrence Pattern: Single Run

Start: 15.05.2019, 22:22:02

Parameters

Parameter Section

Posting Parameters   Test Run Parameters

*Company Code: Test Run: ☑

*Fiscal Year: Asset:

*Posting Period: Subnumber:

Accounting Principle:

Figure 9.33: App F1914—schedule asset accounting jobs, depreciation posting run

You can also set a recurring task, for example POST DEPRECIATION, although users may prefer to confirm all additions and disposals are complete each period before triggering the depreciation to be run when ready.

RECALCULATE DEPRECIATION, as the name implies, this recalculates the planned depreciation, but it does not post anything until you run the post-depreciation job. This transaction is also found in app F1914 SCHEDULE ASSET ACCOUNTING JOBS and is based on GUI transaction AFAR. (Its predecessor, also based on AFAR, was app F1376 RECALCULATING VALUES). It is usually run at year end, or each period if you are using unit of production depreciation, but can be run at any time.

Once a scheduled asset job has been run, you will see the results in the overview page and can check the items in the LOG or RESULTS columns for further information (see Figure 9.34). An example log for a RECALCULATE DEPRECIATION run is shown in Figure 9.35, and the RESULTS button may take you to the spool files (where relevant) for the full report of what has been proposed or posted.

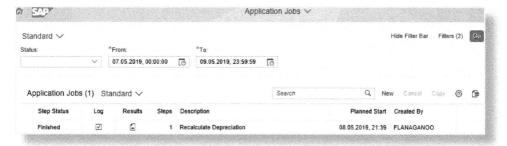

Figure 9.34: App F1914—schedule asset accounting jobs, overview

Log Details	Standard ∨		Search				
Message Type	**Description**						**Time Stamp**
☑ Success	Company code 1210, AP LG: 1 fixed assets processed						08.05.2019, 21:39

Figure 9.35: App F1914—schedule asset accounting jobs, logs

The depreciation run should pick up any manual, unplanned, and planned depreciation (plus any revaluation adjustments).

9.11   Asset drill down and reporting

9.11.1 Asset explorer

App ASSET VALUES is based on the classic GUI transaction AW01N, known as the ASSET EXPLORER. There is also an on-premise SAP Fiori app, F1684 MANAGE FIXED ASSETS. We will cover both; although they show similar data, they are in slightly different formats. The initial screen of the ASSET EXPLORER (see Figure 9.36) shows all the available depreciation areas on the top left and clicking on each one will display the values for that depreciation area on the right-hand side.

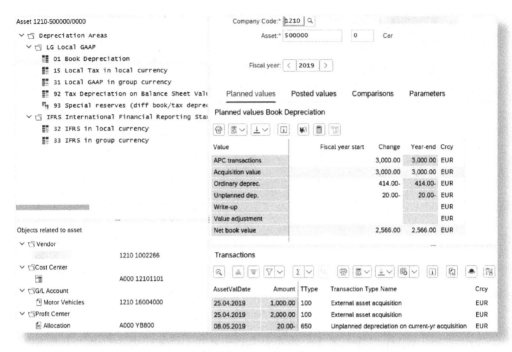

Figure 9.36: Transaction AW01N—asset explorer

Also, at the top left are buttons to jump to the asset master data, translate currency amounts, jump to other asset reports, and switch on simulation. There is also a legend button to see what all the other buttons represent. On the bottom left, you have related master data objects, such as G/L account, cost center, supplier, and so on.

In the bottom right-hand corner are the posted transactions, usually acquisitions, disposals, settlements, unplanned depreciation, revaluations, and so on. You can double-click on the transactions to see the accounting document or use the RELATIONSHIP BROWSER button, ▦All, in the planned values tab to see the documents behind each transaction. See the example in Figure 9.37.

In Figure 9.38, we show an extract of the first four months from the bottom section of the POSTED VALUES tab of the asset explorer. You select the year at the top of the screen (not shown) and the tab shows the planned and unplanned amounts of depreciation and revaluation to be posted each month for that year. When the depreciation is fully posted, the yellow triangle in the status column becomes a green square to indicate the posting is complete. There is also a different status button to show values from a legacy system.

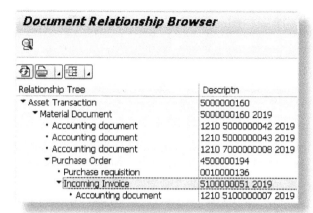

Document Relationship Browser

Relationship Tree	Descriptn
▼ Asset Transaction	5000000160
▼ Material Document	5000000160 2019
• Accounting document	1210 5000000042 2019
• Accounting document	1210 5000000043 2019
• Accounting document	1210 7000000008 2019
▼ Purchase Order	4500000194
• Purchase requisition	0010000136
▼ Incoming Invoice	5100000051 2019
• Accounting document	1210 5100000007 2019

Figure 9.37: Transaction AW01N—relationship browser with asset documents

Depreciation posted/planned

Status	Status	Per	ΣOrd. Dep.	ΣUplnd Dep.	ΣReserves	ΣRevaluat.	Crcy
Posted	Posted	1	15.00-	0.00	0.00	0.00	GBP
Planned	Planned	2	15.00-	0.00	0.00	0.00	GBP
Planned	Planned	3	15.00-	0.00	0.00	0.00	GBP
Planned	Planned	4	15.00-	0.00	0.00	0.00	GBP

Figure 9.38: Transaction AW01N—asset explorer posted/planned depreciation

Figure 9.39 shows the COMPARISONS tab with the asset history for each year in the columns, and the years in the rows.

Book Depreciation:2019 -2024

Fiscal year	Σ	APC transactions	Acquisition value	Σ	Ordinary deprec.	Σ	Unplanned dep.	Net book value	Acquisitio
<2019									EUR
2019		3,000.00	3,000.00		414.00-		20.00-	2,566.00	EUR
2020			3,000.00		600.00-			1,966.00	EUR
2021			3,000.00		600.00-			1,366.00	EUR
2022			3,000.00		600.00-			766.00	EUR
2023			3,000.00		600.00-			166.00	EUR
2024			3,000.00		166.00-				EUR
•		3,000.00		•	2,980.00-	•	20.00-		EUR

Figure 9.39: Transaction AW01—asset comparison values tab by year

Figure 9.40 shows the comparison tab again, but with a different layout. The asset history is shown by year in the rows, and you can add the depreciation areas you want to compare to the columns by clicking on the numbered buttons above the display (not shown in figure).

Comparison of several depreciation areas:2019 -2024

Value	Fiscal...	01 Book D...	15 Local Tax i...	31 Local G...	32 IFRS in...	33 IFRS in gr...
APC transactions	2019	3,000.00	3,000.00	3,000.00	3,000.00	3,000.00
Acquisition value	2019	3,000.00	3,000.00	3,000.00	3,000.00	3,000.00
Ordinary deprec.	2019	414.00-	414.00-	414.00-	375.00-	375.00-
Unplanned dep.	2019	20.00-	20.00-	20.00-	20.00-	20.00-
Net book value	2019	2,566.00	2,566.00	2,566.00	2,605.00	2,605.00
Acquisition value	2020	3,000.00	3,000.00	3,000.00	3,000.00	3,000.00
Ordinary deprec.	2020	600.00-	600.00-	600.00-	496.00-	496.00-
Net book value	2020	1,966.00	1,966.00	1,966.00	2,109.00	2,109.00
Acquisition value	2021	3,000.00	3,000.00	3,000.00	3,000.00	3,000.00
Ordinary deprec.	2021	600.00-	600.00-	600.00-	496.00-	496.00-
Net book value	2021	1,366.00	1,366.00	1,366.00	1,613.00	1,613.00
Acquisition value	2022	3,000.00	3,000.00	3,000.00	3,000.00	3,000.00
Ordinary deprec.	2022	600.00-	600.00-	600.00-	496.00-	496.00-
Net book value	2022	766.00	766.00	766.00	1,117.00	1,117.00

Figure 9.40: Transaction AW01N—comparison values tab by depreciation area

In the PARAMETERS tab of the asset explorer, you have the depreciation key, useful life, expired useful life, and depreciation start date.

Figure 9.41 shows an example of a 360-degree asset factsheet in app F1684 MANAGE FIXED ASSET.

You can move through the screens and tabs to see similar information to the asset explorer plus a graphical representation of the life cycle of the asset and net book value.

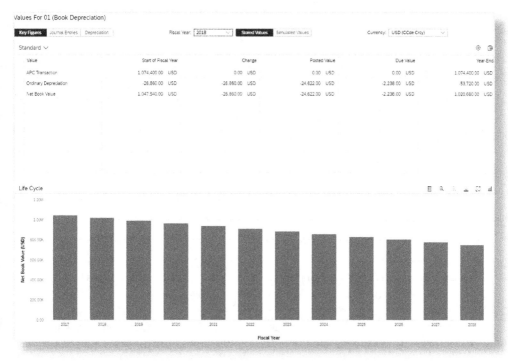

Figure 9.41: App F1684—manage fixed asset app

9.11.2 Reporting

In this section, we show a few examples of reporting using SAP Design Studio multidimensional apps. Although we only show a few examples, the reports can be run by many different dimensions and key figures. More detail about multidimensional reporting is shown in section 10.1.

Asset balances

App F1617A Asset Balances is fairly self-explanatory, a straightforward list showing opening APC, (also known as gross book value), less depreciation, giving the net book value. You can sort, filter, and summarize by many different criteria, including account determination, acquisition year, cost center, asset class, and so on, as well as by asset number and subnumber. Figure 9.42 shows app F1617A Asset Balances sorted by asset class and then by asset number.

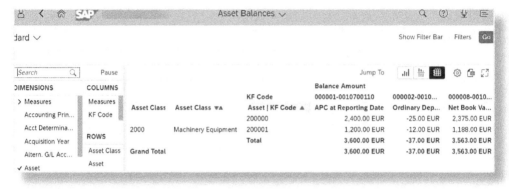

Figure 9.42: App F1617A—asset balances

Asset history

App F1615A ASSET HISTORY SHEET is very similar to the asset balance report, but shows opening balances, plus all the transactions in the year (additions, disposals, transfers, revaluations, depreciations, and so on), to give the closing balances and net book value at the reporting date. You can sort, summarize, and filter by similar criteria to the asset balances. Figure 9.43 gives an overview of the asset history by cost center and then by asset class as an example of two dimensions.

Asset Cost Cent	Asset Class ▲	Balance Amount ▾▲	Balance Amount '	Balance Amount ▾▲	Balance Amount ▾▲
12101101	4000	10.000.00 EUR	2.200.00 EUR	12,200.00 EUR	0.00 EUR
	Result	218,500.00 EUR	21,500.00 EUR	240,000.00 EUR	-99,376.00 EUR
	1000	2.000.00 EUR	0.00 EUR	2,000.00 EUR	0.00 EUR
	1100	2.000.00 EUR	0.00 EUR	2,000.00 EUR	-144.00 EUR
12101102	2000	28.000.00 EUR	0.00 EUR	28,000.00 EUR	-8,093.00 EUR
	3000	2.000.00 EUR	0.00 EUR	2,000.00 EUR	-592.00 EUR
	3200	2.000.00 EUR	0.00 EUR	2,000.00 EUR	-1,201.00 EUR
	Result	36,000.00 EUR	0.00 EUR	36,000.00 EUR	-10,030.00 EUR
12101201	2000	0.00 EUR	2,250.00 EUR	2,250.00 EUR	0.00 EUR
	3210	15.000.00 EUR	0.00 EUR	15,000.00 EUR	-10,051.00 EUR
	4000	0.00 EUR	0.00 EUR	0.00 EUR	0.00 EUR
	Result	15,000.00 EUR	2,250.00 EUR	17,250.00 EUR	-10,051.00 EUR

.nce Amount ▾▲	Balance Amount ▾▲	Balance Amount ▾▲	Balance Amount ▾▲	Balance Amou
0.00 EUR	0.00 EUR	0.00 EUR	10,000.00 EUR	12,200.00 E
-99,376.00 EUR	-1,652.00 EUR	-101,028.00 EUR	119,124.00 EUR	172,183.00 E
0.00 EUR	0.00 EUR	0.00 EUR	2,000.00 EUR	2,000.00 E
-144.00 EUR	-7.00 EUR	-151.00 EUR	1,856.00 EUR	1,916.00 E
-8.093.00 EUR	-238.00 EUR	-8,331.00 EUR	19,907.00 EUR	22,179.00 E
-592.00 EUR	-29.00 EUR	-621.00 EUR	1,408.00 EUR	1,660.00 E
-1,201.00 EUR	-57.00 EUR	-1,258.00 EUR	799.00 EUR	1,301.00 E
-10,030.00 EUR	-331.00 EUR	-10,361.00 EUR	25,970.00 EUR	29,046.00 E
0.00 EUR	0.00 EUR	0.00 EUR	0.00 EUR	2,250.00 E
-10,051.00 EUR	-426.00 EUR	-10,477.00 EUR	4,949.00 EUR	8,715.00 E
0.00 EUR	0.00 EUR	0.00 EUR	0.00 EUR	0.00 E
-10,051.00 EUR	-426.00 EUR	-10,477.00 EUR	4,949.00 EUR	10,965.00 E

Figure 9.43: App F1615A—asset history by cost center and asset class

Figure 9.44 shows an extract of the same report by profit center.

Profit Center	Asset	Balance Amount Acquisition, Cu...	APC at Reporting ...	Depreciation,...	Acc. Depr. at R...	Net Book Value at Reporting
	Plant1	2,400 EUR	2,400 EUR	-25 EUR	-25 EUR	2,375
YB600	Plant2	1,200 EUR	1,200 EUR	-12 EUR	-12 EUR	1,188
	Total	3,600 EUR	3,600 EUR	-37 EUR	-37 EUR	3,563
YB700	AUC	0 EUR	0 EUR	0 EUR	0 EUR	0
	Total	0 EUR	0 EUR	0 EUR	0 EUR	0
Grand Total		3,600 EUR	3,600 EUR	-37 EUR	-37 EUR	3,563

Figure 9.44: App F1615A—asset history by profit center

9.12 Asset year-end closing

There are several steps to the asset closing process, in addition to ensuring all the relevant acquisitions, retirements, transfers, depreciation, revaluations, and any other documents are posted.

9.12.1 Open new year

This is now included in the general ledger carryforward transaction explained in section 11.4. In previous versions of SAP, there was a separate transaction specifically for asset accounting, but this is no longer the case. It is described as carryforward, but it effectively opens the new year so that further postings are carried forward automatically. You cannot run any transactions or reports in asset accounting once you are physically in the new year without opening the new year. With this transaction, the earliest you can open the new year is anytime in the last period of the previous year.

9.12.2 Close old year

This should be done when the old year is complete, often after the auditors have been in and audit adjustments made, but must be completed before you open the following year because you can only have a maximum of two years open at any one time. For on-premise releases (and Cloud up to 1902), the year can be closed by selecting the template YEAR-END CLOSING

ASSET ACCOUNTING in app F1914 SCHEDULE ASSET ACCOUNTING JOBS, based on GUI transaction AJAB.

Asset year-end closing in SAP S/4HANA Cloud

In SAP S/4HANA Cloud, app MAKE COMPANY CODE SETTINGS—ASSET ACCOUNTING SPECIFIC, based on GUI transaction FAA_CMP, now has added functionality to close or reopen the fiscal year. You select the company code and ledger, click on the select entry button, ⬚ᴋ, and you will see the screen on the right-hand side where you can perform the close or reopen the year. See Figure 9.45. You can close everything else and leave, for example, a tax depreciation area open for adjustments, or open one depreciation area later if there are audit adjustments after the close.

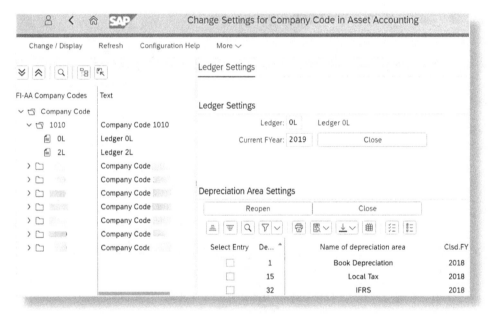

Figure 9.45: Transaction FAA_CMP—close or reopen asset year in ledger settings

If you are using investment management and internal orders or projects, there may be additional steps to carryforward commitments, budgets, etc.

220

9.13 Asset migration

The key change from previous versions of SAP is that asset accounting has a much tighter integration with finance, so instead of posting a value to the asset and then later updating finance with a separate journal, everything is done simultaneously. You can create the master data first and then post the values manually if you only have a few assets, but generally you would fill the legacy migration templates with all the master data and transactional data and upload it all in one go. In this case, the system creates the asset master record and posts the journal to update the asset values and general ledger at the same time.

Prior to the migration, you have to ensure that the company code settings are correct and enter the migration date. The app for this is MAKE COMPANY CODE SETTINGS—ASSET ACCOUNTING-SPECIFIC, based on GUI transaction FAA_CMP, and the date can be entered on the legacy data transfer tab. See Figure 9.46.

Figure 9.46: Transaction FAA_CMP—company code settings for asset transfers

If you have only a few assets, you can create the initial master data with a special legacy data app, CREATE ASSET MASTER RECORD—FOR LEGACY ASSET, based on GUI transaction AS91. Although historically you could also enter values in this transaction, this has now been blocked and you need to use a separate transaction to post the asset and the G/L account values together. You can also set up AUC master records and assets with this transaction.

Creating the asset master data for a legacy item is fairly similar to creating a normal asset, but you will need to enter the original capitalization date from the legacy system.

Next, you can enter the values with app POST TRANSFER VALUES—FOR LEGACY ASSET, based on GUI transaction ABLDT, or TRANSFER OPEN ITEMS OF AuC—FOR LEGACY ASSET, based on GUI transaction ABLDT_OI.

As you can see in Figure 9.47, you simply enter the relevant values for each depreciation area. If you enter the depreciation amount, it will automatically add the negative sign.

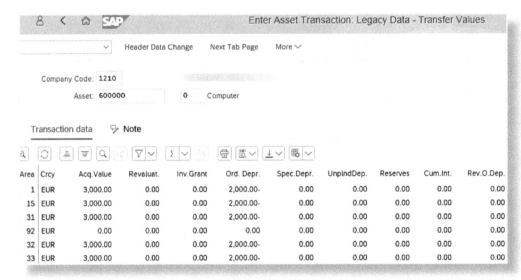

Area	Crcy	Acq.Value	Revaluat.	Inv.Grant	Ord. Depr.	Spec.Depr.	UnplndDep.	Reserves	Cum.Int.	Rev.O.Dep.
1	EUR	3,000.00	0.00	0.00	2,000.00-	0.00	0.00	0.00	0.00	0.00
15	EUR	3,000.00	0.00	0.00	2,000.00-	0.00	0.00	0.00	0.00	0.00
31	EUR	3,000.00	0.00	0.00	2,000.00-	0.00	0.00	0.00	0.00	0.00
92	EUR	0.00	0.00	0.00	0.00	0.00	0.00	0.00	0.00	0.00
32	EUR	3,000.00	0.00	0.00	2,000.00-	0.00	0.00	0.00	0.00	0.00
33	EUR	3,000.00	0.00	0.00	2,000.00-	0.00	0.00	0.00	0.00	0.00

Figure 9.47: Transaction ABLDT—transfer of legacy asset opening balances

In Figure 9.48, you can see the simulation of the asset posting. The APC of the asset is debited and the accumulated depreciation is credited with the balance, and the net book value is debited to the migration account set in the configuration.

Line items

Type	Period	Ledger Grp	AccP	DocumentNo	Item	PK	Segment	Profit Ctr	G/L Acc	Short Text	ε	Amount	Crcy
UE	3	OL	LG	$ 1	1	70	1000_A	YB800	16007000	000000600000 0000		3,000.00	EUR
UE	3	OL	LG		2	75	1000_A	YB800	17007000	000000600000 0000		2,000.00-	EUR
UE	3	OL	LG		3	50	1000_A	YB800	39913000	Initial FI-AM offset		1,000.00-	EUR
				$ 1							•	0.00	EUR

Figure 9.48: Transaction ABLDT—simulation of legacy asset posting

10 Reporting

Some of the display and reporting apps have been covered in the related chapters, but we have kept the remainder together as there are a lot of similarities, particularly with the SAP Design Studio multidimensional reporting apps. It also made sense to group some reports together, particularly for accounts payable and receivable apps.

10.1 Multidimentional reporting apps

Examples of some multidimensional reporting apps that have the same functionality are: F0996A—TRIAL BALANCE, F2843—CASH FLOW STATEMENT, F1615A—ASSET HISTORY, F1617A—ASSET BALANCES, F0956A—JOURNAL ENTRY ANALYZER, as well as many internal orders and cost and profit center reports. You will recognize the format as soon as you open an app, as they all behave in a similar way, but with different measures, dimensions, and key figures. Note that some of the apps also have an *accessible* Web Dynpro version in a more tabular format that may be easier to work with, but should have the same figures and dimensions.

10.1.1 Selection screen and layout

Selection screen

First, you will see a selection screen, with the heading PROMPTS. Here you might typically select, or restrict, the report to a company code and a date range, among other things, but the relevant fields vary with each app; some require a financial statement version, for example. You can easily get back to this screen once inside the report, as it is one of the first options when you click on the settings ⚙ button. Note that the OK button at the bottom of the selection screen will remain grayed out until all the mandatory fields are completed.

Layout

Below is a list of the things that you can do with the type of layout shown in Figure 10.1.

▶ Show or hide the filter bar; choose fields to show on the bar and filter on them

▶ Drag and drop dimensions into rows or columns

▶ Sort by clicking on ascending or descending triangles in the column headers

▶ Save your choices either as a variant (STANDARD button top left) or as an SAP Fiori tile

▶ JUMP TO other transactions in a new screen

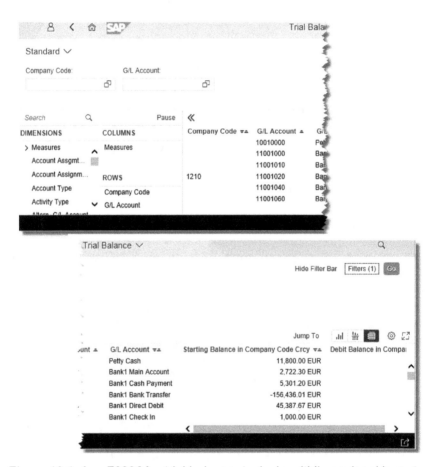

Figure 10.1: App F0996A—trial balance, typical multidimensional layout

Explanation of buttons in Figure 10.1

The ACTIONS button 📝 at the bottom right of the screen, gives you the option to EXPORT TO MS EXCEL, SEND E-MAIL, or SAVE AS TILE. You can use the 🔄 to expand the data area and hide the dimension columns, and there is also a button with arrows pointing inwards to return to the original screen.

The three buttons ⏹ ⏹ ⏹ allow you to toggle between a chart, a table, or both together, although not all reports make sense in chart form. Figure 10.2 illustrates the concept and shows the trial balance in mixed format, with a chart on top and table below.

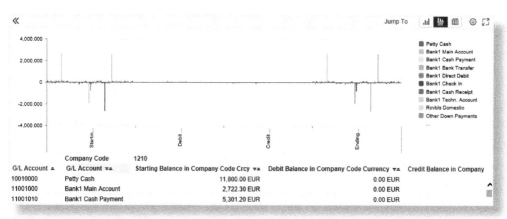

Figure 10.2: App F0996A—trial balance shown in chart and table form.

10.1.2 Body of the report—dimensions

If you right-click on a dimension in a line of the report, you have a number of options (see Figure 10.3) depending on where you are in the body of the report, but relating specifically to that dimension.

G/L Account ▲	G/L Account ▼▲	Starting Balance in Company Code Crc
10010000	Petty Cash	0.00
1100 Sort	✓ Key Ascending	10,700.00
1100 Display	Key Descending	2,000.00
1100	Text Ascending	0.00
1100 Attributes		0.00
1100 Hierarchy	Text Descending	0.00
1100 Totals	Sort by Hierarchy	-10,000.00
1210		33,900.00
1256 Filter		-64,000.00
1260 Suppress Zeros in Rows		0.00
1260 Jump To		0.00

Figure 10.3: Functions in the body of a multidimensional report

225

Sort

You have the option to sort by Key Ascending, Text Ascending, Key Descending, Text Descending, or Sort by Hierarchy, where applicable. Using the G/L account as an example, the key is the G/L account number and the text is the description.

Display

Here you can change the way a field is displayed. For example, the key, code, or both; or the text, description, or both. In Figure 10.1, for example, we have chosen to show only the company code number and not the name, but we are showing the G/L account description as well as the code.

Attributes

Depending on the dimension selected, different attributes from the master data will be available to show in the next column. For example, if you select the attributes for a G/L account, you could choose G/L Account Type, which would then add a column next to the G/L account indicating whether each G/L account is a type Balance Sheet, Primary Costs or Revenue, Secondary costs, or Non-operating Expense or Income.

Hierarchy

If you are using flexible hierarchies, (see section 4.1.3), you can select, expand, and collapse them here as well as re-order the lower-level nodes.

Totals

You can choose to show or hide totals on the top or bottom of the section, and you can also choose to only show totals if there is more than one item.

Filter

You have several options, Filter Member, Filter Member and Remove From Axis, and Drill Down.

Suppress zeros in rows

As the name implies, only rows with a value not equal to zero are shown in the report.

Jump to

You can jump directly to other apps, depending upon what has been set up and your authorizations.

10.1.3 Body of the report numbers

If you right-click on a number in the body of the report, you will see a pop-up box with options NUMBER FORMAT, DEFINE CONDITIONS, and JUMP TO, but if you click on the header of a number column, you will see the five options, as shown in Figure 10.4.

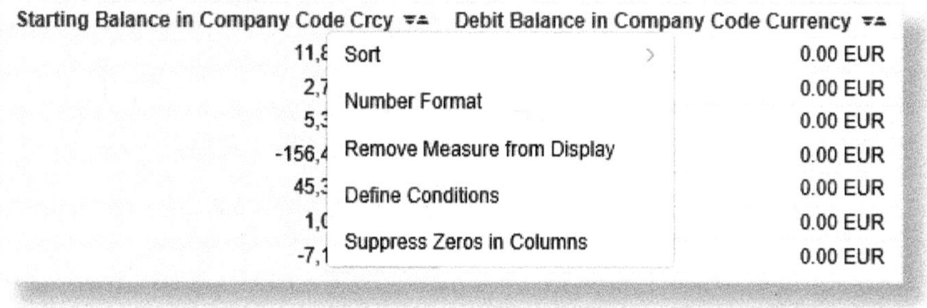

Figure 10.4: Multidimensional report body, number column options

Define conditions

As shown in Figure 10.5, you can create various conditions, based on different key figures. For example, you can select the accounts in the Trial Balance with the Top 20 Highest closing balances. You can also create the TOP N or BOTTOM N by sum, percentage, or value and add conditions with AND, OR, and various other options.

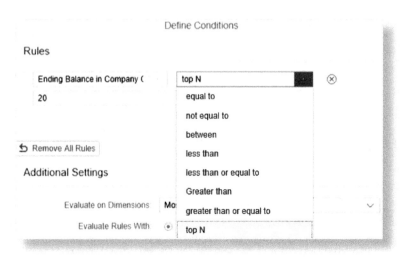

Figure 10.5: Multidimensional report, define conditions

Suppress zeroes in columns

As the name implies, only columns with a value not equal to zero are shown in the report. This is not the same as SUPPRESS ZEROES IN ROWS mentioned earlier in this section, as you can swap the axes, and suppress a whole column. Figure 10.6 shows the opening balance, debits, credits, and closing balance in the rows and all the G/L accounts in the columns. To swap the axes in this case, we dragged the G/L account from ROWS into COLUMNS and the measures from COLUMNS into ROWS.

G/L Account	10010000	11001000	11001010	11001020
G/L Account	Petty Cash	Bank1 Main Account	Bank1 Cash Payment	Bank1 Bank T
Starting Balance in Company Code Crcy	11,800.00 EUR	2,722.30 EUR	5,301.20 EUR	-156,436,
Debit Balance in Company Code Currency	0.00 EUR	0.00 EUR	0.00 EUR	0
Credit Balance in Company Code Currency	0.00 EUR	0.00 EUR	0.00 EUR	-946.
Ending Balance in Company Code Currency	11,800.00 EUR	2,722.30 EUR	5,301.20 EUR	-157,382

	11001020	11001040	11001060	11001080
.ent	Bank1 Bank Transfer	Bank1 Direct Debit	Bank1 Check In	Bank1 Cash Receipt
EUR	-156,436.01 EUR	45,387.67 EUR	1,000.00 EUR	-7,122.30 EUR
EUR	0.00 EUR	0.00 EUR	0.00 EUR	0.00 EUR
EUR	-946.86 EUR	0.00 EUR	0.00 EUR	0.00 EUR
EUR	-157,382.87 EUR	45,387.67 EUR	1,000.00 EUR	-7,122.30 EUR

Figure 10.6: Rows and columns swapped around

Sort

In the number format or amount format of the report body, SORT has two options, KEY FIGURE VALUE ASCENDING and KEY FIGURE VALUE DESCENDING.

Number format

If you select NUMBER FORMAT, a pop-up will appear with the options to choose a scaling factor and decimal places. For example, the petty cash balance from Figure 10.1, which was 11,800.00, will be shown as 12 with a scaling factor of 1,000 and zero decimals. You may have to wait briefly while the system recalibrates everything.

Remove measure from display

As the description implies, selecting REMOVE MEASURE FROM DISPLAY will remove the measure from either the column or the row (depending where you have the measures), completely.

10.1.4 Other options

Filters and key figure functionality

You can add fields to the filter bar by clicking on the FILTERS button at the top right of the screen (different to right-clicking in the report) and then selecting the box to the right of the field you want to add.

If you scroll down to the bottom of the filters box, you will see an option for MEASURES. You can add back any options removed by mistake when using REMOVE MEASURE FROM DISPLAY.

Click on the dropdown in the MEASURES field and you will get a new pop-up titled KEY FIGURES. Here you will find many options in global and transaction currencies, plus the freely defined currencies. See Figure 10.7.

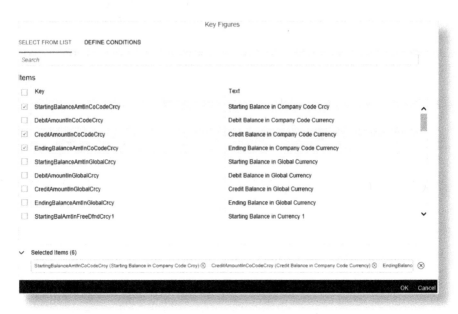

Figure 10.7: Key figures and currencies in the filter area

Settings

Using ⚙, you can also change chart settings and swap axes, as well as manage the totals fields.

10.2 General ledger reporting

10.2.1 Trial balance

App F0996A TRIAL BALANCE, used as an example in section 10.1, is used here in Figure 10.8, to show a clearer example of a multidimensional report.

App F2767 TRIAL BALANCE COMPARISON allows you to compare two periods or years. See Figure 10.9, where we have also dragged the COST CENTER dimension into the ROWS section.

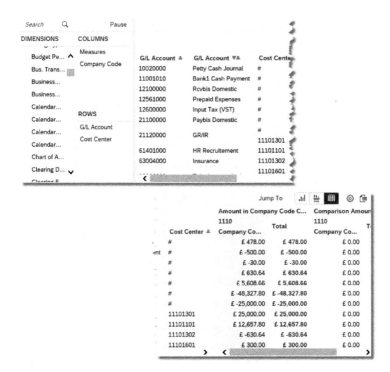

		Compa	G/L Account ▲	G/L Account ▼▲	Starting
Search	Pause		10020000	Petty Cash Journal	
DIMENSIONS	**COLUMNS**		11001010	Bank1 Cash Payment	
Chart of Ac... ∧	Measures		12100000	Rcvbls Domestic	
Clearing Date			12561000	Prepaid Expenses	
Clearing En...			12600000	Input Tax (VST)	
Clearing Fis...			21100000	Paybls Domestic	
✓ Company C...		1110	21120000	GR/IR	
Company C...	**ROWS**		61401000	HR Recruitement	
Controlling...	Company Code		63004000	Insurance	
Cost Center	G/L Account		63006000	Telephone and other	
Cost Object			63008000	Building PerSer	
Country CoA			65100000	Office Supplies	
				Total	

Jump To

Starting Balance i	Debit Balance i	Credit Balance in	Ending Balance in
£ -30.00	£ 530.00	£ -52.00	£ 448.00
£ 0.00	£ 0.00	£ -500.00	£ -500.00
£ 0.00	£ 0.00	£ -30.00	£ -30.00
£ 0.00	£ 630.64	£ 0.00	£ 630.64
£ -5,600.00	£ 5,608.66	£ 0.00	£ 8.66
£ 0.00	£ 0.00	£ -48,327.80	£ -48,327.80
£ 0.00	£ 25,000.00	£ -25,000.00	£ 0.00
£ 0.00	£ 12,657.80	£ 0.00	£ 12,657.80
£ 0.00	£ 0.00	£ -630.64	£ -630.64
£ 0.00	£ 570.00	£ 0.00	£ 570.00
£ 0.00	£ 1,500.00	£ 0.00	£ 1,500.00
£ -28,000.00	£ 28,043.34	£ 0.00	£ 43.34
£ 0.00	£ 74,540.44	£ -74,540.44	£ 0.00

Figure 10.8: App F0996A—trial balance

		G/L Account ▲	G/L Account ▼▲	Cost Cente
Search	Pause	10020000	Petty Cash Journal	#
DIMENSIONS	**COLUMNS**	11001010	Bank1 Cash Payment	#
Budget Pe... ∧	Measures	12100000	Rcvbls Domestic	#
Bus. Trans...	Company Code	12561000	Prepaid Expenses	#
Business...		12600000	Input Tax (VST)	#
Business...		21100000	Paybls Domestic	#
Calendar...	**ROWS**	21120000	GR/IR	#
Calendar...	G/L Account			11101301
Calendar...	Cost Center	61401000	HR Recruitement	11101101
Calendar...		63004000	Insurance	11101302
Chart of A...				11101601
Clearing D... ∨				

Jump To

	Amount in Company Code C...		Comparison Amoun
	1110		1110
Cost Center ▲	Company Co...	Total	Company Co...
#	£ 478.00	£ 478.00	£ 0.00
#	£ -500.00	£ -500.00	£ 0.00
#	£ -30.00	£ -30.00	£ 0.00
#	£ 630.64	£ 630.64	£ 0.00
#	£ 5,608.66	£ 5,608.66	£ 0.00
#	£ -48,327.80	£ -48,327.80	£ 0.00
#	£ -25,000.00	£ -25,000.00	£ 0.00
11101301	£ 25,000.00	£ 25,000.00	£ 0.00
11101101	£ 12,657.80	£ 12,657.80	£ 0.00
11101302	£ -630.64	£ -630.64	£ 0.00
11101601	£ 300.00	£ 300.00	£ 0.00

Figure 10.9: App F2767—trial balance comparison

10.2.2 Financial statement version

To report on the organization's results for the year, you can use app F0708 DISPLAY FINANCIAL STATEMENT. You need to choose the required FINANCIAL STATEMENT VERSION in the selection screen. You can show comparison periods (see Figure 10.10) and there is also a button to download the whole statement in PDF format. Click on items in blue to link or drill down to other apps such as display G/L balances or display G/L line items. You can choose different tabs for ALL ACCOUNTS, BALANCE SHEET, PROFIT & LOSS, or UN-ASSIGNED ACCOUNTS.

You can add in G/L accounts, profit centers, and segments and their descriptions by clicking the ⚙ button. You can also filter on different objects or add in additional filter options by clicking on the ADAPT FILTERS button.

Description	Period Balance	Comparison Balance (Actual)	Absolute Difference	Relative Difference
∨ ASSETS	3,389,227.06 EUR	196,438.00 EUR	3,192,789.06 EUR	1,625.3
∨ Fixed Assets	233,469.00 EUR	234,538.00 EUR	-1,069.00 EUR	-0.5
⟩ Intangible Assets	8,765.00 EUR	19,109.00 EUR	-10,344.00 EUR	-54.1
∨ Tangible Assets	224,704.00 EUR	215,429.00 EUR	9,275.00 EUR	4.3
⟩ Land	11,466.00 EUR	11,768.00 EUR	-302.00 EUR	-2.6
⟩ Buildings	34,394.00 EUR	35,829.00 EUR	-1,435.00 EUR	-4.0
⟩ Technical Installations, Equipment ...	154,089.00 EUR	133,727.00 EUR	20,362.00 EUR	15.2
∨ Other Tangible Assets	12,553.00 EUR	24,105.00 EUR	-11,552.00 EUR	-47.9
⟩ Gross Amounts	29,000.00 EUR	29,000.00 EUR	0.00 EUR	0.0
☑ Depreciations / Provisions	-16,447.00 EUR	-4,895.00 EUR	-11,552.00 EUR	-236.0
Accumulated Depreciation - Motor Vehicles	-3,718.00 EUR	-1,196.00 EUR	-2,522.00 EUR	-210.9
Accumulated Depreciation - Furniture and Fixtures	-10,350.00 EUR	-3,505.00 EUR	-6,845.00 EUR	-195.3
Accumulated Depreciation - Computer Hardware	-2,379.00 EUR	-194.00 EUR	-2,185.00 EUR	-1,126.3
⟩ Tangible Assets in progress	12,202.00 EUR	10,000.00 EUR	2,202.00 EUR	22.0
∨ Current Assets	3,155,758.06 EUR	-38,100.00 EUR	3,193,858.06 EUR	8,382.8
∨ Inventory and in process	3,234,993.10 EUR	0.00 EUR	3,234,993.10 EUR	0.0
⟩ Raw Materials, Other Procurement	57,062.17 EUR	0.00 EUR	57,062.17 EUR	0.0
⟩ Work-in-Progress (Goods and Services)	81,536.32 EUR	0.00 EUR	81,536.32 EUR	0.0
⟩ Semi-Finished and Finished Goods	2,853,188.61 EUR	0.00 EUR	2,853,188.61 EUR	0.0

Figure 10.10: App F0708—display financial statement version

Figure 10.11 shows the financial statement design in app MANAGE FINANCIAL STATEMENT VERSION, based on GUI transaction OB58. This transaction also gives you the option to assign a G/L account to a different FSV item, depending on whether it is an asset or a liability, although in the figure, the bank accounts are linked only to current assets (indicated by the X next to the G/L account numbers).

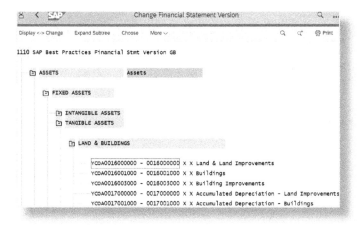

Figure 10.11: Transaction OB58—financial statement version, design

10.2.3 Journal entry analyzer

App F0956A JOURNAL ENTRY ANALYZER can be used to analyze journal entries with similar flexibility to the trial balance app, see Figure 10.12, which includes journal entry type, posting keys, dates, and line item numbers in the ROWS section.

Search	Pause	Journal Entry ▲	Journal Entry Type ▲	Posting
DIMENSIONS	**COLUMNS**			01
Partner Project ∧	Measures	90000038	RV	50
Partner Sales Doc.				
Partner Segment				01
Partner WBS Ele...		90000039	RV	50
Personnel Number	**ROWS**			01
Plant	Journal Entry	90000040	RV	50
✓ Posting Date	Journal Entry Type			
✓ Posting Key	Posting Key			01
✓ Posting View Item	Posting Date	90000041	RV	50
	Posting View Item			

		Jump To		
▲	Posting Key ▲	Posting Date ▲	Posting View	Amount in CC Crcy ▼▲
	01	04.12.2018	1	3,550.37 EUR
	50	04.12.2018	2	-2,983.50 EUR
			3	-566.87 EUR
	01	04.12.2018	1	5,638.82 EUR
	50	04.12.2018	2	-4,738.50 EUR
			3	-900.32 EUR
	01	04.12.2018	1	208.85 EUR
	50	04.12.2018	2	-175.50 EUR
			3	-33.35 EUR
	01	04.12.2018	1	5,638.82 EUR
	50	04.12.2018	2	-4,738.50 EUR
			3	-900.32 EUR

Figure 10.12: App F0956A—journal entry analyzer initial screen

233

You can drill down into each journal entry, but not perhaps as you might expect, by double-clicking. One method is to right click on the item that you want to drill down into and select FILTER • DRILL DOWN and then choose a dimension from the dropdown, as shown in Figure 10.13.

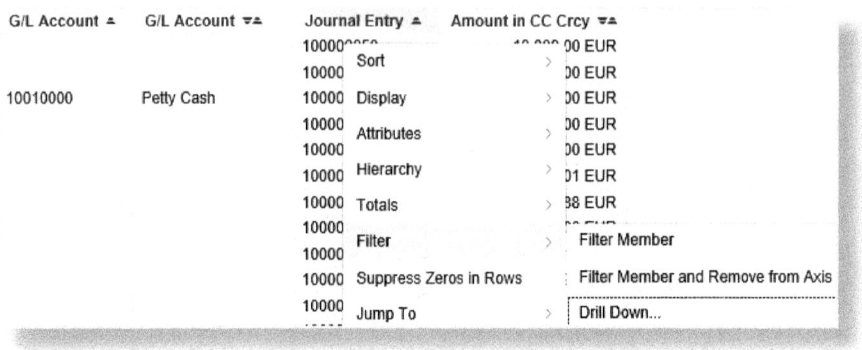

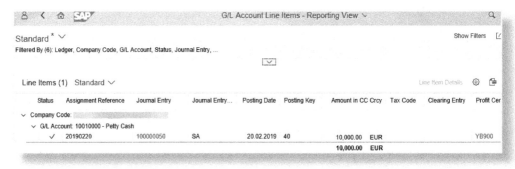

Figure 10.13: App F0956A—journal entry analyzer drill down

Or you can click on the JUMP TO button and select another app to display the journal there. For example, we jumped to app F2217 DISPLAY G/L ACCOUNT LINE ITEMS—REPORTING VIEW shown in Figure 10.14, and from there we clicked on the journal number to go to app F0717 MANAGE JOURNAL ENTRIES.

Figure 10.14: App F0956A—jump from journal entry analyzer to G/L line

10.2.4 Cash flow reporting

With app F3076 CASH FLOW STATEMENT INDIRECT METHOD, you need to first select a financial statement version in the selection screen. See the example in Figure 10.15.

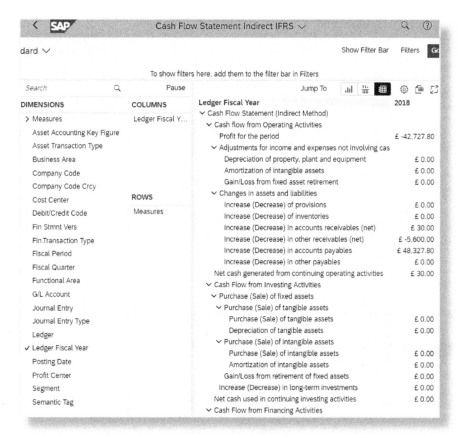

Figure 10.15: App F3076—cash flow statement indirect IFRS

10.2.5 Audit journal

App F0997 Audit Journal, (Figure 10.16), has a Compact Journal tab and a Journal tab. The Compact Journal tab groups the journal entries by period and by type, whereas the Journal tab shows them by posting date and journal number.

You can group by Period, Created by, Document Type, etc., or drill down to individual journals and export them to a spreadsheet. You can use Display Journal Entry Changes, (bottom bar) if text, payment terms, or payment methods have been changed, (you can't change fields such as accounts, cost or revenue objects, amounts, or dates). Check Gaps in Journal Entry Numbering is critical for countries where gaps are not allowed. Check Multi-Referenced Invoices displays documents on the same vendor or customer account with the same reference, including those with different amounts or dates.

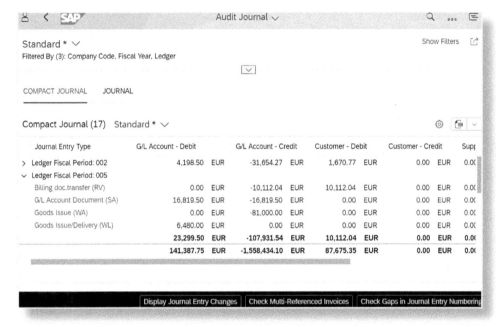

Figure 10.16: App F0997—audit journal grouped by period totals

10.2.6 Line item and G/L account balances

Figure 10.17 shows the G/L account balances main screen (APP F0707 DIS-PLAY G/L ACCOUNT BALANCES).

You can select (filter by) ledger, company code, G/L account number, fiscal year, and period, if relevant. The apps F2218 DISPLAY G/L ACCOUNT LINE ITEMS—POSTING VIEW and F2217 DISPLAY G/L ACCOUNT LINE ITEMS—REPORTING VIEW have similar layouts, but the reporting view includes document splitting items. The layout for both of them is shown in Figure 10.18.

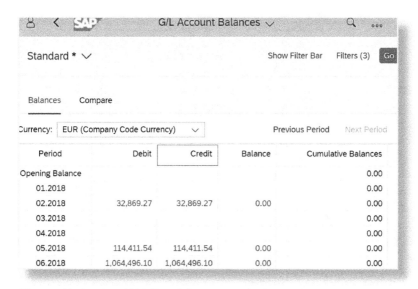

Figure 10.17: App F0707—G/L account balances

Accounting Documents (386)   Standard * ∨

Status	Journal Entry	Journal Entry Type	Posting Date	Posting Key	Amount in CC Crcy	Transaction Code
> Company Code: 1010 - Company Code 1010					0.00 EUR	
∨ Company Code: 1110 - Company Code 1110						
∨ G/L Account: 10020000 - Petty Cash Journal - postings automatic only						
∨ Item Type: 1 - Normal Items						
☐ ✓	1300000000	SK (Cash Document)	01.01.2019	40	500.00 GBP	FBCJ
☐ ✓	1300000001	SK (Cash Document)	01.01.2019	50	-15.00 GBP	FBCJ
☐ ✓	1300000002	SK (Cash Document)	01.01.2019	50	-20.00 GBP	FBCJ
☐ ✓	1300000003	SK (Cash Document)	01.01.2019	50	-17.00 GBP	FBCJ
☐ ✓	1400000000	DZ (Customer Payment)	31.12.2018	40	30.00 GBP	FBCJ
					478.00 GBP	
> G/L Account: 11001010 - Bank 1 - Cash Payment					-500.00 GBP	
∨ G/L Account: 12100000 - Trade Receivables Domestic						
∨ Item Type: 1 - Normal Items						
☐ ○	1400000000	DZ (Customer Payment)	31.12.2018	15	-30.00 GBP	FBCJ
> G/L Account: 12561000 - Prepaid Expenses					630.64 GBP	
> G/L Account: 12600000 - Input Tax (VST)					5,366.32 GBP	
> G/L Account: 21100000 - Trade Payables Domestic					-46,873.76 GBP	
> G/L Account: 21120000 - Goods Received/Invoice Received					0.00 GBP	
> G/L Account: 61401000 - HR Recruitement					12,657.80 GBP	

Figure 10.18: App F2217 and App F2218—display G/L line Item entries

10.3 Accounts payable/receivable reports

Many of these reports often exist as almost identical apps in both accounts payable and receivable. The main differences between reports such as overdue payables and overdue receivables is the name and the fact that one covers suppliers and the other customers, which is why we have put them together in one section. There are many permutations and options available for all the reports, so to avoid repetition, we will not demonstrate each feature with each report. Instead, we will show one or two different features for each report, using different combinations of charts such as vertical and horizontal bar charts, line charts, pie charts, water fall charts, and tables.

Most of them are also smart business KPI apps, showing some data on the tile itself, for example, in Figure 10.19. Although you can't always display the SAP Fiori reference number easily in the app itself, we still give it, as they usually have a number in the SAP Fiori apps library, if you want further information.

Figure 10.19: Examples of smart accounts receivable apps

10.3.1 Receivables and payables reporting

App F1748 total receivables

Figure 10.20 shows the basic report by due period, and you can change the intervals in APP F1748 TOTAL RECEIVABLES. You can use the toggle filter button ⊟ to see the intervals and the add filter button ▽₊ to add fields to filter by.

Figure 10.20: App F1748—total receivables by due period

Clicking on ⚙ gives you a number of additional measures and dimensions so you can rearrange the categories, series, and axes, as shown in Figure 10.21. (In some releases/reports, you can expand the measures in the dimensions column to see what is available and selected).

View Settings		
Chart		Sort
Stacked Column Chart ∨	Search 🔍	Show Selected ≫ ∧ ∨ ≫
☐ Select all (6/21)	Type	Role
☑ Net Due Interval	Dimension	Category ∨
☑ Future Amount	Measure	Axis 2 ∨
☑ Amt 1st Due Period	Measure	Axis 2 ∨
☑ Amt 2nd Due Period	Measure	Axis 2 ∨
☑ Amt 3rd Due Period	Measure	Axis 2 ∨
☑ Amt 4th Due Period	Measure	Axis 2 ∨
☐ Account group	Dimension	Category ∨
☐ Accounting Clerk	Dimension	Category ∨
☐ Company Code	Dimension	Category ∨
☐ Company Code Crcy	Dimension	Category ∨
☐ Country Key	Dimension	Category ∨
☐ Customer	Dimension	Category ∨

Figure 10.21: App F1748—total receivables settings options

Overdue receivables

The two apps for customers are F1747 OVERDUE RECEIVABLES TODAY and F2539 OVERDUE RECEIVABLES BY RISK CLASS. In Figure 10.22 you can see the top ten receivables by customer. You can change the three due periods (shown in different colors) to however many days you want.

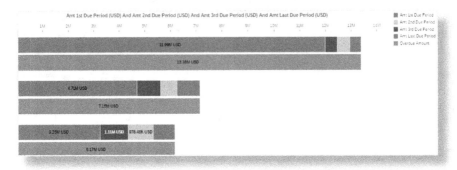

Figure 10.22: App F1747—top ten overdue receivables by due period

Overdue payables

App F1746 OVERDUE PAYABLES, similar to app F1747 OVERDUE RECEIVABLES TODAY, allows you to compare overdue supplier amounts in various ways. See Figure 10.23 and Figure 10.24.

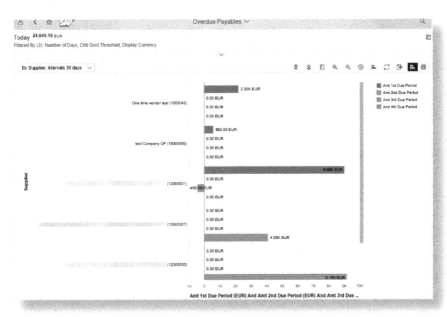

Figure 10.23: App F1746—overdue payables in intervals

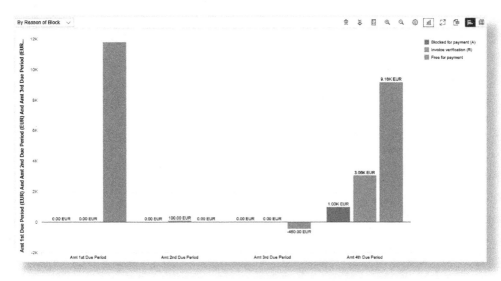

Figure 10.24: App F1746—overdue payables by reason of block

Future payables

For app F1743 Future Payables, shown in Figure 10.25, we have added Item Payment Block in the dimension drilldown.

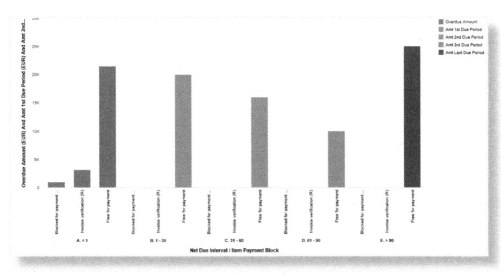

Figure 10.25: App F1743—future payables by item payment block

There are two similar receivables apps, F1744 FUTURE RECEIVABLES TODAY and F1748 TOTAL RECEIVABLES—TODAY. Figure 10.26 shows the future receivables in table format.

Figure 10.26: App F1744—future receivables in table format

10.3.2 Receivable and payable KPIs

This section covers some accounts receivable and payable KPIs.

Days sales outstanding (DSO)

Figure 10.27 shows app F1741 DAYS SALES OUTSTANDING—LAST 12 MONTHS. You can refresh the report by clicking on the ⟳ now in the bottom left corner and you can go to other apps by clicking the OPEN WITH button in the bottom right corner.

By clicking ⟱ you can, for example, split customers by *Accounting Clerk, Company Code, Country, Display Currency*, etc. See Figure 10.28.

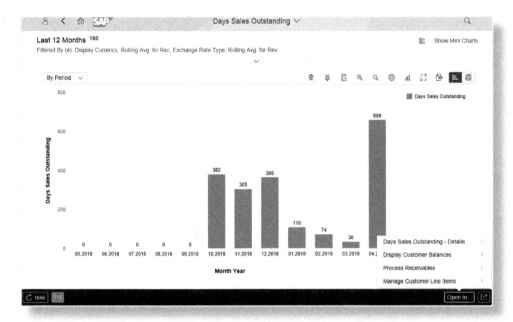

Figure 10.27: App F1741—days sales outstanding by period

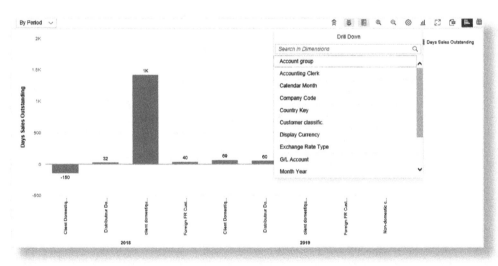

Figure 10.28: App F1741—DSO dimension drilldown by year by customer

Days payable outstanding

In app F1740 DAYS PAYABLE OUTSTANDING—LAST 12 MONTHS, you can use the SELECTED CHART TYPE button to choose different chart types. This button is to the right of ⚙ and shows a mini example of the current chart |≰. Figure 10.29 shows days payable as a line item chart.

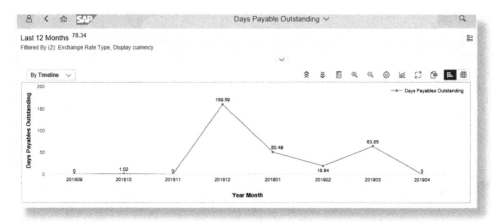

Figure 10.29: App F1740—days payable outstanding, timeline line chart

Figure 10.30 shows the days payable by the top ten suppliers.

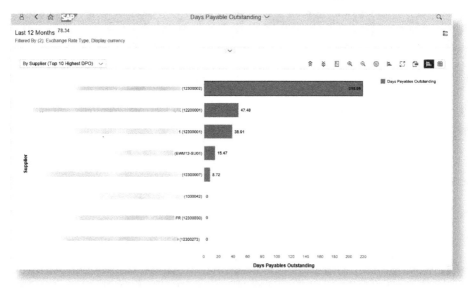

Figure 10.30: App F1740—top ten days payable outstanding

In Figure 10.31, we used the dimension drill down to select the supplier region and pie chart.

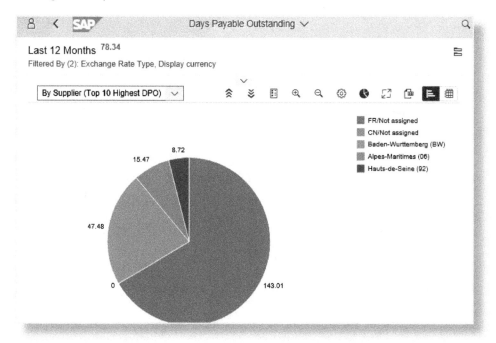

Figure 10.31: App F1740—DPO drill down by supplier region

Days beyond terms

In app F1739 DAYS BEYOND TERMS—LAST 12 MONTHS, we used the condition shown in Figure 10.32 to restrict the chart to 7 months and chose a waterfall chart, as shown in Figure 10.33.

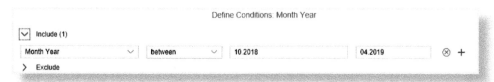

Figure 10.32: App F1739—days beyond terms for 7 months

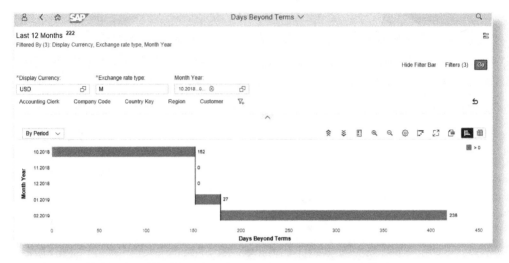

Figure 10.33: App F1739—days beyond terms as waterfall chart

10.3.3 Aging analysis

App F1733 AGING ANALYSIS PAYABLE AMOUNT shows items aged by different intervals. You can see one or more suppliers, add columns, and export to a spreadsheet. As you can see in Figure 10.34, you can change the width and numbers of the aging grids as required.

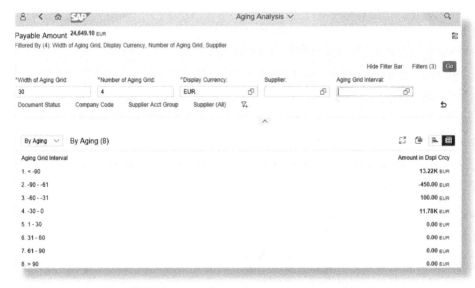

Figure 10.34: App F1733—supplier aging analysis as table

10.3.4 Discounts

App F1735 CASH DISCOUNT FORECAST allows you to forecast what cash discounts are going to be available and if there are any discounts on blocked invoices that should be looked at urgently if you want to claim the discount in time. App F1736 CASH DISCOUNT UTILIZATION shows what percentage of cash discounts offered were actually taken. See Figure 10.35.

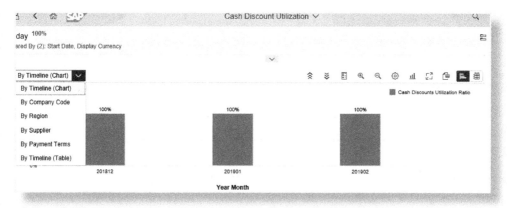

Figure 10.35: App F1736—cash discount utilization

10.3.5 Change logs

App F2681 DISPLAY ITEM CHANGE LOG can appear in both accounts receivable and accounts payable catalogs. Depending where you run it from, you will see either suppliers or customers in the filter bar. The log shows the details of any changes to journal entries and invoices, such as text changes, payment blocks, and changes to payment methods, terms, and discounts. Figure 10.36 shows the supplier version, but the customer version is almost identical.

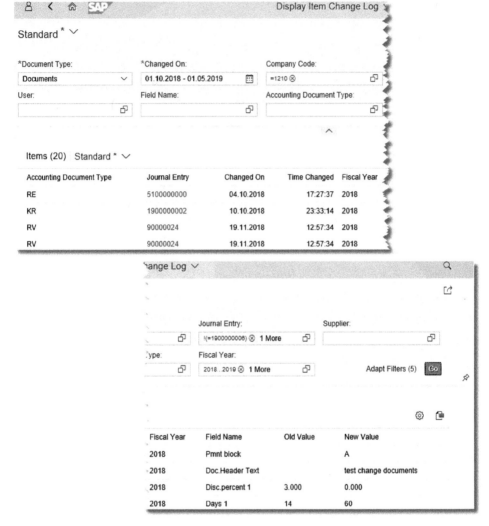

Figure 10.36: App F2681—display changes to supplier documents

10.4 Overhead cost reports

The cost center, profit center, internal order, projects, functional area, and several other reports are all multidimensional reporting apps and four different apps exist for each one with the measures below:

- ▶ ACTUALS

- ▶ PLAN/ACTUALS

- ▶ PLAN/ACTUAL YTD

- ▶ PLAN/ACTUAL CRCY TRANS

We have shown an example of a cost center and functional area actuals report in Figure 10.37 and Figure 10.38.

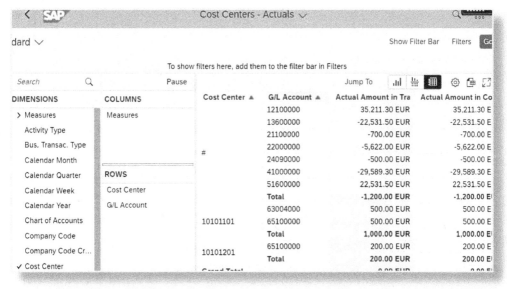

Figure 10.37: App F0940A—cost centers actual report

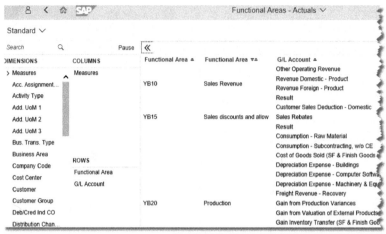

Figure 10.38: App F1583B—functional area actuals

11 Closing

In this chapter, we will start with some definitions, and then explain how the periods are set up in SAP S/4HANA. We will then go on to explain some of the period- and year-end processes and the closing cockpit.

11.1 Related definitions

The following are some key definitions relating to period and year ends.

Fiscal year variant

Each company code is assigned a *fiscal year variant*. The default is *K4*, which means that the company has 12 standard calendar periods plus four special periods for your own adjustments and the audit adjustments at the year end. However, you can set up other variants based on calendar, for example 52 periods in a year, or you can set up non-calendar periods, but the maximum of special periods is four. Some companies have 4-week periods for two months of a quarter and 5 weeks for the third, so that the period always ends on the same day of the week. You can also configure a shortened fiscal year for companies starting up or closing down.

Posting period variant

A *posting period variant* is a group of one or more company codes that share the same physical close. A posting period variant can be created separately for each company code so that each can close when ready, or it can be centrally controlled with one variant so that the head office can close all company codes at once. You could also have a separate variant by region, or for temporary use by new company codes (who might need to keep an earlier period open longer to complete the migration). The related SAP Fiori app, shown in Figure 11.1, to manage the variants account ranges and authorization groups is F2581 MANAGE POSTING PERIOD VARIANTS in SAP S/4HANA Cloud and from 1809 on-premise release.

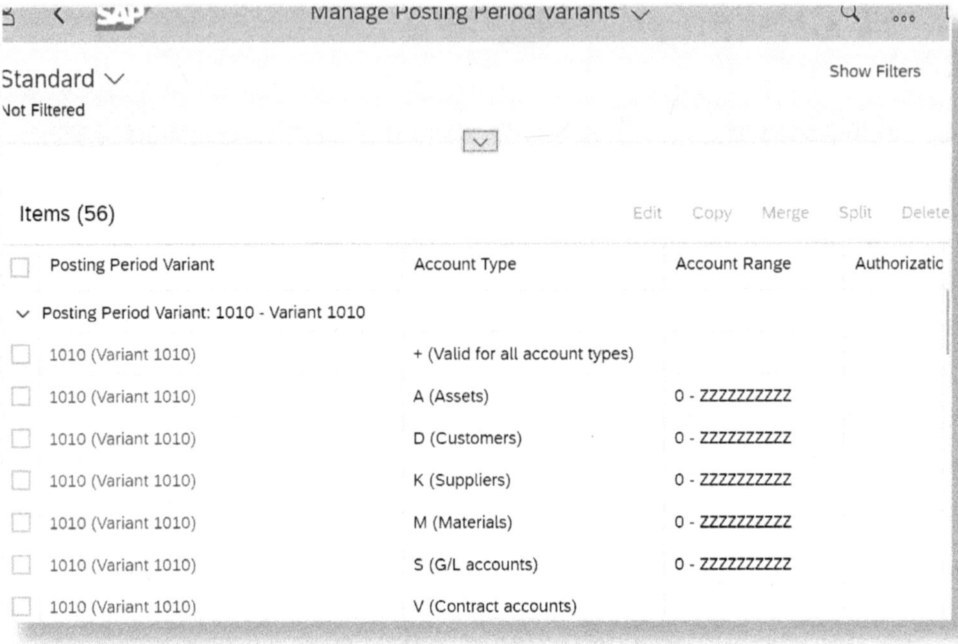

Figure 11.1: App F2581—manage posting period variants

App F2293 MANAGE POSTING PERIODS replaces app F0806 OPEN POSTING PERIODS, to open and close the periods, see Figure 11.2. It also includes scheduling. If you choose company code view, you can see and maintain each ledger separately (by scrolling down).

There are a number of *account types* that can be used in the posting period variant. These same account types can be used elsewhere, for example, to restrict a document type to certain account types. You can change the open periods all at once, or you can close, for example, MM periods, but keep finance open, and you can also open and close different account types or ranges within the account type. You must always have a global type + (valid for all account types) which overrides the others. So, for example, if S is open for period 12, you must have + open for at least period 12 as well in order to post to a G/L account.

To open a period, first select which item(s) you want to change, then click on the SET POSTING PERIODS button on the bottom right and choose OPEN PERIODS. A pop-up will appear with separate tabs for NORMAL PERIODS, ADJUSTMENT PERIODS, and CO-RELATED PERIODS. See Figure 11.3.

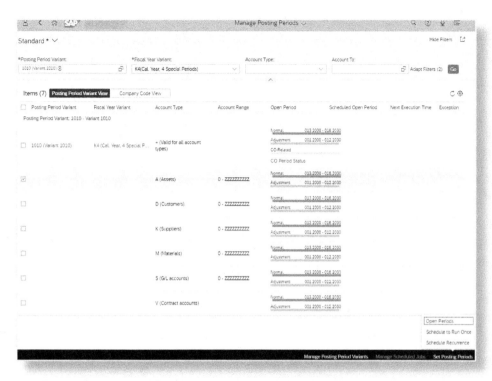

Figure 11.2: App F2293—manage posting periods

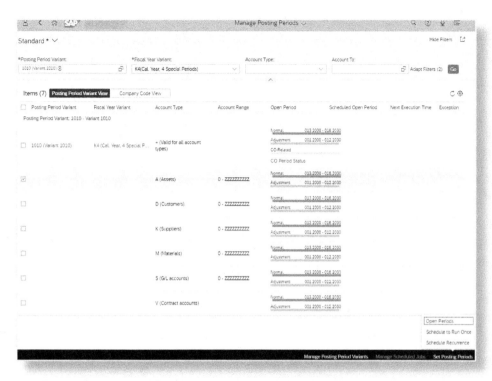

Figure 11.3: App F2293—set posting periods

If you go to the CO-RELATED PERIODS tab and select SET CO PERIODS you will see a list of business transactions, which allows you to further refine your selection by transaction. See Figure 11.4. You could, if you wanted, close most controlling transactions and leave one or two transactions open.

Select: Bus.Transaction

Hide Advanced Search Go

Bus.Transact...
Text:

Items

	Bus.Tr...	Text
☐	COIN	CO Through-postings from FI
☐	CPPA	ABC Actual process assessment
☐	GPDP	Distribution Primary Costs
☐	GPDS	Distribution Secondary Costs

Figure 11.4: App F2293—CO periods by controlling business transactions

Once closed, it is technically possible to reopen earlier periods, but not good accounting practice to allow any changes to be made once reporting for the period is completed.

Closing postings from logistics

Logistics closing covers areas such as sales, purchasing, and manufacturing postings and is usually closed earlier than the finance periods, ideally around midnight on the last day of the period, and once closed should not be re-opened, particularly where you have stock valuations involved. Most postings in these areas usually take the current date, so will post into whatever period is opened. However, you can choose to allow postings into previous periods. The transaction itself is similar to the GUI transaction MMPV and you can also schedule it, for example, as shown in Figure 11.5 and Figure 11.6.

Figure 11.5: App F1240—application jobs scheduler

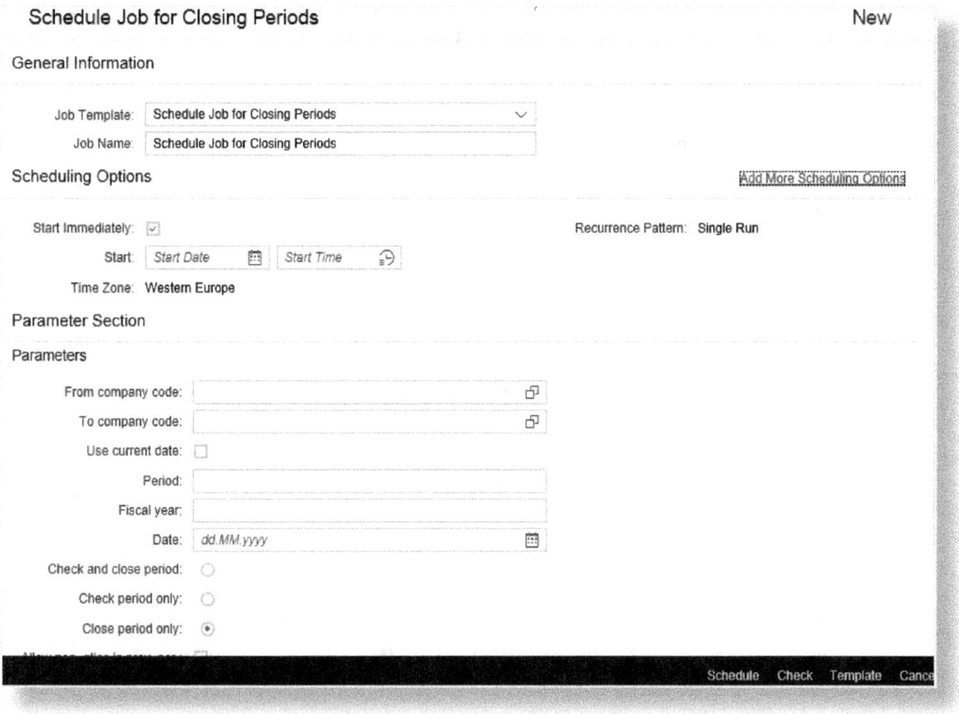

Figure 11.6: MM period close using the scheduler

11.2 Period-end closing

This section covers the different tasks run at the period end. In SAP S/4HANA, many items are processed during the period instead of at the period end, and due to the speed of the SAP HANA database, a lot of transactions run faster anyway. We will run through some of the key tasks. Note that some closing tasks were included in the relevant section where it made sense, for example, we included the GR/IR closing tasks in the section where we explained the GR/IR in accounts payable.

11.2.1 Preclosing activities

Typically, you would open the new periods in FI and MM (logistics) first thing on the first day of the new period to allow sales and goods receipts to be posted with the current date. Depending on the complexity of the organization, you could schedule the opening of the periods to open automatically at one minute after midnight, but if there are tasks that need to be completed first, you may prefer to do this manually (particularly where stock valuations are involved).

However, you would not close finance immediately, especially at a quarter end. You would usually keep two periods open temporarily because there are likely to be a number of tasks that belong in the period to be closed and are still incomplete or can only be prepared at the end of the period. This would include payroll journals, accruals, recurring journals, provisions, fixed asset depreciation, foreign currency valuation, and so on. In addition, you will want to reconcile certain accounts and post adjustments and corrections. Accounts receivable may only receive information about incoming payments after the last day of the period. Accounts payable will also want to post as many invoices as possible that relate to the previous period to reduce the number of accruals required.

Some closing activities have already been covered, for example, balance confirmations and reclassifications under accounts payable, and valuation adjustments under accounts receivable. Some, like foreign currency revaluation apply equally to the general ledger as well as accounts payable and receivable as you could have items posted in a foreign currency in all three areas.

11.2.2 Foreign currency revaluation

Most organizations revalue balances held in foreign currencies on a regular basis as required by International Accounting Standard (IAS) 21, as well as most local authorities.

Regulations vary between countries and for different requirements. For example, group reporting may require the use of a group exchange rate which differs from the local requirement to use the national bank rate; some countries post certain items to the balance sheet whereas others post them to the P&L, and so on. To incorporate the different requirements, different *valuation areas* can be defined and assigned to different accounting principles, which are in turn assigned to different ledgers as required. Most organizations post the revaluation on the last day of the period and reverse it on the first day of the following period. Some countries, such as Hungary and Korea, don't allow the revaluation to be reversed at the year end, but instead post a delta amount.

Figure 11.7 shows some of the parameters that can be entered. You can run the transaction for multiple company codes (assuming they share the same valuation area), but you need to select a VALUATION AREA and a VALUATION KEY DATE, which determines the date up to which items are included, as well as the reversal date. You can run it in test mode or reverse mode (VALUATION RESET). Simulation settings apply only if you have a simulation ledger set up. The OUTPUT/TECHNICAL SETTINGS tab gives you more information about keeping a log.

Figure 11.7: Transaction FAGL_FCV—foreign currency valuation initial screen

If you choose *Save Log*, (see Figure 11.8), then, even if it was only a test run, a LOG button will appear and you can drill down to the detail of the planned or actual revaluation and postings at a later date.

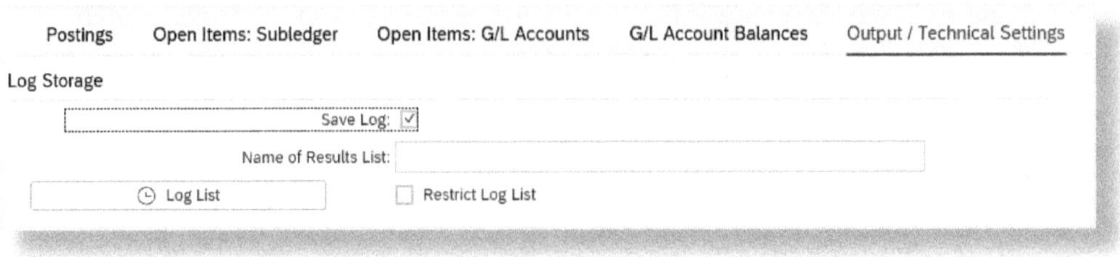

Postings	Open Items: Subledger	Open Items: G/L Accounts	G/L Account Balances	Output / Technical Settings

Log Storage

Save Log: ☑

Name of Results List: _____

🕐 Log List   ☐ Restrict Log List

Figure 11.8: Transaction FAGLFCV—foreign currency revaluation, save log list

The same GUI transaction FAGL_FCV, or SAP Fiori app based on this transaction, is used to revalue the subledgers (debtors and creditors) and general ledger accounts, such as banks held in foreign currency, accruals (GR/IR account), and intercompany G/L accounts. G/L accounts can be open-item managed such as GR/IR accounts or line item, such as the main bank accounts, although you will probably also have open-item managed bank control accounts.

Figure 11.9 shows the different tabs for subledgers, G/L account open items, and G/L account balances. You can run the valuation for everything in one run, or, for example, accounts payable can run the valuation for suppliers and accounts receivable for customers, without waiting for other areas to be completed.

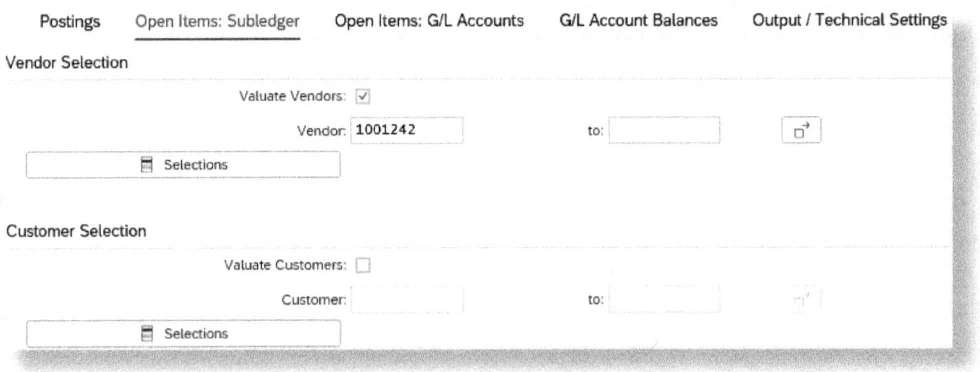

Postings	Open Items: Subledger	Open Items: G/L Accounts	G/L Account Balances	Output / Technical Settings

Vendor Selection

Valuate Vendors: ☑

Vendor: 1001242   to: _____   ▢

🗄 Selections

Customer Selection

Valuate Customers: ☐

Customer: _____   to: _____   ▢

🗄 Selections

Figure 11.9: Transaction FAGL_FCV—currency valuation open items subledger

When revaluing a customer or supplier account, the revaluation is not post-ed back to the subledger, but to an adjustment account that reports in the same area in the balance sheet. Figure 11.10 shows the test results of re-valuing a supplier document for US$122.40 which was originally valued at €136.00 with an indirect exchange rate of 0.90000, but is now revalued with a direct exchange rate of 0.960000, giving an amount of US$117.50 (not shown) and difference of €18.50 to be posted to the adjustment account. You would never use a mix of direct and indirect quotations, but we wanted to show what both types look like on the screen.

AccTy	G/L	Account	DocumentNo	Amount in FC	Crcy	Amount in LC
<	21200000	1001242	5100000002	122.40-	USD	136.00-
	21200000			122.40-	USD	136.00-
				122.40-	USD	136.00-

Amount in LC	LCurr	Revaluat.	Exch. Rat	Typ	Amount Posted
136.00-	EUR	0.96000	/0.90000	RE	18.50
136.00-	EUR				18.50
136.00-	EUR				18.50

Figure 11.10: Transaction FAGL_FCV—showing results of revaluation

Even running the report in test mode will produce a button to click on for the postings. Figure 11.11 shows the posting for the supplier revaluation (from a different example).

```
Valuation Area IF/30.04.2019/Posting Proposal

Ledger Grp CoCd DocumentNo Document Header Text      Typ
Itm PK G/L           Amnt in CC Amnt in Gl. Crcy

2L           1210          FC Valuation
  1 50 72540000              18.50           18.50
  2 40 21202000              18.50           18.50

2L           1210          Reverse posting
  1 40 72540000              18.50           18.50
  2 50 21202000              18.50           18.50
```

```
Typ Pstng Date Crcy  LCurr LCur2 Free   Text
        AmntCrcy1 Text

    30.04.2019 USD   EUR   EUR
                 21200000 - Valuation on 20190430
                 21200000 - Valuation on 20190430

    01.05.2019 USD   EUR   EUR
                 21200000 - Valuation on 20190430 Reversal
                 21200000 - Valuation on 20190430 Reversal
```

Figure 11.11: Transaction FAGL_FCV—revaluation postings

11.2.3 Post currency adjustments

App F1606 POST CURRENCY ADJUSTMENTS is shown in Figure 11.12. This transaction is usually quite rare as most postings should be made automatically with the correct exchange rate. This is only required where a foreign currency posting has an incorrect amount in one currency (for example, group currency or a second local currency), and needs to be adjusted without affecting the document currency, or, for example, environments with volatile exchange rates. When you first enter the transaction, the field DEBITS/CREDITS CUR: has a dropdown available where you can choose the currency you want to correct, (depending on what is set up in your system), for example, we have chosen the company code currency. You complete the rest of the journal as usual and you can hold, simulate, or post.

Figure 11.12: App F1606—post currency adjustment

11.2.4 Regrouping receivables/payables

This includes, for example, reclassifying customer credit balances, supplier debit balances, items outstanding longer than one year, and reclassifying capex items for some countries, and is covered under accounts payable in section 6.6.2.

11.2.5 Taxes

VAT

Countries with very complicated taxes may elect to have a separate tax system, although SAP S/4HANA does include tax procedures for most countries. In Europe, for example, most countries are required, by law, to add value added tax (VAT) to domestic sales (depending on the type of product some sales may also be exempt or zero-rated). The customer pays the full amount of the invoice to the organization that then pays over the VAT portion to the tax office. At the same time, the organization receives invoices from suppliers which includes VAT. The organization then deducts this VAT from their overall payment to the tax office. There are special rules for inter-EU VAT (as different countries have different rates) and also for international sales and purchases. In SAP S/4HANA, a tax code is entered for each line item and VAT is calculated based on the percentage configured in the tax code (or it can be entered manually if necessary).

The full amount of the invoice is posted to the customer or supplier, the net amount is posted to revenue or expenses, and the VAT is posted to a VAT account, either input (purchases) or output (sales). For reverse-charge VAT, the same amount is posted to both the input and output VAT accounts. By reverse-charge, we mean the customer does not charge VAT on the sales invoice and the supplier posts and reports both the input and output tax on the incoming invoice and on their declaration.

In some instances, VAT can only be recovered when payment has been made against the invoice, so it is posted in SAP S/4HANA with a specially configured tax code. Then a report is run which checks each invoice for whether payment has been made and if it has, it then transfers the tax to a standard tax code, to be included in the final declaration.

The VAT accounts have a special setup, for example, in the G/L account master record, the input tax account has a tax category < and output tax has >, which prevents manual posting to this account. At the end of the period, the input and output tax are netted off and either paid over or reclaimed from the tax office, which means that the G/L accounts normally would be zero, barring timing differences, if the final posting is in a different period.

Tax posting

 The tax G/L account should not be cleared with an ordinary journal, as you have to enter tax codes which update the tax reports as well, and you won't be able to check historic amounts.

There are two options, you can use a special type of journal (app F1597 POST TAX PAYABLES) or run the clearing automatically. Postings made using either of these ways do not need tax codes, and therefore update the G/L accounts without updating the tax report totals. Some organizations report manually, but you can also send the tax declarations electronically, in fact, in some countries, electronic is mandatory. Typically, the amounts are cleared to a control account so that any manual adjustments can be taken into account prior to transferring a single balance to the tax office supplier account for payment via the automatic payment program. Alternatively, a manual payment may be made or the tax collected automatically via direct debit.

App F1597 POST TAX PAYABLES does not require you to enter a tax code or tax base, but otherwise behaves like a normal journal entry allowing you to use a document/journal entry type and G/L account of your choice. In Figure 11.13, the net amount, which is reclaimable, is posted to a G/L account that is not a reconciliation account and the incoming payment can then be posted there to clear it, or the balance transferred to a supplier account to pay with the automatic payment program.

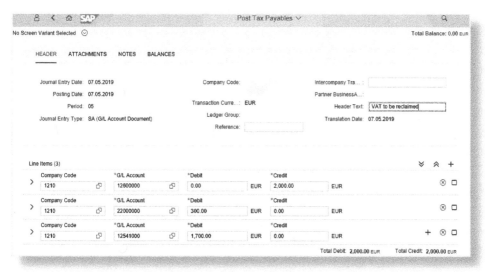

Figure 11.13: App F1597—post tax payables

The other app that users from previous SAP versions will be familiar with is CREATE ADVANCE RETURN ON SALES/PURCHASE TAX, based on GUI transaction S_ALR_87012357. This can be used both for checking and posting the VAT. After entering the company code and date range, you can open up the FURTHER SELECTIONS to restrict by tax code, input or output tax, G/L account, and so on. The TAX PAYABLE POSTING can be opened to select criteria to post the tax. Important in the OUTPUT CONTROL section is the READ ADDRESS DATA field, which, when selected, allows you to display more information about each supplier or customer from the master records in the detailed VAT report.

On the display screen, once the report is run, there is no option to change the columns and filter, total, etc., so you have to do this beforehand for each section (input, output, line item, and summary) of the report separately in the OUTPUT LISTS on the selection screen. Here (see Figure 11.14) you can create and configure your own layouts by selecting the ⊞ button and moving fields that you want to add from right to left.

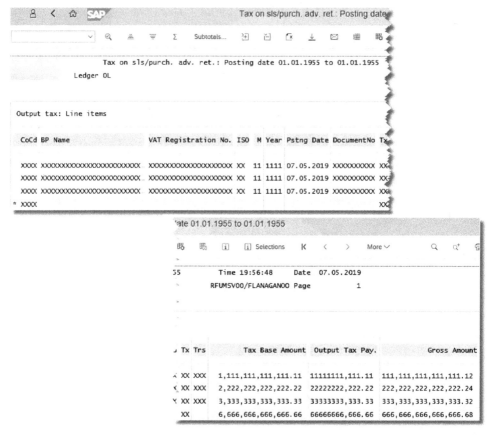

Figure 11.14: Create advance return on sales/purchase tax layout

Figure 11.15 shows the layout you can use for checking. The combination of BP NAME (although anonymized in the figure), VAT REGISTRATION NO., and ISO (country) should assist you in carrying out some checks. For example, if you are in the EU and selling to another EU country and there is a VAT registration, you are allowed to not charge VAT, but if there is no VAT registration, then VAT must be correctly charged if the product is vatable, otherwise you will get a warning message.

```
Output tax: Line items
```

CoCd	BP Name	VAT Registration No.	ISO	M	Year	Pstng Date	DocumentNo	Tx	Tr
1210			FR	5	2019	03.05.2019	90000032	AU	MWS
1210			FR	5	2019	07.05.2019	90000033	AU	MWS
* 1210								AU	

Tx	Trs	Tax Base Amount	Output Tax Pay.	Gross Amount
AU	MWS	29.10-	8.73-	37.83-
AU	MWS	776.00-	155.20-	931.20-
AU		1,788.07-	363.45-	2,151.52-

Figure 11.15: Create advance return on sales/purchase tax checks

There are also a number of apps to aid reconciliation, such as F2096 TAX DECLARATION RECONCILIATION (Figure 11.16) which shows the total of each TAX CODE and you can then drill down to the journal entries. In the DIFFERENCE AMOUNT column, it shows the amount that the tax amount differs from the percentage that is in the tax code configuration so you can investigate further.

8	<	⌂	SAP	Tax Declaration Reconciliation ⌄				Q

Standard * ⌄
Filtered By (1): Tax Code

Tax Boxes and Tax Codes (2) Standard * ⌄

Tax Box ID	Tax Code	Percentage	Transaction	Amount in LC	Calculated Tax	Difference Amount	Posting period	
X	Input VAT 20 % V6	20.000	VST	7,366.66 EUR	1,473.33 EUR	53.33 EUR	3	>
X	Input VAT 20 % V6	20.000	VST	15,056.67 EUR	3,011.33 EUR	0.00 EUR	4	>

Figure 11.16: App F2096—tax declaration reconciliation

App F2095 TAX RECONCILIATION ACCOUNT BALANCE shows the amount of tax posted to each tax G/L account and allows you to drill down to the details. See Figure 11.17.

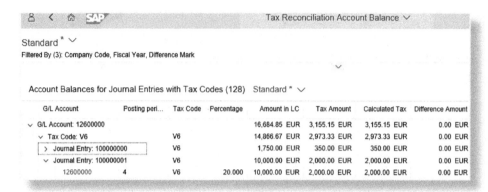

Figure 11.17: App F2095—tax reconciliation account balance

Advance compliance reporting

Advanced compliance reporting (best practices scope item 1J2 ADVANCE COMPLIANCE REPORTING) deals with the regular statutory submissions of an organization. Once you have set up the reports in F2131 DEFINE ADVANCED COMPLIANCE reports, you can run them from the F1515 ADVANCED COMPLIANCE REPORTING app, as shown in Figure 11.18.

Some examples of compliance reports are withholding taxes, U.S. 1099 reports, sales tax/VAT returns, Intrastat declarations, and EC sales lists.

Withholding taxes

Some authorities require withholding taxes to be reported or deducted from certain types of suppliers, usually where the government wants to ensure they receive the taxes in a timely manner. Examples may be non-corporate suppliers, such as self-employed plumbers or handymen, overseas suppliers, or receivers of royalties. Taxes can be deducted at the invoice or payment stage, depending on the country rules. Withholding tax information is set up in the supplier business partner under the company code role. Depending on the local regulations, withholding tax may be posted when the invoice is posted or when the automatic payment program deducts the tax from the payment to the supplier. The tax is posted to a separate account and paid over to the relevant tax office.

Advanced Compliance Reports (5)

Reporting Status	Submission Due Date	Report Name	Reporting Year	Reporting Period	Current Reporting Phase
Overdue 26 Days	31.01.2019	USA Withholding Tax - 1099 MISC	2018	01.01.2018 - 31.12.2018	Declaration
Overdue 26 Days	31.01.2019	USA Withholding Tax - 1099 K	2018	01.01.2018 - 31.12.2018	Declaration
Overdue 26 Days	31.01.2019	USA Withholding Tax - 1099 INT	2018	01.01.2018 - 31.12.2018	Declaration
Overdue 26 Days	31.01.2019	USA Withholding Tax - 1099 G	2018	01.01.2018 - 31.12.2018	Declaration
Overdue 26 Days	31.01.2019	USA Withholding Tax - 1042 S	2018	01.01.2018 - 31.12.2018	Declaration

Current Reporting Phase	Reporting Progress	Current Activity Name	Reporting Entity Name	Actions
Declaration	0 of 1	None	US Reporting Entry	>
Declaration	0 of 1	None	US Reporting Entry	>
Declaration	0 of 1	None	US Reporting Entry	>
Declaration	0 of 1	None	US Reporting Entry	>
Declaration	0 of 1	None	US Reporting Entry	>

Figure 11.18: App F1515—advanced compliance reporting, U.S.

11.2.6 Accruals or deferrals

An *accrual* is where a cost has been incurred, but has not been properly booked into the accounts. Typically, this would be where the goods have been received, but the full posting, including the invoice is not complete.

Accruals are registered automatically in SAP S/4HANA as part of the procurement process. GRs and invoices received are posted to the GR/IR account and as the GR is generally received first, any balance on this account usually represents an accrual. The details of this account were covered in section 6.1.4.

However, in some cases, manual accruals need to be made for an expense that has been incurred in a financial period, but not yet charged to the accounts, perhaps because it was not possible to post a goods or service receipt for whatever reason, or because the exact value is not yet known and must be estimated, for example, utilities or telephone bills.

Although there are different ways to record accruals, the SAP best practice is to debit expenses and credit the accruals account in the balance sheet at the end of one period and reverse the posting at the beginning of the next period.

Probably the easiest way to do this is using the journal upload program (see section 5.2.5) to upload the initial accrual, selecting the document or journal type *AD.* Then when you want to reverse them, you can quickly select all *AD* documents for the relevant period and reverse them all in one go. In app F0717 MANAGE JOURNAL ENTRIES, you will see tab RELATED DOCUMENTS, which will show the reversal if you are in the original accrual, or the original accrual if you are in the reversal.

In GUI transaction FBS1, or GUI-based app ENTER ACCRUAL/DEFERRAL JOURNAL ENTRY, you can also post a journal similar to a normal journal, except on the first screen you assign a reversal reason (05 ACCRUAL/DEFERRAL POSTING) and date, as shown in Figure 11.19.

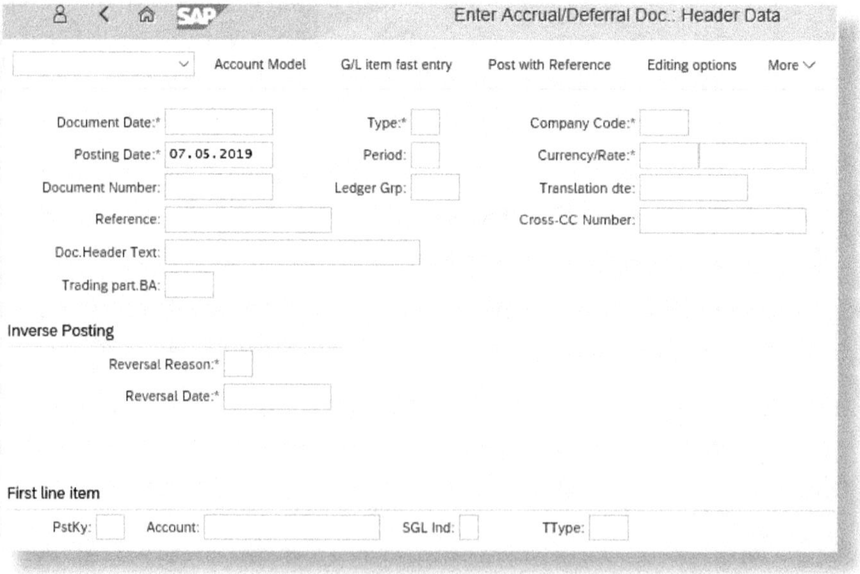

Figure 11.19: Transaction FBS1—accrual journal

You then reverse the transaction the following month with app REVERSE ACCRUAL/DEFERRAL JOURNAL ENTRY, based on GUI transaction F.81, which has the advantage of having a test run so you can check what you are reversing. You can run it for a wide range of documents or restrict it by document number, document type, dates, references, users, etc.

Purchase order accruals

 Best practices scope item 2VB PURCHASE ORDER ACCRUALS is available for purchase order accruals without goods receipt, but only in SAP S/4HANA Cloud.

11.3 Closing cockpit

The closing cockpit, as the name implies, provides a central control over all the closing tasks. Closing cockpits have existed in SAP for a while, sometimes included in the license and sometimes not. Currently, there are some GUI-based transactions and apps, as well as a completely new set of apps only available in SAP S/4HANA Cloud.

Essentially, you can create user groups, assign users to them, and then assign a template of tasks which you can add to or change as required. The tasks can be in a hierarchy, for example, each company code or plant may have its own set of tasks and you can review the status by company code and check which tasks are completed and which are still outstanding. Some tasks can be automatically scheduled, but still need confirmation that the task was carried out without error. Figure 11.20 illustrates the steps.

Figure 11.20: Closing cockpit steps

Each transaction will have a planned start and end date and dependencies. In some cases, you can launch the transaction from the closing cockpit, in other cases, you may want to include a task that is not directly in the system. For example, you may want to include checks carried out in external systems, or reports/calculations transferred to Microsoft Excel. You can also use approval flows.

App F2693 FINANCIAL CLOSE OVERVIEW, only available in SAP S/4HANA Cloud at the moment, is covered in best practices scope item 2V8 ADVANCED FINANCIAL CLOSING. It shows cards with information on the face of the card about delayed tasks, open tasks, tasks to be approved, completion rate (i.e., percentage of tasks still open) by organizational units, as well as by overdue days and number of errors.

Some users may be using the GUI-based apps DISPLAY FINANCIAL CLOSING COCKPIT (FCLOCO) and DEFINE USER SETTINGS (FCCO_USER_SETTINGS), but the following are the apps related to the scope item 2V8:

▶ DEFINE USER GROUPS—FCCO_USER_GROUPS

▶ F2690 APPROVE CLOSING TASKS

▶ F2694 DEFINE CLOSING TASKS

▶ F2695 PROCESS CLOSING TASKS

▶ F2693 FINANCIAL CLOSING OVERVIEW

▶ F3344 CLOSING TASKS COMPLETION

▶ F3946 CHANGE LOG—FINANCIAL CLOSING

11.4 Year-end closing

The year-end closing includes all the tasks covered in the period-end closing, often in more detail, and in some cases may include, for example, stock-takes or fixed asset inventories, unless these are done on a rolling basis. In addition, there are some transactions specific to the year end, and although you may revalue periodically for group purposes, it may be that you only revalue the local ledger (using different rules) at the year end.

App F1596 CARRY FORWARD BALANCES implies that it carries forward only existing postings and would need to be redone with each new journal. In fact, it opens the new year for the postings to flow through into the new year, even those made after the carryforward is completed. Historically, it was not too critical when it was run, other than not showing the opening balances in some transactions. However, since the asset accounting carryforward has now been combined into the general ledger carryforward, it is necessary to run it in a timely manner, otherwise, no asset reports or transactions can be run. In addition, it now carries forward the balances for customers and vendors.

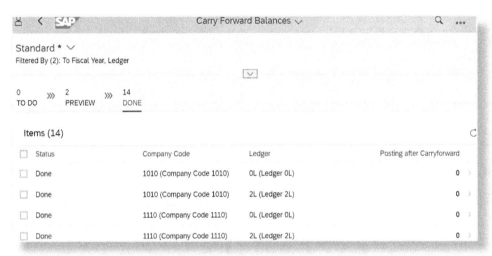

Figure 11.21: App F1596—carryforward balances

The carryforward can be run at any point during the last period of the previous year, but not before, and you can only ever have two years open. You can see the status of each company and ledger in Figure 11.21. You can preview the balances to be carried forward (see Figure 11.22) and you can check the postings afterwards. There is also a rerun button at the bottom of the screen (not shown).

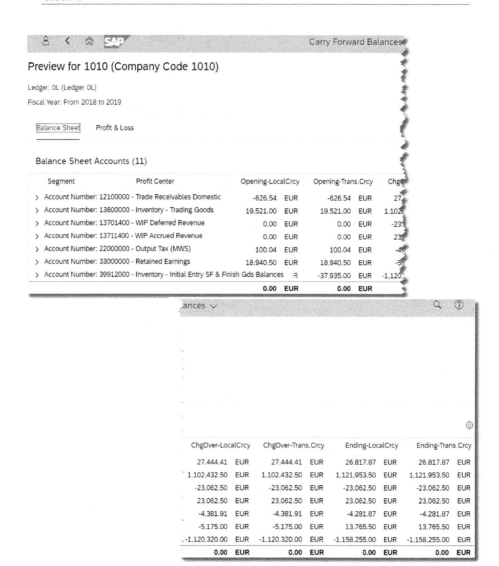

Figure 11.22: App F1596—preview for year-end closing

Preview for 1010 (Company Code 1010)

Ledger: OL (Ledger OL)

Fiscal Year: From 2018 to 2019

Balance Sheet | Profit & Loss

Balance Sheet Accounts (11)

Segment	Profit Center	Opening-LocalCrcy		Opening-Trans.Crcy		Chg
> Account Number: 12100000 - Trade Receivables Domestic		-626.54	EUR	-626.54	EUR	27
> Account Number: 13600000 - Inventory - Trading Goods		19,521.00	EUR	19,521.00	EUR	1,102
> Account Number: 13701400 - WIP Deferred Revenue		0.00	EUR	0.00	EUR	-23
> Account Number: 13711400 - WIP Accrued Revenue		0.00	EUR	0.00	EUR	23
> Account Number: 22000000 - Output Tax (MWS)		100.04	EUR	100.04	EUR	-4
> Account Number: 33000000 - Retained Earnings		18,940.50	EUR	18,940.50	EUR	-5
> Account Number: 39912000 - Inventory - Initial Entry SF & Finish Gds Balances	R	-37,935.00	EUR	-1,120	
		0.00	EUR	0.00	EUR	

ChgOver-LocalCrcy		ChgOver-Trans.Crcy		Ending-LocalCrcy		Ending-Trans.Crcy	
27,444.41	EUR	27,444.41	EUR	26,817.87	EUR	26,817.87	EUR
1,102,432.50	EUR	1,102,432.50	EUR	1,121,953.50	EUR	1,121,953.50	EUR
-23,062.50	EUR	-23,062.50	EUR	-23,062.50	EUR	-23,062.50	EUR
23,062.50	EUR	23,062.50	EUR	23,062.50	EUR	23,062.50	EUR
-4,381.91	EUR	-4,381.91	EUR	-4,281.87	EUR	-4,281.87	EUR
-5,175.00	EUR	-5,175.00	EUR	13,765.50	EUR	13,765.50	EUR
-1,120,320.00	EUR	-1,120,320.00	EUR	-1,158,255.00	EUR	-1,158,255.00	EUR
0.00	EUR	0.00	EUR	0.00	EUR	0.00	EUR

11.5 Summary

New innovations from SAP are changing things in ways not seen before and are released much faster in the cloud with the quarterly releases. With the increase in automation, it is said that we are moving from the age of *digital transformation* into the age of the *intelligent ERP*.

There is machine learning with SAP Leonardo, for example, in the areas of cash allocation and the GR/IR account reconciliation process, which historically have both been quite manual and cumbersome. There is predictive analysis; better multibank connectivity; *SAP CoPilot*, SAP's new intelligent digital assistant; and much more in progress and already being seen in 2019.

This book has covered most of the standard financial processes and hopefully helped you understand a bit better how things fit together and how to get the best out of some of the key transactions. Don't forget that there is a lot of additional information, more scope items, test scripts, and process flows in SAP Best Practice Explorer *https://rapid.sap.com/bp*, plus the country-specific items.

You have finished the book.

A The Author

Oona Flanagan is an Anglo/Irish freelance SAP FICO and SAP S/4HANA certified application professional, as well as a qualified accountant and published author. She has over 20 years of global implementation experience across multiple industries (pharma, fashion, food, beverages, consumer goods, media, packaging, shipping containers, banking, and transportation) as well as many years' accounting experience.

Oona loves languages and has worked in multiple countries during her SAP career. Oona owns her own company Jazzmore Solutions Limited, has an MBA, and is a Fellow of both the Chartered Institute of Certified Accountants and the British Computer Society.

B Index

C Disclaimer

This publication contains references to the products of SAP SE.

SAP, R/3, SAP NetWeaver, Duet, PartnerEdge, ByDesign, SAP Business-Objects Explorer, StreamWork, and other SAP products and services mentioned herein as well as their respective logos are trademarks or registered trademarks of SAP SE in Germany and other countries.

Business Objects and the Business Objects logo, BusinessObjects, Crystal Reports, Crystal Decisions, Web Intelligence, Xcelsius, and other Business Objects products and services mentioned herein as well as their respective logos are trademarks or registered trademarks of Business Objects Software Ltd. Business Objects is an SAP company.

Sybase and Adaptive Server, iAnywhere, Sybase 365, SQL Anywhere, and other Sybase products and services mentioned herein as well as their respective logos are trademarks or registered trademarks of Sybase, Inc. Sybase is an SAP company.

SAP SE is neither the author nor the publisher of this publication and is not responsible for its content. SAP Group shall not be liable for errors or omissions with respect to the materials. The only warranties for SAP Group products and services are those that are set forth in the express warranty statements accompanying such products and services, if any. Nothing herein should be construed as constituting an additional warranty.

More Espresso Tutorials Books

Anurag Barua:

First Steps in SAP® Fiori

▶ SAP Fiori fundamentals and core components
▶ Instructions on how to create and enhance an SAP Fiori app
▶ Installation and configuration best practices
▶ Similarities and differences between SAP Fiori and Screen Personas

http://5126.espresso-tutorials.com

Ann Cacciottolli:

First Steps in SAP® FI Configuration

▶ Get an overview of SAP Financials configuration
▶ Explore fundamental aspects of FI-GL, FI-AR, and FI-AP configuration
▶ Learn how to create, define, and assign company codes and chart of accounts
▶ Obtain hands-on instruction based on examples and screenshots

http://5137.espresso-tutorials.com

Janet Salmon & Claus Wild:

First Steps in SAP® S/4HANA Finance

► Understand the basics of SAP S/4HANA Finance

► Explore the new architecture, configuration options, and SAP Fiori

► Examine SAP S/4HANA Finance migration steps

► Assess the impact on business processes

http://5149.espresso-tutorials.com

M.Larry McKinney, Reinhard Müller, Frank Rothhaas:

Practical Guide to SAP® FI-RA— Revenue Accounting and Reporting

► ASC 606 statutory requirements

► Integration between SAP SD, PS, FI-RA, and FI-GL

► Troubleshooting data migration challenges

► BRFplus in revenue accounting

http://5174.espresso-tutorials.com

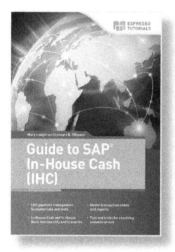

Mary Loughran, Lennart Ullmann:

Guide to SAP® In-House Cash (ICH)

▶ SAP payment management fundamentals and tools

▶ In-House Cash and In-House Bank functionality scenarios

▶ Useful transaction codes and reports

▶ Tips and tricks for resolving common errors

http://5191.espresso-tutorials.com

Mary Loughran, Praveen Gupta:

Cash Management in SAP® S/4HANA

▶ Principle areas of Cash Management powered by S/4HANA

▶ Comparison between ECC and SAP S/4HANA functionality, including an overview of release 1809

▶ Deployment options and implementation steps

▶ SAP Cash Management implementation tips and tricks

http://5281.espresso-tutorials.com

Marjorie Wright:

Credit Management in SAP® S/4HANA

- ▶ Basic configuration settings
- ▶ Integration points with FI-AR and SD
- ▶ Organizational structure and master data
- ▶ Business Partner master record

http://5300.espresso-tutorials.com

Oona Flanagan:

Delta from SAP ERP Financials to SAP® S/4HANA Finance

- ▶ Key changes to financial accounting and structure in SAP S/4HANA Finance
- ▶ New general ledger structure in the universal journal
- ▶ Master data changes in G/L accounts and the business partner
- ▶ SAP S/4HANA preparation and migration tools

http://5321.espresso-tutorials.com